JDS
Grad. Student
Phil. Depart.
Indiana,
Univ.

1961

Prof. Phil. Chr. Doct.

Lincoln Chr. Seminary

1967

The Household of Faith

The Story of Unity

JAMES DILLET FREEMAN

UNITY SCHOOL OF CHRISTIANITY
LEE'S SUMMIT, MO.
1951

The Household of Faith

was first published in 1951.
This is the first printing.

FOREWORD

The publication of this book, *The Household of Faith,* which tells the story of Charles and Myrtle Fillmore and of Unity, has been a project dear to me. Those of you who have been helped by my father and mother may have some understanding of how much they meant to me. I lived with them. I felt their love and was inspired by their faith. My reading this book has been like a visit with them. It brings back many memories.

With the passing of Charles Fillmore in 1948, it was my privilege to become president of Unity School of Christianity. When I think of what a vast organization Unity is and of how much responsibility is mine, I sometimes have misgivings about my ability to do the job. And then, I recall the time in 1907 when my father asked me to take over the duties of office manager. Although I felt unqualified, my father insisted. "Have faith. You can do it," he said. "If something comes up, I will help you." So today when misgivings arise, I know that our heavenly Father is here as He has always been, and He is saying, "Have faith. You can do it. If something comes up, I will help you."

The spirit of faith, of willingness to trust in God and to follow His leading expressed by all my co-workers has been chiefly responsible for the great growth of Unity.

When I went to work as Unity's office boy in 1899, the office force consisted of two persons besides myself. The office was a small room in a rented house in Kansas City, Mo.

What changes have come to Unity! Where there were three office workers, today there are hundreds. Where there were a few thousand subscribers, today there are more than a million. Where perhaps a hundred letters came to Unity each week, today there are more than thirty thousand.

Where perhaps a few hundred persons looked to Silent Unity for help through prayer, today there are many more than half a million. What is more, Unity has entered fields of service that were not even thought of in 1899. There are radio programs. There are centers. There are new magazines. There is a vast variety of books and other literature, much of it published in foreign languages. Streams of Unity literature pour out free of charge to hospitals and prisons, to the blind and other needy individuals throughout the world.

Yet there is one way in which Unity has not changed. This book about my father and mother has made me realize this once again: whether located in a small rented house or in many buildings spreading out over twelve hundred acres, Unity has always been a household of faith—faith in God as the source of every good, faith in our Father as the one presence and one power in all the world.

Lowell Fillmore

Lee's Summit, Mo.
June, 1951.

CONTENTS

CHAPTER I

The Faith of the Fillmores

"According to Your Faith"

I N THE MIDDLE OF THE SPEECH, the fire in the stove went
out. When the speaker noticed this, he did not stop his
speech—he went right on—but he came down from
the platform and picking up a stick of wood took out a
knife and began to whittle kindling. With this kindling
he re-lighted the fire. As he worked, he kept on speaking
calmly, occasionally emphasizing his remarks by gesturing
with the stick of wood from which he was whittling.
When he had the fire going once more to suit him, he re-
mounted the platform, speaking all the while.

A boy in the congregation had attended other religious
meetings but never had he been to one like this, where the
minister built a fire and made a speech at the same time.
The simple act seemed to light a fire inside the boy. He was
so impressed that he volunteered, during the time that he
was in Kansas City, to come to all the meetings that the
man conducted and keep the fire going.

Fifty years later, he wrote to Unity to tell about the
incident, for the speaker had been Charles Fillmore, a co-
founder of Unity School. The fire in the stove burned to
ashes half a century ago but the fire that was lighted in the
boy's heart and mind is today still burning as brightly as
ever.

Charles Fillmore lighted many fires in many minds. He
was a fire-bringer, a carrier of the Promethean spark. He
was highly developed spiritually, yet his spirituality was

7

salted by a sense of practicality. He was an original and creative thinker and moved boldly into new realms of thought, yet he never lost the common touch. He was always trying to light fires in people's minds, but if the fire in the stove that warmed their bodies went out, he attended to that also. His head was in the clouds, but his feet were on the ground. He was gifted with uncommon sense but he had an uncommon lot of common sense. There was about him the divine simplicity that must have characterized Jesus and some of the great philosophers of ancient times. You might imagine Socrates lighting the fire, if it went out in the middle of one of his discourses with his students. Charles Fillmore was such a man.

Probably few men have spent more hours in prayer than he. He lived for ninety-four years, and the last sixty of those years were for him almost a constant prayer. His life had one purpose—the unfoldment of his own spiritual qualities so that he might help others to find and unfold the Spirit within them.

Afflicted with a physical handicap that kept him more or less in pain, he might have settled for half a life. But he was not content to take life and half live it. He had the divine intuition that life is meant to be something grand and wonderful. He felt that life is good and that it should be full of joy, not suffering; that evil is only the result of man's failure to understand and to apply the truth about himself. He felt that men develop only a fraction of their inherent powers. He spent much of his lifetime praying and thinking and laboring to develop those powers within himself.

Perhaps it was because he himself needed physical help so much that he was not content with a religion that merely taught him to endure his pain. Religion to him was not an artist's subtle drawing to be hung up on the temple wall and occasionally admired, it was a set of working drawings that he could carry about with him in the back pocket of his mind and apply to any situation that might arise. He sought for a religion that would heal.

He felt that it is as right for men to have an alert mind, a healthy body, and prosperity in their affairs as it is for them to be spiritual. He felt that men are meant to live abundantly on all levels of their being; that it is God's will for them to be strong and vigorous and rich and successful and happy. He never had much sympathy with religions that emphasize the spiritual to the exclusion of the other needs of men. You might say of him, as Jesus said of Himself: "I came that they may have life, and may have *it* abundantly."

Charles Fillmore came to men and women who had been taught that God is far away and hard to approach, that God is a stern judge, and this life is meant to be a trial and a vale of tears; and he proved to them by his own way of living that none of these things is true.

To Charles Fillmore, God was his personal friend. He spent many hours every day in simple conversation with Him. He loved God, and God loved him, and they met together frequently and talked matters over in prayer. Charles took his affairs and his needs to God, and God gave him what he asked. He wrote of God:

> "Never be formal with God. He cares no more for forms and ceremonies than do the principles of mathematics for fine figures or elaborate blackboards.
> "You cannot use God too often. He loves to be used, and the more you use Him the more easily you use Him and the more pleasant His help becomes. If you want a dress, a car, a house, or if you are thinking

of driving a sharp bargain with your neighbor, going on a journey, giving a friend a present, running for office, or reforming a nation, ask God for guidance, in a moment of silent soul desire."

He did not believe that God gives us everything we ask for, good or bad; neither did he believe that there is anything that we should not take to God in prayer. One time a saloonkeeper came to him for prayers for healing and was helped. The saloonkeeper then said: "I also need prayers for prosperity, but of course you could not pray for a man in my business to prosper."

Charles Fillmore replied: "Certainly. God will help you to prosper. 'If ye shall ask anything of the Father, he will give it you in my name,' does not exclude saloon-keepers." He prayed for prosperity for the man, just as he would have prayed for anyone else, and learned afterward that the man had gotten out of the saloon business and had found prosperity in other lines of work.

Because Charles Fillmore was a man of prayer, but a practical man as well, thousands of people today have health of body, success in their affairs, and happiness in their lives that they would never have had except for him.

Never an issue of *Unity* or *Weekly Unity* appears that does not contain the stories of those who have changed their life by the application of the ideas taught by the Fillmores. In the column, "Because Someone Prayed," in the copy of *Weekly Unity* that happened to be published as these words were being written, this story appears:

"*Dear Unity:* A year ago this month, I came down with what the doctors diagnosed as multiple sclerosis. I was in the hospital for about a week; then my parents took me home in a wheel chair. The doctors had given me up, but the superintendent in the hospital told my mother, 'All the physicians have given your daughter up, but the greatest physician of all has not. Turn to Him in prayer.'

"I was taken home and put to bed. I tried each day to walk, but my legs were very weak. Then came a day when I stayed in bed all day. Mom brought her ironing and stayed very close to me.

"One morning early, I had the radio on. I was unable to talk very well, but Mom could make out that I said, 'Unity.' She said, 'Yes, I must write to Unity.' She did write, and a neighbor mailed the letter to you. One hour later, I tried to tell Mom that I wanted to go to the bathroom. She said she would put me on the bed pan, but I said, 'No, I want to walk,' and walk I did, although it took a long time to get to the bathroom.

"Today through faith and effort, I am walking, talking, and seeing God's beauty.

"I went back to school on October 24, 1949. Everyone was glad to see me, and all my friends tried very hard to believe that I was all right. It took a while, but gradually my ability to walk and talk came back, and finally I was completely well.

"During the time I was ill, Mom spent hours reading to me God's beautiful words from the Bible, and also reading *Unity* and *Daily Word*.

"I graduated this past June from the printing department of Girls' Trade High School in W——.

"I was able to run presses while in high school, and I became editor of the school paper. This past year, I sang in the church choir and also taught Sunday school. I am now working at the H—— Press in W——. I am what is known as a copyholder. I hope someday to be a proofreader or commercial artist. I enjoy both types of work.

"I owe all my good fortune to our heavenly Father and to my dear parents, who worked and prayed along with me. The prayers of all our friends and you people out there, who help each and every person who needs

His loving care, have helped in my restoration to health.
Today I have no signs of multiple sclerosis whatsoever.
I am in perfect health, both mental and physical. May
He who watches over us bless you and keep you for
ever and ever.—*B. J.*"

Because someone prayed! Because Charles Fillmore
prayed! Because he and his wife Myrtle Fillmore dedicated
their lives to prayer, and to the service of their fellow man!

Charles and Myrtle Fillmore worked together to build
Unity. It was Myrtle Fillmore who first accepted the idea
of divine healing; it was Charles Fillmore who edited the
first magazine. It was Myrtle Fillmore who first led Silent
Unity; it was Charles Fillmore who named the work Unity
and developed it into the world-wide organization it is
today. It was Myrtle Fillmore who led the people in meditation and prayer; it was Charles Fillmore who made speeches
and wrote books. They worked together as heart and head
work together, and from their united efforts grew the great
movement that is Unity. If Mrs. Fillmore supplied the
original impetus, it was her husband who supplied the
greater part of the energy that carried it forward.

Charles and Myrtle Fillmore had a simplicity about
them that endeared them to all who knew them. They soared,
but they lived simply. They founded a faith that reaches
around the world, yet their humility was as great as their
accomplishments. It was Unity, not Charles and Myrtle
Fillmore, whose success they worked to forward. There was
no pretense about these two. They never took a title to
themselves and they were such unassuming people that no
one else felt like calling them by a title either. Among their
workers and close friends, there was almost a family feeling,
and many of these called them "Papa Charley" and "Mama
Myrtle." They were the kind of people who, when they

12

went to the vegetarian cafeteria that Unity built on the corner of Ninth and Tracy in Kansas City, stood in line, took their turn, and paid for their meals just as everyone else did.

Charles and Myrtle Fillmore believed that the most important thing in their lives was their ideas and their works, the good they did for others; they were teachers. Those who came to Kansas City after 1906 and studied under them remember them always as they appeared on the platform at 913 Tracy Avenue before the congregation of the Unity Society of Practical Christianity on a Sunday morning. Myrtle Fillmore, wearing her white hair like a crown, gentle, smiling, sitting silent with a look not wholly of this world, and Charles Fillmore standing at the rostrum leaning slightly to one side with his hands braced before him and making in his calm, deliberate style some observation like the following:

> "God is the health of His people. God is infinite life. Let us hold to the Spirit of God, demonstrating itself in life everywhere. That is what the scientific world is preaching today, and we cannot get away from this proposition of the omnipresence of the one life. There is nothing else to come but the Spirit of Truth. We do not look for another. We know that the Spirit of Truth is here. It has always been here, but we have turned our face in another direction. We have looked somewhere else rather than to the Spirit of Truth. The Spirit of Truth is in the midst of you. It is in you, and you will never have peace of mind, you will never have success in any way, you will never have health of body, you will never have anything satisfactory until you demonstrate its presence and its power in your life."

Charles Fillmore was always a student and a teacher, seeking, always seeking, for further insight into the mysteries of life. He spent years poring over the Bible, working out his volumes of interpretation, trying to uncover the hidden meaning of the Scriptures in terms of human life and affairs. He spent years on years in prayer and thought, seeking a knowledge of the mysteries wrapped up in his own being, slowly working out his doctrine of the twelve powers of man, seeking in the silence to unfold and quicken these powers in his own body, working night after night into the early morning hours to send his word down into the cells of his body, to quicken and regenerate them to eternal life.

Charles and Myrtle Fillmore were more than teachers. They were healers. They were not content merely to have ideas or even to tell others of the ideas. They took the ideas and worked to demonstrate them in their own lives and bodies. The very heart of the Unity teaching has to do with healing the ills of mind, body, and affairs. Unity began with the healing of Myrtle Fillmore. Its first fruits were the healing of her friends and neighbors, accomplished by her realization of the Christ power within. The heart of Unity today is the Society of Silent Unity, which sends its message of healing to hundreds of thousands of persons throughout the world each year. In the anteroom outside the Fillmores' offices each day, people waited their turn to have these two teachers, who had touched God's power and whom God's power had touched, utter a healing prayer for them.

Charles and Myrtle Fillmore were builders, too. Go out to Unity School today and walk down the shady lanes or stand and gaze at the buildings that house Unity and you get a sense of what they built. It was their son Rickert who erected the buildings at Unity Farm, but it was they who envisioned such a spiritual center; and it was they who from nothing but an idea and faith in that idea, in half a century built the Unity work of which the buildings are but a visible expression.

Today the presses in the vast Unity printing building are rolling out literature in a dozen languages to be sent to millions of people in most of the countries of the earth. On the radio from scores of stations in the United States and other countries, the Jesus Christ message as interpreted by Charles and Myrtle Fillmore goes out to more than three million people. Teachers and Truth lecturers in hundreds of Unity centers are every day expounding the ideas of these two pioneers to thousands of eager students.

Charles and Myrtle Fillmore had many abilities. They were practical people: teachers, ministers, healers, builders. But they had vision, too. They worked to turn their ideas into magazines and buildings, into restored bodies and renewed minds and illumined lives. But their ideas soared even beyond their accomplishments. They had the vision of the perfect man in God, and this perfection was their goal. They aimed at the highest, and how high they mounted! They aimed at eternal life, and how much of life they won, not only for themselves but for how many others! Because they lived close in thought and aspiration to God, there was about them an atmosphere of spirituality that those who were near them felt.

About Myrtle Fillmore, there was always an unworldly quality that once made her husband say of her, "Myrtle belongs on another planet." She was not much concerned with worldliness. Almost all the writing that she did was in private letters, most of which have disappeared. Her speaking rarely consisted of formal addresses, but was more likely to consist of the inspiration that came to her at the moment. When she spoke, thought moved through her as a butterfly moves through a field of summer flowers, lighting on an idea, hovering for a moment, tasting its sweetness, then moving on to another. Little that she said was ever written down. Yet though most of the words she uttered have vanished, their effect has not vanished from the hearts and minds of those who heard them and were lifted up, nor from the flesh of those who heard them and were healed. Unity itself is the ever-living, ever-growing expression of her spirit.

About Charles Fillmore, there was something of the prophet. He lived simply and he lived very close to God and he felt very strongly that God was speaking to him, using him to convey divine ideas. Like Joseph and Daniel, he felt that God came to him in dreams and visions of the night and revealed to him much of the Truth about which he wrote and spoke. He was always looking forward. He foresaw radio and talked about it in sermons and articles. He foresaw that the atom would be split and become a source of power. His mind was always ranging far ahead of most persons', even ahead of his fellow workers.

The mother of one of the editors at Unity School recalls that the first time she ever went to hear Charles Fillmore speak she thought he talked about such "crazy things, such as talking through the ethers and harnessing the ethers to do our work for us" that she almost never went back.

Once one of his editors questioned an article Mr. Fillmore had written about atomic energy. Years later, the first atomic bomb was detonated in New Mexico.

Charles and Myrtle Fillmore followed the "visionary gleam." They were pioneers of mind and spirit. They were never bound by limited conceptions about life but were always striking out into the new. They were people with the courage to step out on faith. "Judge not according to appearance," said Jesus, and Charles and Myrtle Fillmore took Him at His word. Appearances might say, "You cannot do it," but Charles and Myrtle Fillmore did not believe in appearances. "If you need something," said Mr. Fillmore, "go ahead and get it, do something about it."

Charles and Myrtle Fillmore were a man and woman of faith. In the word faith is summed up the story of their life and works—and the story of Unity. They did their works through faith. They soared beyond their works through faith. They were teachers through faith. They were healers through faith. They were builders through faith. They were overcomers through faith.

Many, many times in the history of Unity they came to a place where it seemed that they could not go on, yet they went on through faith.

They taught that God is a help in every need and they prayed in this simple faith. Over and over when they were in need, they went to God to prove that what they taught is true. All that they thought and wrote and did they wrought through faith. Through faith, they turned to God in the beginning. Through faith, they healed their bodies. Through faith, they brought healing to others. Through faith, they founded Unity. Through faith, they persevered in their idea when everything seemed to say that they were destined for failure. Through faith, they built a work that rings the world around with faith and prayer.

They never lost faith.

Once Unity was in serious financial straits. Bills that had to be paid were piling up, and there did not seem to be money enough to meet the pay roll. The Fillmores called their staff together to pray about the matter. One of the staff said, "Let us pray that the money holds out."

"Oh, no," whispered Myrtle Fillmore, "let us pray that our faith holds out."

CHAPTER II

Charles Fillmore's Early Years

"Youth and the Dawn of Life"

C HARLES FILLMORE was born into this present itinerary on August 22, 1854, at 4 a. m., on an Indian reservation just outside the little town of St. Cloud, Minnesota, in a log cabin that his father Henry had built by a ford over the Sauk River. He was christened Charles Sherlock Fillmore. He never used his middle name.

Charles Fillmore once wrote about one of his ancestors, John Fillmore: "As a boy of thirteen he was kidnapped on the coast of England by pirates. He was on the pirate ship for eighteen years. Finally he and a companion tied the pirates while they were under the influence of liquor and sailed the ship into Boston harbor, where the pirates were executed. This little incident in my family history has often reminded me of what a lecturer on heraldry once said about his family tree: that he was somewhat timid about looking it up because he might find something hanging to it. A facetious member of the audience queried, 'By the neck or the tail?' "

Millard Fillmore, thirteenth President of the United States, was Henry Fillmore's second cousin. An uncle of Henry's, Glezen Fillmore, was the first ordained Methodist Episcopal Minister in New York State and established the first Methodist Episcopal Church in Buffalo, New York.

Charles's father Henry was born and reared in Buffalo. After receiving a common school education, he left the city for the wilderness of Minnesota. In Minnesota, he became a trader with the Chippewa Indians and settled on a small reservation located just north of St. Cloud.

Young Fillmore, the Indian trader, had been in Minnesota only a few months when he met and married Mary Georgiana Stone, the eighteen-year-old daughter of a millwright. Born in Nova Scotia of Welsh and English ancestry, she had been brought West by her father when she was a child.

Charles Fillmore was born in a log cabin where the only protection against the forty-degree-below-zero cold of the Minnesota winters was the huge fireplace, which devoured logs at a rate that kept Charles and his younger brother Norton busy throughout the winter.

When Charles was seven, his father Henry left home. He had managed to acquire some land about ten miles north of the cabin where the boys lived with their mother and there he built another cabin for himself. From then on, the boys spent part of their time with their mother and part with their father.

As Charles Fillmore later wrote, his childhood was "romantic but crude and unprofitable." It was a kind of Huckleberry Finn existence. Hunters and trappers came and went, roving bands of Chippewa and Sioux Indians passed by the cabin. Charles spent a great deal of time wandering in and out of the Indian lodges and tepees as freely as did the Indian children. In this way, he and his mother learned some words of the Chippewa tongue, and years later Grandma Fillmore taught these to Rickert and Lowell. When a member of that tribe visited Unity School long afterward, one of the boys was able to repeat a few words in the Chippewa language, which the Indian seemed to understand.

The Indians were nearly always on the warpath, not only with one another but sometimes with the whites. When

Charles was less than two years old and he and his mother were alone in their cabin, a band of painted Sioux rushed up. The leader, a towering medicine man fantastically painted and decked in the full regalia of his profession, strode into the cabin, tore little Charles out of his mother's arms, and rode away with him. It was evening before the warriors brought him back to his distracted mother. Where they had taken him and what they had done with him, Charles could not remember, but he always had a feeling that they had used him in some mystical ceremony.

Charles attended a log-cabin school where there was one schoolmaster for all the students and the school term was only for the three mid-winter months of the year. He went to this school for only a few years, so he did not have much formal education. Neither did he have many opportunities to go to church.

Though the family was not rich, there was never any dire lack of food in the house. Food in Minnesota in the 1850's was easy to obtain. Wild game and berries of all kinds were plentiful. Many times in the winter and early spring, Charles and his brother would go down to a nearby creek or pond and break the ice to find cranberries frozen under it, or perhaps to fish. In the fall, there was an abundance of wild rice and Charles would go out in a canoe, just as the Indians did, and bending the rice blades into his canoe, he would beat off the grain with a stick and bring it home to dry and store.

It was the mother, Mary Georgiana Fillmore, who was to be the chief force in shaping Charles's destiny. Life had never been easy for Mary Fillmore—or "Grandma Fillmore," as she came to be known to the Unity workers— but she had never asked for ease. Like her son Charles, she was one of those persons who have a rich zest for life. She

21

was not afraid to live. Neither the natural wilderness in which she was reared nor the economic wilderness in which she found herself by the necessity of having to raise a family singlehanded ever daunted her.

Mary Fillmore was a strong character. She wrapped herself in an imperious manner and developed a tenacity of will with which she could press forward through poverty or inharmony, or whatever obstacle she faced, until her goal was reached.

Mary Fillmore needed her tenacity of purpose to raise her family in the wilderness. At twenty-five, she found herself alone with two children to feed and care for; the oldest, seven; the youngest, five. She lived in a crude cabin four miles outside the nearest town, surrounded by half-savage Indians and half-civilized whites, mostly French traders and trappers who spoke a foreign tongue. The people were hospitable, however, and she managed to make enough money as a dressmaker to keep the three of them clothed and fed. The food was simple, but with the magic known only to those who have to do it, Mary Fillmore had learned how to take a small bag of beans and a soup bone and turn them into a week's meals for three.

After five years of this struggle, one of the members of the little family, Norton, ran away from home and never returned to live with them. He disappeared into the West and out of the life of Charles Fillmore except for occasional contacts.

It was a short time after his brother left that Charles Fillmore met with the accident that was probably the determining incident of his life. His hip was dislocated in a skating accident. A doctor decided that rheumatism had set in and treated the boy for that. There was no improvement; instead the leg grew steadily worse. A succession of doctors produced a succession of diagnoses, but no improvement in the patient. In the words of Charles Fillmore, himself, "I was bled, leached, cupped, lanced, seasoned, blistered, and roweled. Six running sores were artificially produced on my leg to draw out the diseased condition that was presumed to be within. Physicians of different schools were employed, and the last one always wondered how I ever pulled through alive under the treatment of the 'quack' that preceded him; and as I look back at it now it's a miracle to me how I ever got away from them all with the little bundle of bones and sinews that I found in my possession after they had finished their experiments."

By that time, the hip socket had been destroyed, the leg had stopped growing, and could not be moved. For more than two years, the disease ran its course in the leg, sometimes seeming to disappear only to return with increased violence. Many times during the course of the sickness, Charles did not believe that he was going to come through. Often he must have wondered why he was making the struggle. It was a titanic struggle. But there was a titan in the little body, and the struggle was made. Whenever he could be, he would be up and about on a pair of handmade crutches, hopping around the cabin, doing what he could to help. When the disease would bring his body down again, it did not bring him down in spirit. He never gave up.

This boy did not know what it meant to give up—to sickness, to poverty, to discouragement. Probably the spirit of the mother, by this time a veteran of hardship, helped him more than anything else, for she fired the son with her courage, which, if it had no power to stop the infection in the leg, did have power to stop the infection from spreading to the boy's spirit. The spirit remained whole, and as is very often the case under such conditions, even grew stronger.

Qualities of the heart and mind are like physical qualities, they are developed by exercise. Often we make no effort to acquire them unless life forces demands for them upon us; but once we have them, they are ours to use. For two years, merely to keep the thin flame of life flickering in his body, Charles Fillmore had to call on all the energy he could command; he had to build the will to live, or die. He had to build courage. He had to build resourcefulness. When the struggle ended in victory, these qualities remained and were his to put to other purposes.

When after two years the disease had run its course, it left a withered leg. But it left something else, too—a spirit that would not give up, a spirit that was not daunted by pain, a vital, determined, courageous spirit. It was this robust spirit that was to shape the life of the man.

Youth is the time of life when men engage most actively in physical pursuits, but this activity was denied Charles Fillmore. Here were an alert, swift, vital mind and a bold, self-reliant, enterprising spirit lodged in a body incapable of much physical activity. This mind and this spirit had to find an outlet for their energy. Charles Fillmore did not have less energy than others; he had more. The two-year struggle he had made against disease had released tremendous quantities of energy within him. Now he had to put this energy to use.

He started back to the one-room schoolhouse, but his difficulty in getting about made it hard for him to go to school; moreover, in a short time he had to go to work to help his mother.

His first job was as a printer's devil in St. Cloud. Here he learned some of the printer's trade that was to be of use to him thirty years later when he came to publish the magazine *Unity*. After that, he worked in a grocery store and in a bank.

Charles worked hard in the grocery store and the bank, but his work could not begin to absorb his energies. He had a mind that demanded more vigorous use than he could put it to in his work.

At this time, an army officer named Edgar Taylor happened to be stationed in St. Cloud. His wife Caroline had gone through college, a rare attainment for women of that time. This woman had a genuine love for classical literature. Also she had a son, Edgar, a boy of Charles's age, to whom she was devoted and she was determined that this boy should amount to something. At the time when young Charles met her and was drawn to her, she happened to be busy teaching her son, much against his will, the classical literature that she herself loved so much.

Here was a woman who had read and thought; her mind was full of knowledge. She was familiar with many books, most of which probably the young son of an Indian trader had never even heard of. But Charles had a curious and avid mind, a spirit ready for books and learning, and however Edgar reacted to literature, Charles was happy to make its acquaintance. Shakespeare, Tennyson, Emerson, Lowell, and we do not know how many others, were poured one after another into the active ferment of his imagination. Edgar Taylor might have preferred to be out running around with other boys, but Charles, who was unable to do this, reveled in the books that Mrs. Taylor introduced him to. He learned to love the beautiful language and exalted ideas of Shakespeare and Tennyson. They made such a deep impression on the boy's mind that all his life his writings were embellished with quotations from their works. So much did the American writers, James Russell Lowell and Ralph

Waldo Emerson, come to mean to him that later when he was married he and his wife Myrtle, who was also a great admirer of the writers, gave each of their first two sons Lowell Page and Waldo Rickert, the name of one of those two great New England transcendentalists. Later Charles Fillmore was to write an article on the metaphysics of Shakespeare; and numerous quotations by Emerson were to appear in the pages of *Unity*.

Not only did Mrs. Taylor teach him to read great literature, but she also taught him the rules of grammar and gave him writing exercises to perform. Many an evening when he came home from the grocery store or the bank, he and she together would pore over something he had written while she pointed out mistakes and assisted him with his rhetoric. Besides her interest in literary matters, she was interested in the new ideas that, seeping out of New England, were making people here and there question the concepts of orthodox theology, and she helped to stimulate an interest in those new ideas in the young man who had turned to her for learning.

Above all, however, by teaching him grammar and acquainting him with the beautiful phrasing and noble ideas of the great English and American poets and essayists, she was helping him to prepare himself to express ideas of his own when at last they should come to him. When, three decades later, he felt the urge to express the new thoughts that were unfolding in his mind, the small amount of formal schooling he had obtained would have equipped him but poorly for the task that was his; but thanks to Mrs. Taylor, when at last he found something to say, he had the skill with which to say it so that people would stop and pay attention to it.

Meanwhile St. Cloud was growing up. By 1870 it had

a population of 3,000. Had Charles Fillmore stayed there, he might have become in time a prosperous merchant or a banker, for he was to prove later that he had a shrewd business sense; but such a prospect could never have held much allure for a man as imaginative of mind and adventurous of spirit as Charles Fillmore. Among the books he read there were many about the West. Out West, there were marvelous opportunities. There fortunes were being made, mines being discovered, cities being built. It was a young land exploited by young men and it beckoned to the young with hands dripping gold and adventure.

Charles Fillmore had a cousin who lived in the little town of Caddo, located just north of the Texas border in the Indian Territory that is now Oklahoma. One day in the spring of 1874, when Charles was nineteen years old, he packed his clothes, went down to the railroad station in St. Cloud, bought a one-way ticket to Caddo and got on the train.

Caddo was located in what was probably the wildest district in the United States, and Charles Fillmore did not stay there long. He went on to the end of the Missouri, Kansas & Texas Railroad, which had its terminus twenty miles south, across the Red River, in Denison, Texas. In Denison, he managed to make a friend of the chief clerk in the freight office and was hired to check cars in the yard. With a sheet of paper and a pencil, he would go out each day to write down the numbers of all freight cars that were in the vicinity of Denison. All his spare time, he spent in the freight office helping his friend the clerk do his work. His other friends laughed at him for this diligence, but it proved ultimately not to be without profit, for one day the clerk became ill and Charles was the only person who knew how to perform his duties. For the next five years, Charles

Fillmore worked as chief clerk in the freight office of the Missouri, Kansas & Texas Railroad in Denison.

As soon as he was able, he sent for his mother. Charles and his mother were unusually close all their life. She had reared him and supported him. When he had been sick, she had inspired him to live. Later when he and his wife Myrtle were busy founding Unity, she was to take care of the family, cooking the meals, keeping house, making and mending clothes, washing, feeding, and tending the three boys through illness and health, getting them off to school and welcoming them home again; and stretching the few dollars that the founders of Unity were able to provide into food and clothing enough for all. All her life, with doting eyes and loving heart, she was to stand by and look after the needs of the one she called "my boy Charles." Now when he sent for her, she was quick to come to Denison to make a home for him. To help support the home, she once more went to work as a dressmaker.

Among all American pioneers were many of education and refinement. Denison had no small number of these. It was inevitable that they should gravitate together to discuss the literary and philosophic matters that interested them. Charles attached himself to such a group. They were young people who met at one another's homes in the evening, often to read poetry, or if the urge should strike them, to write a few lines.

We know that Charles joined this group, because it was as a member of it in 1876 that he met a red-haired schoolteacher who had come down from Clinton, Missouri, two years before to teach in a private school. The name of this teacher was Myrtle Page.

CHAPTER III

Truth Comes to Myrtle Fillmore

"The Two Shall Become One"

MYRTLE PAGE was next to the youngest of the nine children of Marcus and Lucy Page. She was born in Pagetown, Ohio, August 6, 1845. Her family had been early settlers of the town and were influential citizens. They were members of the Methodist Episcopal Church, and Myrtle became a member as a child. Her religious training was strict. The family frowned upon most forms of amusement, and the children were not permitted even such diversions as playing cards or dancing. Myrtle, however, was the favorite of the father, and in lighthearted moments, when the rest of the family were not around, he taught her how to dance the Highland fling, which she loved to do.

Myrtle had been christened with the name Mary Caroline but she never liked the name. From her infancy she could remember her father calling her by the pet name, "Myrtilee, Myrtilee." As a little girl, she adopted the name Myrtle.

She had a better than ordinary education for young women of her time, for when she was twenty-two, she enrolled at Oberlin College where she took the "Literary Course for Ladies." When she left college, she did not go home but went to live with a brother, David Page, who had moved his family to Clinton, Missouri, a small town about seventy miles southeast of Kansas City. Here she secured a position teaching in the village school.

Myrtle was not a robust person, for she had been brought

up in the belief that she was an invalid and had inherited a tendency to tuberculosis. She did not, however, let this belief interfere with her life. She lived an active life, working hard as a teacher and entering enthusiastically into many of the activities of the local Methodist church. When she was about thirty years of age, she secured a position as a teacher in Denison, Texas. It was here that she and Charles met.

Myrtle had the same literary interests that Charles had. She loved to read poetry and philosophy and she loved to recite. It was through a recitation that she gave that Charles Fillmore first took notice of her. He had gone to spend a literary evening at the home of some friends, and there a good-looking, vivacious, red-haired young woman got up and recited a poem for the group. Charles later told friends that at that first moment, as he watched her and listened to her, something inside him said: "There's your wife, Charles."

In a short time, the two were exchanging books and ideas; and since they were also interested in scientific matters, they often went out into the countryside together, searching for fossils. When, in 1878, Myrtle left Denison and returned to Clinton to teach school there again, Charles wrote to her asking if they could carry on their acquaintance by correspondence. She replied:

> "I was truly pleased to find, when I returned from my visit in the country Thursday, among my other mail, a letter from you. Such a correspondence would prove rather a treat than a burden to me. I shall ever feel grateful to you for contributing so much to my literary enjoyments and for new thoughts and suggestions, yes, and for a kind of sympathy I seldom meet.
> "I have learned many lessons in the past year.

" 'What the world teaches profits to the world.
What the soul teaches profits to the soul,
Which then first stands erect with Godward face,
When she lets fall her pack of withered facts,
The gleanings of the outward eye and ear,
And looks and listens with her finer sense;
Nor Truth nor knowledge cometh from without.'

"You question my orthodoxy? Well, if I were called upon to write out my creed it would be rather a strange mixture. I am decidedly eclectic in my theology. Is it not my right to be? Over all is a grand ideal God but full of love and mercy. And dear to my heart is Christ, the perfect man, who shared our earthly sorrows, yet ever lived blameless, and taught such sweet lessons of patience, forgiveness, and tolerance. Outside of ourselves must we go for a strength to trust and rely on. Trusted, that strength proves a help. Call it by what name you choose, the soul understands it.

"Last Sabbath I had a glorious time. They sent for me to visit down in the country among my old Fairview friends, and Sunday there was a 'basket meeting' 'way off in the woods.' I went. The sermons were quite good, and the spot was divine. Near the preacher's stand rose a great ledge of rock that overhung a small stream. It stretched for a half mile or more. Oh, it was grand! I went up on the top, gathered ferns and mosses—the most beautiful mosses! One's foot sunk down among them, green and silver gray they were. And the most picturesque nooks and grottoes. Oh, to me came the messages then, from the divine Spirit, more direct than through His human messengers!

"The good, simple-hearted country folk enjoyed seeing me enjoy it so and confessed, 'It was mighty nice.' They saw rock and moss, listened decorously to the man of God, while I, in a kind of charmed life, was a part of all I saw—and a part of God. What have I said? But you understand me, you know there are times when we go out and seem to become a part of this great Spirit

31

of the universe. Now, I seldom dare confess to this foolish (?) other life I keep within myself, but I couldn't live without it. And when I try to choke it out, I am the most miserable creature on earth."

Meanwhile Charles continued to work in Denison, but a year later, in 1879, he lost his job with the railroad. This came about over a friend who also worked in the freight office. When a visiting dignitary on the railroad came through Denison and in the presence of Charles made a false accusation against this friend, Charles's sense of fair play and loyalty sprang vigorously to his friend's defense. After a furious argument in which he told the official in no uncertain terms that the accusation was untrue, he was dismissed.

However, for some time before this, Charles had been thinking of leaving Denison. His being a clerk in a freight office had proved to be no more satisfying than his working in a bank or a grocery store had been. His mind was reaching out for something more. He was restless for new enterprises. He did not know just what it was that he wanted to do but he knew that he was not content with the sort of thing that he had found. Out in Colorado, gold and silver had been discovered and people were making fortunes over night, so out to Colorado went Charles Fillmore.

The first work that he secured there was as a mule-team driver. The work was extremely hazardous and required so much stamina that it is difficult to believe that a man with his physical handicap could have done it, but he did. The life of a mule-team driver was the crudest sort of life imaginable and exposed to all kinds of peril. At night, Charles slept under his wagon, the only shelter that he had against the mountain weather. The trails through the passes were scarcely trails at all, and it was sometimes all that he and the six mules he drove could do to get the wagonload of freight to its destination. "Once," he told a friend, "mules, wagon, and all went off the edge of a precipice." But he was able to fling himself from the wagon seat to safety.

One of the towns to which Charles drove his team was Gunnison, Colorado. This was a brand-new boom town when he went there in 1879. Buildings were going up on every side as fast as men and materials could be brought in to build them, and new mines were being discovered every day. Charles looked about him, discovered that Gunnison held much better prospects than driving a mule team over the mountain trails, and stayed. Here he learned to be an assayer and for the next two years engaged in the mining and the real-estate business. Some of the partners that Charles had at this time became important figures in the early development of Colorado.

With all his arduous activities, however, he did not forget the titian-haired schoolmistress in Clinton, Missouri, with whom he had so many ideas and interests in common. His correspondence with her continued and increased in ardor. In the spring of 1881, he took a trip back to Clinton, and there on March 29, in the little Methodist church, he and Myrtle were married. The Pages were well-liked in Clinton; Myrtle had many friends there; on the day of her marriage the little church was full.

Especially prominent among those who attended the wedding, were the pupils of the fourth-grade class that Myrtle had been teaching. They came in a body and sat in the front rows of the church. They had loved their teacher so much that some of them wept at the thought of losing her. Years later, one wrote to Unity, "We did not like Charles Fillmore then at all because he was taking our beloved teacher away from us." To this day letters are received at Unity School in which the writer proudly states, "I was one of the pupils of Myrtle Fillmore when she was a teacher. She was a wonderful teacher."

That night, Charles and his bride got on the train for Colorado and set out on the great adventure of their life together. Three weeks later, Myrtle was writing excitedly back to her sister:

"This is the first work my pen has done since I crossed the 'delectable mountains.' (Charles smiles at my name for the Continental Divide.)

"Of the three weeks since *the day,* one was spent on the road, one in resting, and this last one in taking in the situation. Gunnison, like all rapid growths, has not stopped for the extras. We all live in one dooryard fenced in by the mountains. Children and burros seem to have spontaneous growth here and belong to no one in particular but rove round over the unfenced wastes, creating a melody that makes one unconsciously shield his ears.

"Three weeks ago, we left you. I seem to have an unsorted jumble of mountains, snow and strange experiences in my mind to fill up this space between now and then. Our journey was delightful—I might fib a little to include our trip over the range. We remained at Poncha Springs, the end of the rails, two days, resting for our stagecoach trip. We left Poncha in a stagecoach at 7 in the morning (Monday). At 11 we had a layover at a ranch till 8 o'clock at night, waiting for the snow to freeze on the mountains. We had Mark Twain's typical driver, by name 'Jack.' When we were finally transferred to sleigh runners, such an experience as we had. There were eleven men, I the only lady.

"The roads or passes were in such fearful condition that the men were obliged to walk the greater part of the way up. It was grand. The moon hung above, the stars seemed to crown the higher peaks. Constant changes seemed taking place, mountain on mountain

34

piled on one side, water pouring down in cataracts among the pines far, far below. Again fields of snow would rise till the stars seemed to have them for background. On the other hand one misstep would have landed us hundreds of feet below where the snow was pierced by the dark needles of the pines.

"It was a very dangerous ride. We were two days and one night getting through and had to contrive all manner of ways to get through at all. We had several breakdowns. Sometimes the men had to use all their strength to steer the sled clear of some steep precipice.

"I enjoyed it the first day and night, it was all so new and sublime. We reached the summit at midnight. Old Mount Ouray lay at our right covered with snow and crowned with stars. The moon, that had seemed to us to set two or three times, rose again and gave us light. We commenced our descent. The roar of the waters that seemed to make the road their bed gave a new touch to the sublime.

"I wasn't aware at the time that I was doing anything remarkable by keeping cool during all this journey of hairbreadth escapes, but 'Jack' seemed to have conceived a great respect for me and laid aside all his adjectives and even compromised himself enough to enquire after the comfort of 'the lady.' I learned that I gained quite a reputation for bravery among the masculine part of our adventurers, who seemed to have discussed the subject and agreed 'that not one lady in a thousand would have shown such coolness and bravery.'

"We got into Gunnison about 6 o'clock Tuesday afternoon. The Halls had been worrying about us, having heard fearful reports of the treacherous mountain roads. And it was fortunate we got through when we did, for almost a week passed before the next coach got through."

The two adventurers did not stay in Gunnison long. Charles's enterprises there did not turn out favorably.

Pueblo, Colorado, was in the midst of a real-estate boom, so it was there that the enterprising young man took his bride.

When he arrived in Pueblo, Charles had exactly ten cents in his pocket but he had in his head and heart that which made up for his lack of money—he had courage, self-reliance, and intelligence. The first thing he did was go to a grocery store and order some groceries to be sent to the rooms where he had left Myrtle. Since he had no money, he told the grocer to send the order C.O.D.; but when the food was delivered and Myrtle had no money to pay for it, the delivery boy took it back. In the meantime, Charles had met a friend on the street and borrowed ten dollars with which he returned to the grocery store to pay for the groceries, giving the grocer the impression that he was outraged at having been embarrassed over such a trifling sum. He had observed that the grocer was not using all the space of the store and he talked the man into letting him use part of this space to open up a real-estate office for himself.

In the real-estate business in Pueblo, Charles Fillmore prospered. He was always a person of original ideas and he had ideas about how to sell real estate as he had about everything else. An early-day history of Kansas City was to write about him in regard to his real-estate activities there a few years later: "Fillmore & Company have always been governed by ideas original with themselves and have been eminently successful." Among the things he did in Pueblo to attract business—this was at a time before such methods of advertising became common—he fitted out a pony and wagon with huge signs made out of red letters on yellow cloth to advertise his business and drove the pony and wagon around the streets of Pueblo.

In Pueblo, two sons were born to the Fillmores, Lowell Page in 1882 and Waldo Rickert in 1884. Shortly after the birth of this second son, the real-estate boom ended. Charles's partner at that time was Charles Small, brother-in-law of Nona Brooks, who later founded Divine Science. The two men struggled along for a time to make a living, but their income grew less and less and at last they decided to break up the business.

Charles Fillmore was never one to be content with mediocre success. Since at the moment, he could see no place in Colorado where there was much prospect of immediate prosperity, he decided to move on. He paused briefly in Omaha, Nebraska, but in the winter of 1884 went on with his family to Kansas City and opened up a real-estate business there.

In 1884, there was no better spot in the nation than Kansas City for an enterprising real-estate operator. The town at the confluence of the Kaw and Missouri Rivers was just beginning to grow, and in the next four years an extraordinary real-estate boom was to take place there. The whole community was seized with the spirit of expansion. Real-estate values doubled, tripled, soared out of sight. Office buildings were sold, re-sold, and re-sold again in a single day, each time at a profit. When new subdivisions were opened up, people stood in line waiting for an opportunity to invest their money in a lot. It was a great period of growth. Downtown values rose and rocketed. Outlying farms sold at downtown prices. Population swelled. By 1887, the real-estate transactions of Kansas City were exceeding in value those of Chicago.

In the midst of this boom, Charles Fillmore brought his family and opened up his business. His experience in Pueblo had equipped him to move capably in conditions like these and, in a short time, he was more prosperous than he had ever been before. He acquired some land in the northeast section of the city and laid out a real-estate subdivision that he named Gladstone Heights, the name it still bears.

Charles Fillmore was a shrewd businessman. He had abundant energy and original ideas and he put them to work for him. He bought and sold, and sold and bought, and he made money. Once he even sold the building in which he had his offices and made $10,000 on the deal. In a short time, he had accumulated a nice sum and had played a part in the development of Kansas City. To this day, some of the streets of that city still bear the names he gave them, among them Myrtle Avenue, which he named for his wife, and Norton Avenue, which he named for his brother.

During this time, Charles continued his interests in mining. He was a partner in a silver mine outside Silverton, Colorado, and one summer took his wife and oldest son there, leaving Rickert with "Grandma" Fillmore in Kansas City. For three months, Charles and Myrtle and Lowell lived in a tent high up on Red Mountain, with some crude furnishings that they had managed to contrive and one or two items that they had brought in on the backs of burros. Nearly every night, even in mid-summer, snow would fall and cover the tent. In the morning, they would beat the snow off the tent. It would melt as the sun rose in the heavens, but the next night everything might be covered by snow again. The boy, Lowell, played about the camp, and all three of them roamed among the mountains while Charles prospected for silver. The simple life and healthful mountain air must have been especially beneficial to Myrtle, who had been suffering from tuberculosis. The family was able to remain there for only a few months, for although at first it had appeared that the mine was going to be a rich one, the vein of silver failed unexpectedly, and in the fall the three went back to Kansas City.

A period of depression now set in in the affairs of the Fillmores. The failure of the mine was followed shortly by the collapse of the real-estate boom in Kansas City. Charles and his family were left with no financial resources at all and were actually in debt. In the meantime, Myrtle underwent a spell of severe sickness. From her earliest childhood, she had been taught to think of herself as an invalid. In her early years, tuberculosis that she had been brought up to fear had developed in her, and in Clinton she had also contracted malaria. In the mountains, her condition had improved, but now, when the family was having its hardest financial struggle, the tuberculosis returned more virulently than ever.

At that time, Myrtle had great faith in medicine, and tried all sorts of medical remedies. Her son Lowell recalls that the medicine cabinet was always full to overflowing with pills and nostrums with which she was continually dosing herself and all the other members of the family. But doctors told her that if she remained in Kansas City she would probably have only a short time to live; there was nothing that they could do for her.

The Fillmores considered returning to Colorado. There seemed to be many reasons why they should make such a move. The mountain climate might alleviate Myrtle's condition. They had many friends in Colorado. Charles had excellent business connections there. It would be easy for him to re-establish himself. Yet in spite of all these reasons, they stayed in Kansas City. For at this time, Charles Fillmore had an unusual experience.

"I had," he wrote, "a strange dream. An unseen voice said, 'Follow me.' I was led up and down the hilly

39

streets of Kansas City and my attention called to lo-
calities I was familiar with. The Presence stopped and
said: 'You will remember having had a dream some
years ago in which you were shown this city and told
you had a work to do here. Now you are being reminded
of that dream and also informed that the invisible
power that has located you will continue to be with you
and aid you in the appointed work.' When I awoke, I
remembered that I had had such a dream and forgotten
it."

Charles Fillmore had always been interested in religion,
though his approach to it was an unorthodox one. He had
occasionally gone to church with his mother, who had been
reared as an Episcopalian and knew the litanies by heart.
But it was not from the standpoint of one who has been
reared in a doctrine from childhood and simply accepts it as
part of his life, that Charles approached religion. His approach was from a philosophic standpoint. Charles Fillmore
was born to yearn after God, to seek Him with all his heart.
He had an instinctive urge to seek out the meaning of life
and he was the kind of person who had to find the meaning
in his own soul. He had to find God for himself. Other
persons might point the way, others might give him hints
and clues, but he would have to test their ideas for himself
and prove them in his own mind and his own life before
they would have validity for him.

It is easy to imagine him as a young man poring by
candlelight over the lines of masters like Shakespeare and
Emerson, reading them over and over to himself, but he
was not passively accepting what they said. He had his own
thoughts about their conclusions. Charles Fillmore was innately religious in the highest sense. He was born with a
curious and capable mind that was intended to inquire into
Truth and into the nature of many things. His was a mind

on fire to know the Truth, and he sought for it everywhere. The statement that Myrtle Page had written of herself, "I am decidedly eclectic in my theology" could be even more aptly applied to Charles Fillmore. If he rejected anything, it was never arbitrarily; he had examined it, tested it, and decided that it was wanting in value. He studied many philosophies and religions.

As a young man, one of Charles's first interests had been spiritualism. He had a friend who felt that he had the powers of a medium, and the two of them had spent many evenings together in the dark facing each other silently across the table, their fingers pressed lightly against the table top to see if they could not waft it mysteriously into the air. Later Charles Fillmore repudiated spiritualism, but only after having thoroughly looked into it.

From the first issues of his magazine *Modern Thought,* we know that Charles Fillmore also had a knowledge of such teachings as Buddhism, Brahmanism, Theosophy, and Rosicrucianism, as well as of Christianity. In one of the early issues of the magazine, he wrote of himself and his wife: "We have taken more than forty courses (in metaphysical subjects), some of them costing as much as $100." Besides all this, he had a considerable understanding of the teachings of many Christian denominations.

Many years later, a Catholic friend was visiting him. The friend expressed a desire to go to Mass but had no means of getting to church from Charles's home. Charles said that he would take her. So they drove to the little Catholic church in Lee's Summit. Afterward Charles astonished his friend by explaining to her the symbolical meaning of every part of the ritual of the Mass.

Charles and Myrtle Fillmore sought Truth freely wherever they could find it. They were not limited in their beliefs and were no respecters of labels. Perhaps it is this early eclecticism of theirs that is responsible for Unity's love for and appreciation of all religious teachings. To this day when Unity School receives a letter from someone who wants to argue about his belief, there is still only one answer:

"We see the good in all religions and we want everyone to feel free to find the Truth for himself wherever he may be led to find it." Unity does not stress the differences, but the points of agreement.

At any rate, when Charles Fillmore had this dream in which he was shown that Kansas City was the town where he should remain because he had a work to do there, the dream did not fall on unfertile soil. Years of study and meditation and an inquiring and receptive mind had prepared him to obey the promptings of the Spirit in him.

At about this same time, another important event happened. A lecturer named Dr. E. B. Weeks came to Kansas City and delivered a series of talks on a subject that was then being referred to by such names as "New Thought," "Christian Science," "Divine Science." Doctor Weeks was sent to Kansas City from Chicago as a representative of the Illinois Metaphysical College, which had been founded shortly before by Emma Curtis Hopkins.

Emma Curtis Hopkins was one of the most unusual figures that has appeared in the whole metaphysical movement. Originally she had been associated with Mary Baker Eddy as an editor of the Christian Science Journal, but as the two had not seen eye to eye on many questions, Mrs. Hopkins left the Eddy School of Christian Science. From Boston, she went to Chicago where she founded a school of her own, which was probably the most influential school of its kind at the time. Emma Curtis Hopkins was a teacher of teachers. Many founders of metaphysical movements learned their fundamental principles from her. Besides Charles and Myrtle Fillmore there were: Charles and Josephine Barton, who published the magazine "The Life" in Kansas City and had a Truth movement of their own; Melinda Cramer, the first president of the International Divine Science Association; Dr. D. L. Sullivan, who taught Truth classes in St. Louis and Kansas City; Helen Wilmans, editor of "Wilmans Express" and a very influential New Thought teacher at the turn of the century; the popular writer, Ella Wheeler Wilcox; Paul Militz and Annie Rix Militz, who founded the Homes of Truth on the West Coast; Mrs. Bingham, who taught Nona Brooks, founder of the Divine Science movement in Denver; C. E. Burnell, a popular lecturer throughout the country for many years; H. Emilie Cady, who studied under Mrs. Hopkins on one of her trips to New York; and many others.

Charles and Myrtle Fillmore took several courses of study under Mrs. Hopkins and became her fast friends. They were among her favorite pupils. Later she was often to write to them when she had cases for healing that seemed unusually difficult to her, for she felt that the Fillmores had superior ability as healers. Once she wrote to them from New York: "Please, please keep on praying for John. I cannot believe that it is merely a coincidence that he always rallies at the times when I know you are praying for him." It was this teacher who had sent Doctor Weeks to Kansas City.

The Fillmores went to the lecture by Doctor Weeks out of curiosity and need. How closely their experience in finding Truth parallels the experience of thousands since then in finding Unity! For over and over the letters that come to Unity declare: "We had tried everything. We had given up hope. We did not know where to turn, and a friend told us about you, so now we are writing to you."

That was the way it was with Charles and Myrtle Fillmore. One evening, in the spring of 1886, when Myrtle was desperately sick and they did not know where to turn, they went to hear Doctor Weeks, who had been recommended by a friend who had been studying this "New Thought," as it was called and felt that Myrtle might get help from it for her physical condition. They did not know much about the subject but they had tried everything else that they knew about, and all had failed. They had reached the place where they were willing to try anything. Charles Fillmore came away from that lecture long ago feeling no different than when he had gone, but the woman who walked out of the hall on his arm was not the same woman who had entered it. A new, a different, a liberating, a transforming conviction was blazing in her heart and mind. Everyone has gone to hear a lecturer and had the experience of having some statement of the lecturer's stand out so vividly in his mind that he has felt, "He said that especially for me." That is the way it was with Myrtle Fillmore that night. As she walked from the hall, one statement repeated itself over and over in her mind:

"I am a child of God and therefore I do not inherit sickness."

Over and over in her mind the words tolled like a bell:

"I am a child of God and therefore I do not inherit sickness."

In one hour, Myrtle Fillmore's whole outlook toward herself and her life had been changed. Like a revelation— and surely such it was—this simple and divine idea that she was a beloved child of God and that God's will for her could only be perfect life and wholeness filled her mind and possessed her being. The old belief that she was an invalid, that she had been born to be an invalid, was as waters that have passed away. Even as she stepped out of the doors of the hall this new, this divine realization was working in her, not only in her mind but in the very cells of her body:

"I am a child of God and therefore I do not inherit sickness."

Like the little leaven that leavens the whole loaf, this thought was to work in her until it had made her every whit whole. It was not to let her go until through her thousands had been made whole, too. It was not to let her go until she and her husband, who was soon set afire with it too, had founded a faith that reached around the world and blessed the lives of millions who with her would joyously declare:

"I am a child of God and therefore I do not inherit sickness."

CHAPTER IV

The Founding of Unity

"In the Beginning"

A FEW YEARS LATER, Myrtle Fillmore wrote one of the most popular articles that have ever appeared in *Unity* magazine—the story of her healing.

"I have made what seems to me a discovery. I was fearfully sick; I had all the ills of mind and body that I could bear. Medicine and doctors ceased to give me relief, and I was in despair when I found practical Christianity. I took it up and I was healed. I did most of the healing myself, because I wanted the understanding for future use. This is how I made what I call my discovery.

"I was thinking about life. Life is everywhere—in worm and in man. 'Then why does not the life in the worm make a body like man's?' I asked. Then I thought, 'The worm has not as much sense as man.' Ah! intelligence, as well as life, is needed to make a body. Here is the key to my discovery. Life has to be guided by intelligence in making all forms. The same law works in my own body. Life is simply a form of energy, and has to be guided and directed in man's body by his intelligence. How do we communicate intelligence? By thinking and talking, of course. Then it flashed upon me that I might talk to the life in every part of my body and have it do just what I wanted. I began to teach my body and got marvelous results.

"I told the life in my liver that it was not torpid or inert, but full of vigor and energy. I told the life in my stomach that it was not weak or inefficient, but energetic, strong, and intelligent. I told the life in my ab-

47

domen that it was no longer infested with ignorant thoughts of disease, put there by myself and by doctors, but that it was all athrill with the sweet, pure, wholesome energy of God. I told my limbs that they were active and strong. I told my eyes that they did not see of themselves but that they expressed the sight of Spirit, and that they were drawing on an unlimited source. I told them that they were young eyes, clear, bright eyes, because the light of God shone right through them. I told my heart that the pure love of Jesus Christ flowed in and out through its beatings and that all the world felt its joyous pulsation.

"I went to all the life centers in my body and spoke words of Truth to them—words of strength and power. I asked their forgiveness for the foolish, ignorant course that I had pursued in the past, when I had condemned them and called them weak, inefficient, and diseased. I did not become discouraged at their being slow to wake up, but kept right on, both silently and aloud, declaring the words of Truth, until the organs responded. And neither did I forget to tell them that they were free, unlimited Spirit. I told them that they were no longer in bondage to the carnal mind; that they were not corruptible flesh, but centers of life and energy omnipresent.

"Then I asked the Father to forgive me for taking His life into my organism and there using it so meanly. I promised Him that I would never, never again retard the free flow of that life through my mind and my body by any false word or thought; that I would always bless it and encourage it with true thoughts and words in its wise work of building up my body temple; that I would use all diligence and wisdom in telling it just what I wanted it to do.

"I also saw that I was using the life of the Father in thinking thoughts and speaking words, and I became very watchful as to what I thought and said.

"I did not let any worried or anxious thoughts into

my mind and I stopped speaking gossipy, frivolous, petulant, angry words. I let a little prayer go up every hour that Jesus Christ would be with me and help me to think and speak only kind, loving, true words. I am sure that He is with me because I am so peaceful and happy now. . . .

"I want everybody to know about this beautiful, true law, and to use it. It is not a new discovery, but when you use it and get the fruits of health and harmony, it will seem new to you, and you will feel that it is your own discovery."

In two years, Myrtle Fillmore was no longer an invalid. Through her prayers she was made absolutely whole.

"I want everybody to know about this beautiful, true law, and to use it," she wrote; and as she became well many did come to know about it, for her neighbors who knew how sick she had been saw the change that was wrought in her and became curious as to what she had done to bring about such a miracle. People began to come to her for help.

The Fillmores did not deliberately set out to found an organization. Mrs. Fillmore set out first to find healing for herself. Having found that, she wanted to share her discovery with others and she found that people wanted that discovery as much as she wanted to give it to them. People, hearing of the change in her, came to her and asked her for help.

Mr. and Mrs. Fillmore were then living in a house on Wabash Avenue in Kansas City, and one of the first persons who came to Mrs. Fillmore was an Irishman, named Caskey, who lived across the street. He was crippled and had to walk on crutches. It took him a long while to comprehend the idea she was trying to get across to him, for at first he did not believe that he could be healed. The two

49

would discuss her ideas and pray together; then she would tell him to put down his crutches and walk. He would often say, "How do I know I can walk?" But again and again she would give him affirmative statements of prayer and have him repeat them with her. However much he might question and doubt, she knew that he could walk. So one day when she told him to put down his crutches and walk, that is what he did. He laid his crutches down and walked across the room. The crippled condition completely disappeared.

Years later, Lowell Fillmore was walking down a street when an express wagon drove up beside him and the driver jumped down from the street. "Aren't you Lowell Fillmore?" the man inquired and went on to say that he was Mr. Caskey whom Myrtle Fillmore had prayed with many years before.

Other persons began to hear about this woman on Wabash Avenue whose prayers were able to bring about healing.

The colored laundress of the Fillmores had asthma. To her too, Myrtle Fillmore suggested prayer, and in a short time she was whole again.

One day, an agent came to the door. He was selling picture frames and molding. He had a suitcase filled with samples of frames to show. Myrtle Fillmore was the kind of person who never turned people away. In a few minutes, he was inside the house and had his things spread out on the floor. Her son Lowell was there, and he crowded forward to see what the agent had.

"This is my little boy," said Mrs. Fillmore to the agent.

"Well," said the latter, "my little boy will never see again." This, of course, she immediately and vigorously denied. She told him of her own experience with prayer, and after a while he asked her if she would come to see his son who had advanced cataracts on both of his eyes.

When she first saw the boy, Myrtle Fillmore said his eyes looked as though they were covered with something like the white of an egg, but she was not dismayed by these appearances. She worked with him as she had with the others, helping him to realize that he was the beloved child of God, that God loved him, that God's will for him was perfect sight.

The second time she went to see him, he had improved so much that he could come to the door and let her in. In a short time, his eyes were completely healed.

Her fame spread beyond her own neighborhood. People from other parts of Kansas City and even from nearby towns started coming to ask for help. To all of them, she gave the same response: that they were God's beloved children and His will for them was health, that the healing power of the Christ was in them and they too could have perfect wholeness by realizing this Truth.

In the meantime, Charles Fillmore had come but slowly to accept what to his wife had been an instant and overwhelming revelation.

"Although I was a chronic invalid and seldom free from pain, the doctrine did not at first appeal to me," he later wrote.

To Myrtle Fillmore, the realization of the Truth about herself and her relationship to God had come suddenly, in a flash of inspiration. She had a new conviction, a burning flame of faith. Charles Fillmore had a different kind of mind. He thought of himself as a hard-headed businessman, and he had a family to provide for. He was reluctant to let his business friends and associates know that he was interested in a new-fangled religious idea such as his wife had. Still, because he was a practical man, when he saw the living, tangible results of his wife's faith, saw bodies rebuilt, crippled limbs renewed, and sight restored, he could not help but become interested.

Charles Fillmore was not one to take things on blind faith. He had an inquiring, scientific turn of mind. When he saw the healings that were coming as a result of his wife's prayers, he began to question why they should come to pass. If people were being healed, there was a reason for the healings. He commenced to inquire into this reason. He read all the books that he could find on the subject; and where courses were available, he took them. The Fillmores studied with Joseph Adams, who published a metaphysical journal called "The Truth Gleaner" in Chicago, when he came to Kansas City. They went to Chicago to study under Emma Curtis Hopkins.

At first, Mr. Fillmore was mentally disturbed by the many conflicting statements about Truth made by various teachers. He could not understand why there should be so many divisions and schools and such an assortment of opinions about an exact science. "The muddle was so deep," he wrote, "that for a time I was inclined to ridicule, yet I couldn't get away from the evidence of a great power back of the flood of contradictory statements."

There might be a doubt as to which one of the teachers was right, but as to the results there could be no doubt whatever. His eyes could see the results. About his doubt he wrote:

> "I noticed, however, that all the teachers and writers talked a great deal about the omnipresent, omniscient God, who is Spirit and accessible to everyone. I said to myself, 'In this babel I will go to headquarters. If I am Spirit and this God they talk so much about is Spirit, we can somehow communicate, or the whole thing is a fraud.'

"I then commenced sitting in the silence every night at a certain hour and tried to get in touch with God. There was no enthusiasm about it; no soul desire, but a cold calculating business method. I was there on time every night and tried in all conceivable ways to realize that my mind was in touch with the Supreme Mind.

"In this cold, intellectual attitude one can easily understand why I did not seem to get any conscious result, but I kept at it month after month, mentally affirming words that others told me would open the way, until it got to be a habit and I rather enjoyed it.

"However, a time came when I began to observe that I was having exceedingly realistic dreams. For months I paid no attention to them, my business at that time being of the earth earthy—buying and selling real estate. The first connection that I observed between the dreams and my affairs was after closing the purchase of a piece of property I remembered that I had dreamed about the whole transaction some months before.

"After that I watched my dreams closely and found that there was a wider intelligence manifesting in my sleep than I seemed to possess in the waking state, and it flashed over me one day that this was the mode of communication that had been established in response to my desire for information from headquarters. This has been kept up ever since with growing interest on my part, and I could fill a large book with my experiences. Everything which it is necessary for me to know is shown to me, and I have times without number been saved from false steps by this monitor. Again and again, I have had mapped out the future along certain lines for months and years ahead, and the prophecies have so far never failed, although I have sometimes misinterpreted the symbols which are used."

This was the way in which Charles Fillmore came into Truth. Being practical, he sought for something that was an exact science. Being a student, he studied under many teachers. In the end he turned, as must all who seek Truth, to the one true Source.

Perhaps it was because of this experience of his own that he was able to help so many others later on who, just as he had done, set out without much faith to go on— persons who could not accept simple statements simply because their intellect was continually raising doubts. To all these, Charles Fillmore could say because he had proved it by his own experience:

> " 'Belief *cometh* by hearing, and hearing by the word of Christ.' Set aside a time every day, a definite time, and pray whether you believe or not. Take a Truth statement and repeat it over and over. It does not matter that at first you do not believe it to be true. If you will persistently affirm Truth, even though you do not believe it at first, you will find that your prayers have power. Faith is like a mustard seed and it will grow. Pray, pray, and keep praying; affirm, and yet affirm once more. Your persistent prayers will succeed."

Charles Fillmore was never a half-way sort of person. Once he became convinced that he was on the track of Truth, he threw all his mind and energies into its pursuit.

Although he did not immediately discontinue his interests in real estate and mining, his absorption in spiritual matters became greater and greater. "My interest," he wrote, "became so pronounced that I neglected my real estate for the furtherance of what my commercial friends denounced as a fanatical delusion."

At this time, Charles Fillmore took the most important step of his life.

His income was the lowest it had been in years, for a depression was sweeping Kansas City, following the collapse of the real-estate boom. The needs of his family were the greatest they had ever been; in 1889 a third child, Royal, was born. His friends were all telling him that his interest in this spiritual idea was a fanatical delusion. He had had no great amount of formal schooling. He had had no experience whatever in the publishing business. Nevertheless, he decided to publish a magazine.

Charles Fillmore had come to believe in the ideas that he had first learned from his wife. He had studied them and probed them as thoroughly as he was able. He had come to see that they made sense and presented a scientific view of life. He had seen them actually demonstrated as true, for he had seen his wife and others healed by them. "I had applied the healing principle to my own case with gratifying results," he stated. "My chronic pains ceased. My hip healed and grew stronger, and my leg lengthened until in a few years I dispensed with the steel extension that I had worn since I was a child."

Here was something of which he could say without reservations, "This is Truth." Here was something that he could believe in, live by. A timid man might have held back, but Charles Fillmore had the courage of his convictions. Having found a faith, he dared to step out on that faith. Having found something that he felt was worth saying, he said it.

In April, 1889, he brought out the first issue of a magazine that he called *Modern Thought*. It contained sixteen pages. The pages, which were divided into three columns, were about the size of the pages today in *Weekly Unity*. Immediately under the name of the magazine appeared the motto: "Devoted to the Spiritualization of Humanity from an Independent Standpoint." The price was ten cents an issue, one dollar for a year's subscription. In the first number Charles wrote:

"The wave of spiritual thought that is sweeping over the land has created a demand in this vicinity for a publication devoted to its discussion and dissemination. With this object in view, *Modern Thought* had its birth. It is not the organ of any school of thought, but the mouthpiece of all honest souls earnestly seeking for spiritual light."

When Charles Fillmore began *Modern Thought,* he had come to the place where he was sure that there was a divine Principle and a science of Being; he had gained an insight into the nature of Truth; but he had not yet come to the place where he was certain as to the exact terms to be used in this science nor as to the exact approach that should be made to the Principle. He knew absolutely that the secret was hidden in himself, and it was clear from the first issue of *Modern Thought* that he thought of the Bible as a necessary guidebook to the Principle:

"Those who base their forms of worship on the Bible find that the fundamental truths are one. . . . Modern research . . . has thrown such additional light upon the original meaning of the Scriptures that it is not safe to assert positively that a single paragraph of the Bible is understood in our day as it was intended at the time it was written. It is the spirit, rather than the letter of the text, that those worship who have within them the true Christ principle."

In the first number, he had articles by Christian Scientists, Theosophists, and Spiritualists. He also had articles reprinted from occult magazines about the development of psychic power. The Modern Thought Publishing Company advertised and sold books of many kinds. In ensuing issues, there were articles about Buddhism and Brahmanism, and advertisements of periodicals and books written by all the schools of metaphysical thought. Charles Fillmore wrote:

"We want the address of every lecturer and healer working on the Spiritual plane. Our aim is to spread all over this great West the good which we know lies in wait for those who are willing to receive it. We are not wedded to any school of metaphysics, hence shall be strictly impartial in our efforts."

The pages of *Modern Thought* were at first not even limited to metaphysical subjects, but contained articles on cheaper houses for working men, the Haymarket riots that had just taken place in Chicago, and excerpts from such works as Edward Bellamy's "Looking Backward."

This state of affairs did not last long, however. *Modern Thought* soon began to take a direction of its own. Charles Fillmore wrote:

"*Modern Thought* aims to occupy a broad platform, and to sympathize with reform movements of every kind, as we believe them to be all parts of a great forward movement of humanity under the direction of unseen intelligence, but it is not our province to become identified with them all, nor to give them a hearing in these columns."

In a few months, he felt called on to write an editorial divorcing himself and his magazine from spiritualism. Still later he repudiated occultism.

The Fillmores were moving steadily toward the teaching of practical Christianity that is today put forth by Unity School. They were moving away from the isms and the cults that had influenced them. In a short time, they were to write:

"These columns are open to teachers and healers who advocate and practice Pure Mind Healing only. This does not mean magnetism, hypnotism, mesmerism, psychometry, palmistry, nor astrology. Not that we con-

57

demn any system, but . . . we find by experience that concentration is necessary to success and we wish to confine these pages to that specific doctrine, and Holy Ghost power, taught and demonstrated by Jesus Christ."

In April 1890, a year after the publication was begun, the name of the magazine was changed from *Modern Thought* to *Christian Science Thought*. Many persons have wondered if Unity was an offshoot of Christian Science. It was not.

Charles Fillmore declared in the second issue of *Modern Thought:*

> "We are asked if the ideas set forth in these columns are endorsed by Christian Science. In order that persons who are ignorant of the teachings of the new philosophy may not be misled by statements made herein, we deem it a duty to inform them that our views are not those of orthodox Christian Science.
>
> "There are, however, many schools of metaphysical thought sailing under the general name of Christian Science. The initial impetus to the movement is attributed to Mrs. Eddy, of Boston, the author of 'Science and Health.'
>
> "As yet we know but little about this hidden force that is so potent in bringing health and happiness to mankind. Like all powerful agents, it is unseen, and thus affords scope for a universe of theories as to its character and modes. Any and all claims of exact knowledge of its nature are beyond the horizon of proof. However, it is enough to know, in our present condition of ignorance of spiritual things, that such a power for good to the human race is within our grasp, and the momentous question is, through which of the present schools can the people best be reached. Experience proves that Christian Science has outstripped all its competitors in spreading the Truth. It is better organized and reaches the masses more readily than any other

movement for the benefit of mankind. A wise mechanic uses the tools at hand best adapted to the work he has to do. He may often wish that they were not quite so cumbersome, but he finds it expedient to throw his energy into the work, rather than stand around and growl at the tools. On this ground, we are partial to and endorse Christian Science, and *by Christian Science, we mean all the metaphysical schools.* It is doing a wonderful work for humanity; has spread with a rapidity that has no parallel in history. It has kindled a fire in the hearts of men that cannot be extinguished, and is silently finding its way into every household in the land."

In 1890, the name Christian Science was used not only by Mary Baker Eddy, but also by many others who were teaching what we today call Truth, or Christian metaphysics. The Fillmores were never students of Mary Baker Eddy. For their inspiration, the Fillmores had gone, as all great teachers do, direct to God. Mr. Fillmore had written, "In this babel I will go to headquarters." He and his wife never thought of Truth as something to be learned out of books alone or to be absorbed wholly from teachers. They thought of Truth as something that each individual must finally discover for himself in himself.

"The impression is abroad," he wrote, "that each school of Christian Science, mind-healing, mental science, metaphysical healing, psycho-therapeutics, mental cure, spiritual science, pneumatophony, old theology, ontology, Christian metaphysics, mental healing, and so forth, has the power to confer upon the individual certain distinctive qualities not possessed by the other schools, and which qualities are exclusive, God-given and attainable only at denominated shrines. . . .

"Many people are also blinded by a name, and labor under the delusion that because they have taken lessons in Christian Science they are in possession of truths that cannot be obtained anywhere in the universe, unless that magic name is over the door. . . . People of limited spiritual unfoldment are sticklers for names and creeds, and are thus worshipers of idols. . . . They quarrel over names, names, names, vapid, unmeaning names, that never were anything of themselves and do not even represent that which they allege to represent."

There had been a tendency for some time for the leaders of all metaphysical movements, even those most violently opposed to Mrs. Eddy, to include Christian Science in their name; thus it was after Mrs. Hopkins changed the name of her school from the Hopkins Metaphysical Institute to Christian Science Theological Seminary that the Fillmores changed the name of their magazine to *Christian Science Thought*. Neither Mrs. Hopkins nor the Fillmores meant, however, that they were teaching the doctrine taught by Mrs. Eddy. As Charles Fillmore wrote in 1890:

"To the public understanding the name *'Christian Science'* stands for all the different schools of metaphysics regardless of the technical differences by which their leaders try to distinguish them . . . we believe that the word Christ as applied to Truth represents an idea that has behind it the occult power necessary to make it the dominant tone in the great symphony which is to harmonize all the discords of earth."

The name *Christian Science Thought* was retained only for a year. Mrs. Eddy made it known that she felt that the name *Christian Science* was her exclusive property and if the Fillmores wanted to use it they must also follow her teaching. This, of course, they had never done. They and other independent metaphysical leaders decided that it was right that Mrs. Eddy should have exclusive use of the name and since their teaching was not the same as hers, they gave up the name. For the next few years, the magazine was called simply *Thought.* Charles Fillmore said many years later:

> "We have studied many isms, many cults. People of
> every religion under the sun claim that we either be-
> long to them or have borrowed the best part of our
> teaching from them. We have borrowed the best from
> all religions, that is the reason we are called Unity. . . .
> We studied Christian Science. [They studied all the re-
> ligions.] We were also classed as New Thought peo-
> ple, Mental Scientists, Theosophists, and so on, but
> none of these sufficiently emphasized the higher attri-
> butes of man, and we avoided any close affiliation with
> them . . . Unity is not a sect, not a separation of people
> into an exclusive group of know-it-alls. Unity is the
> Truth that is taught in all religions, simplified and sys-
> temized so that anyone can understand and apply it.
> Students of Unity do not find it necessary to sever their
> church affiliations. The church needs the vitalization
> that this renaissance of primitive Christianity gives it."

The name *Thought,* however, was also of brief duration.
The Fillmores were not satisfied with this name. It was too
general a term and did not exactly describe the movement.
As Charles Fillmore had said of *Modern Thought:*

> "The name was not an index to the principles which
> the paper advocated, and we were in consequence inun-
> dated by communications of a nature we did not care to
> publish, and were also constantly obliged to explain our
> exact place in the great maelstrom of modern thought."

In the spring of 1891, he and his wife and a few students
met together one evening to pray. As they were sitting in
the silence, suddenly into the mind of Charles Fillmore
flashed the name UNITY. At the moment, he had not even
been thinking about a name and when it came to him it
startled him.

"That's it!" he cried out. "UNITY!" he told the others.

61

"UNITY! that's the name for our work, the name we've been looking for."

Later he told friends the name came right out of the ether, just as the voice of Jesus was heard by Paul in the heavens. "No one else heard it, but it was as clear to me as though somebody had spoken to me."

Then and there the name UNITY was adopted. It was an apt and fortunate choice. The Fillmores had borrowed the best from all the religions. Where the churches had put the emphasis on controversial doctrinal points that had caused division after division in the Christian world, Charles and Myrtle Fillmore were to put their emphasis on the things that are practical, the things that apply to everyday thinking and living. They were not to found a new religion but were to work within the framework of existing religions and appeal to church members without causing them to divorce themselves from their church. They were to propound a teaching that people of all faiths could study and apply to their lives. They were to be a force for unity in the world. The movement that Charles and Myrtle Fillmore had founded was to live and grow under the name UNITY.

CHAPTER V

The Early Publications

"And He Saith unto Me, Write"

WHERE TODAY the Unity publications encircle the earth, in April 1889 there was only one small magazine of sixteen pages called *Modern Thought,* read by a handful of subscribers. At the end of its first year of publication, there were only a few hundred readers. Today there are more than six hundred workers employed in the production and circulation of the magazines. In 1889, all the work was done by one couple, Charles and Myrtle Fillmore. They had had no experience in the publishing business but they had an idea, an idea that they felt it was important for other persons to know about and they were willing to work as hard and as long as they had to in order to get this idea before the world.

To publish a magazine presenting new religious beliefs was not easy. To support his family, Charles Fillmore had to continue in the real-estate business and because his friends ridiculed his religious works as a fanatical delusion, he tried to keep as quiet as possible about the writing that he was doing in connection with the magazine. For many years, he wrote under the pen name of Leo Virgo. Myrtle Fillmore merely signed her articles M. or M.F.

Charles Fillmore published the magazine from his real-estate office in the old Journal Building, which has since been torn down but was then located at the northwest corner of Tenth and Walnut streets in downtown Kansas City. As the real-estate boom had collapsed in 1888 and business was slow, there was not at first much money to spend on the magazine. Mr. Fillmore had to buy a little at a time the paper on which it was printed, so that today the paper in the bound files of the early issues is not always uniform in color and texture. He would go down to the paper house, pick up the best value he could find for the money, and carry it home with him.

When the magazine was five months old, the office of *Modern Thought* was moved to the Deardorff Building at Eleventh and Main.

In the September-October issue a want ad was inserted:

> "WANTED—We want the services on this paper of a young man or woman who can set type and who is interested in the reforms we advocate. To such a one we will give a home and small wages. Address Chas. Fillmore, Kansas City, Mo., care of MODERN THOUGHT."

The ad produced no results, for in December Charles wrote:

> "We beg the pardon of our contributors and readers for the typographical and other errors that appear in these pages. Could they understand that everything but the typesetting is done by one man, and that that one man also labors in another field for the support of himself and family, they would certainly judge leniently. Our correspondents should also be charitable and not expect prompt responses to their letters—in fact they should consider themselves fortunate if they get any response whatever."

Charles and Myrtle Fillmore were indefatigable workers. There was no limit to the amount of time that the two were willing to spend to promote the teaching of Truth. In the early days, however, the magazine was not always published on time. Once it did not appear at all. Charles

Fillmore merely inserted this terse, self-explanatory notice:

> "Our typographical force is bent on taking a holiday, and the editor having urgent business of a personal nature, we have decided to omit the September number of *Modern Thought.*"

The typographical force at that time consisted of a Mr. Palmer who owned some fonts of type and set up the type for the magazine in his own home, where Mr. Fillmore would take the copy to him. It was several years before the Fillmores were able to buy type and hire their own typographers. This was some years after they had moved into the Hall Building at Ninth and Walnut streets, a move that was made in September 1890. Here Unity rented three rooms, in one of which type cases were later set up. In this room Harry Church, Unity's first hired printer, set the type for the magazine. He had a long brown beard, was a Seventh Day Adventist and a vegetarian.

On Saturdays, the oldest son Lowell Fillmore, who was then in grade school, would go down to the rooms in the Hall Building and help wrap the magazines, for which his father would pay him ten cents.

Charles and Myrtle Fillmore did almost all the work. They wrote most of the articles, edited all of them, wrote and addressed the letters, and took care of the details relating to the handling of subscriptions.

In 1898, the Unity offices were moved to a house on McGee Street. Here the composing room force consisted of two women.

When he finished high school, Lowell went to work for Unity at five dollars a week. He ran the small job press, printed the envelopes and stationery, and helped write letters. The forms were sent out to a printing shop where the magazines were printed. Lowell would hire an express wagon, carry the heavy forms down to it, careful not to spill one and "pie" a page, which would mean that it would have to be reset, lift them onto the wagon, inserting quilts between the forms so that they would not be damaged by the jolting ride, accompany them to the building where the printing shop was located, load them onto the elevator, and carry them into the pressroom. After the magazine was printed, he would take the type back to 1315 McGee. Also Lowell helped mail the printed magazines. The wrapping paper was bought in big sheets, and Lowell cut it into wrappers of the proper length with a hand cutter that was in the back room of the house.

"Many things," wrote Lowell Fillmore, describing the work as it was then carried on, "that I did as a part of the daily routine and that took me just a few minutes to do alone constitute whole departments now."

There were still only a few thousand subscribers. Copies of the mailing list were hung on an upstairs closet door. Every time a new subscription came in the name was written on the bottom of the list.

Only a small stock of bound books ready for sale was kept on hand. Lowell was the order-filling department. "I often found," he said, "that we were out of some of our books, which had been printed but not yet folded or bound. So I would go and get the printed sheets of paper, fold them by hand, get them ready, and stitch them and trim them. We kept our finished stock in the office in the front room; the printed pages, covers, binding materials, and other things in the pantry of the old house. I would wrap and stamp the books and take them to the post office. Often my brother Rick would take them in his pony cart. We had time out to mow the lawn and run errands."

Today in the Unity print shop there are twelve presses,

all many times larger than the original job press on McGee Street. There are linotype machines, folders, stitchers, and binders of the latest types. A force of a hundred men and women operates this array of machinery. A battery of graphotype and addressograph machines is needed to print the names and addresses of subscribers on the labels attached to the magazines. The files that contain these names and addresses fill a large room.

The spirit of unity has always activated the work. It pervades the vast buildings at Unity headquarters where hundreds of people carry on the work as it pervaded the small office in the Journal Building where there were only two people to do what had to be done.

In June 1891, after the name Unity had been selected by Charles Fillmore as the right name for the work, the first issue of *Unity* magazine appeared and the name of the company was changed to Unity Book Company. The magazine *Thought* also continued to be published, but *Unity* was started as a special organ for the Society of Silent Unity, which also began at that time. Most of the articles in it were reprinted from *Thought*.

With the first issue of *Unity* magazine, there appeared across the top of the first page the winged globe that through the years has been Unity's emblem and appears on all the Unity letterheads and literature. Charles Fillmore wrote that the idea of having such an emblem came to him as a revelation:

"It is an ancient Egyptian symbol; and I remember that when I first saw it I felt that I had had something to do with it in a previous incarnation. I went to a local artist by the name of Filleau and described to him what I wanted, and he made it under my directions.

"The winged globe or sun disk, as a religious symbol, had its earliest use in Egypt, but it is found in various forms in the religions of other races. It represents the relation existing between Spirit, soul, and body. Soul gives wings to the body. Spirit is the enveloping principle, like the atmosphere in which both soul and body exist, and from which they draw their original inspiration.

"The winged globe is also a symbol of the earth and its soul. The earth has soul, as have its products of every description. All exist in the ether, the *anima mundi*, the divine mother. When the people of the earth lift up their thoughts to God, the *Animus Dei* or directive Spirit, then the planet takes wings into a higher radiation of universal life—the mortal puts on immortality.

"As man develops spiritual consciousness, he attains the realization of the soul as the wings of the body. Back of the soul is Spirit, which quickens and energizes the soul; that is, gives the soul wings. Artists paint their angels with wings, representing in this way their freedom from physical fetters. But the soul does not have wings like a bird. The life activity of the soul is quickened by Spirit until it rises above the thoughts of matter and floats free in the ether or fourth dimension, which Jesus called the kingdom of the heavens."

Although the Fillmores knew little about the publishing business when they first entered it, they did their best to make *Unity* a magazine that was attractive to the public. They were not afraid to make changes. At first, *Unity* was an eight-page paper, the pages being about the size of those in the present *Weekly Unity*, with two columns of type on a page. After about a year, the number of pages was increased from eight to sixteen. This number was increased through the years. Also the size of the pages was changed. Most of the covers were white. Today color is used generously throughout the magazines published by Unity

School, but when in the 90's the Fillmores tried dressing up the magazine with a colored cover, some of the subscribers wrote in to say that any color except white was inappropriate for a magazine devoted to such a serious subject. For several years, the magazine was published twice a month, and the idea was advanced of making it a weekly. However, Charles Fillmore decided that there were not enough subscribers to warrant a weekly. In 1895, *Thought* and *Unity* were consolidated. By 1898, *Unity* had become a monthly periodical of approximately the size it is today.

One of the outstanding features of the early issues of *Unity* was the advertisements. Sometimes one fourth of the space was given over to advertising. They were not commercial ads. Of these Charles Fillmore had written:

"Do not send us commercial advertisements. This is not a trade publication, and we do not desire to cultivate the cupidity of our readers beyond its present capacity. The world is now stark mad with the money-making thought—it is the most formidable disease we have to heal. Should we give up our pages to descriptions of schemes that will increase this crazy whirl, so potent in paralyzing brain and nerves? We had as well commend the advantages of live arc light and trolley wires as conducive to the health of those who will lay hold of them."

The advertisements were those of healers and other metaphysical publications. Although most of them were simple announcements, some of them made sensational claims.

The June 1894 issue of *Unity* printed this notice:

"To maintain the religious dignity of the doctrine we advocate, we must hold to the pivotal thought that it is a spiritual ministry, and not a new system of healing. . . . The tendency on the part of healers is to give curing too much prominence, and thus the world comes to regard the divine doctrine of Jesus Christ as merely a new departure in materia medica. This feature became so prominent in the advertising columns of *Thought* and *Unity,* and it was so rapidly increasing, that we were compelled to call a halt. We never object to printing the dignified announcements of those who trust to the Spirit of God to do that which is needful for the people whom the Father may draw to them; but we do have qualms of conscience when we give place to alluring bids for healing patronage that smack loudly of patent medicine methods.

"Realizing that by so doing we can raise the standard of the doctrine we advocate, we have decided to discontinue display advertisements, and in their stead print regularly a 'Teachers and Healers Directory.' There will be no specific charge made for the carrying of names in this directory. We leave the compensation to the Spirit of justice working through each one. We want to co-operate with all true, honest, faithful Christian workers and will do any right thing to further the cause. We are one with you in advocating the doctrine of Jesus Christ, and the only title we need is 'Christian Teachers and Healers.' Let us be true to this modest yet dignified title, and impress upon our patients that it is their spiritual welfare that concerns us first, last, and always—that when this is made right the desirable things of the external shall be added."

Even after this announcement, ads crept into the magazines. The Fillmores had numerous friends in the metaphysical movement, friends with whom they had taken classes and attended conventions. These friends wanted to advertise, and it was hard to turn them down. The Fillmores were friendly, and as Truth students they had learned to respect individuality. No matter how much they disagreed with the methods of their friends, they continued to be

70

friendly. It was several years before they were able to reduce the ads to a simple list of the names and addresses of Truth teachers, printed at the back of the magazine.

The Fillmores continually struggled against turning their organization into a commercial venture. For this reason, they changed the name of the Unity Book Company to the Unity Tract Society, by which name the organization was known until it was incorporated in 1914 together with the Society of Silent Unity as Unity School of Christianity. (This organization, which is today located near Lee's Summit, Mo., conducts all the Unity publishing activities as well as the ministry of Silent Unity. It supervises the work of independent Unity centers throughout the world and distributes free literature through Silent-70. Unity School is sometimes confused with the Unity Society of Practical Christianity, which was incorporated in 1903 and conducts the local Unity work in Kansas City from Unity Temple, which was completed on the Country Club Plaza in 1950. Charles and Myrtle Fillmore were the leaders of both organizations; although with the growth of Unity the two aspects of the work were separated, they remain very closely allied, as does Unity School with all other Unity centers.)

"We have changed the name," wrote Mr. Fillmore, "to relieve the Publication Department of the appearance of a commercial venture. The dollar tag has been so persistently hung onto this movement in its various departments that it has become known to the public at large as a new system of therapeutics, with the usual financial appendix, instead of a religion. That people may more fully understand that there is no element of financial gain in our Publication Department we purposely adopted the word 'tract,' which is a synonym of religious literature issued without the idea of gain. *This is not a business but a ministry.*"

71

It was indeed a ministry that the Fillmores conducted. Despite the fact that they were having a constant struggle to find the finances to keep publishing *Unity* and take care of their family, Myrtle Fillmore felt that they could be of still further service than they were. At the very beginning of the Unity movement, she had had a vision. It had seemed to her that she was one of a vast congregation of people, many of whom were children. The children were completely undisciplined; in great confusion they were pushing and squirming through the crowd. As she watched them, the thought came to her that they needed someone to look after them. "Who will take care of the children?" she asked.

Even as she asked the question, it seemed to her as though a tremendous force took hold of her and impelled her to the front of the throng. As she was thus thrust forward, a voice spoke to her and said: "You are to take care of the children; this is your work."

Then she awoke; but the vision remained. As soon as she was able, she began a Sunday school that met before the regular Sunday meetings of the Unity Society, and commenced the magazine *Wee Wisdom*. In August 1893, the first number, a small, eight-page paper, was published.

The publication of *Wee Wisdom* brought new financial problems to the struggling couple. The subscription price was only fifty cents a year, far less than necessary to pay the cost of publication, and the subscribers were few.

"The fact is," wrote Mrs. Fillmore in 1895, "that this little paper costs us more than we get for it, and during the past two years the cash outlay over and above the income has been about seven hundred dollars, not allowing anything for editorial services. It has been a debatable question whether to discontinue its publication, raise the subscription price, or cut its size. We are daily reminded by appreciative letters that it is doing a good work among the little ones, so we dismissed the idea of discontinuing its publication. It was not deemed wise to raise the price, so the one thing is to reduce its expense until it shall at least pay printing bills. The subscription list is steadily increasing, and just as soon as the income is sufficient, the former size will again be issued."

Most persons faced with getting out a magazine that cost more than it brought in would have discontinued publishing it; but Myrtle Fillmore was not in the business of publishing magazines, she was in the business of helping people and serving God.

Several times she had to reduce the size of the magazine. For a short time, it was combined with *Unity*. Once it was sent automatically with a subscription for *Unity*, being treated as a sort of bonus. Nevertheless, the little magazine continued to be published. "You are to take care of the children; this is your work," she had been told.

Today *Wee Wisdom* is the oldest children's magazine in America, and it goes into almost two hundred thousand homes. It is published in Braille for blind children and sent to them free of charge whenever Unity is made aware of a need for it.

The statement, "This little paper costs us more than we get for it," has been true throughout its history, but this has never deterred Unity from publishing it.

Myrtle Fillmore was the editor of the magazine for almost thirty years and contributed many stories and poems to its pages. As a result of her vision as to the purpose of the magazine, *Wee Wisdom* has always presented the Unity idea and expressed a positive Christian philosophy of life, but it has kept its material so free from "preaching" that

73

the majority of parents, teachers, and children do not even class it as a religious publication.

Only one book by Myrtle Fillmore was published during her lifetime. This was *Wee Wisdom's Way*, a story about children. This story originally appeared as a serial in *Wee Wisdom*, its initial installment appearing in the first number of the magazine in August 1893. Not only the children but grownups wrote in to comment on the simple language in which it presented metaphysical ideas. Brought forth as a book, it proved to be one of the most popular of the early day publications of Unity.

As Myrtle wrote the story, she would read it to her oldest son Lowell. When he would tell her, "Boys don't say it that way," she would rewrite it. Years later in a letter to a friend she wrote of the book:

> "I'll send you the little book that I wrote when the boys were little. The healings were all true, the characters, of course, fictitious. Trixie really was my own little girl-self. I loved to keep a journal. Some people love this little story. Lowell, my eldest son, who was my critic, almost cried when I told him I had finished the story, and said, 'O Mama, please write more, nobody can tell it like Aunt Joy or write like Trixie.' "

Sometimes Myrtle Fillmore turned the publication of *Wee Wisdom* over to her sons Lowell, Rickert, and Royal. Usually the boys, who referred to themselves as "Wee editors," would edit the August birthday issue. When they were in charge, all the material in the magazine was provided by *Wee Wisdom* readers.

Nowhere has Unity's wish to maintain a nonsectarian spirit been so clearly displayed as in *Wee Wisdom*. From the beginning, Unity School published the magazine with one purpose in view: to meet the needs of children. It has

refused to use the magazine to advance Unity as a movement. The connection of Unity School with it has always
been kept in the background. A worker at Unity once told
about a neighbor of hers who expressed antipathy toward
Unity School and all its works. Yet one day, the worker
discovered that this neighbor's children were readers of
Wee Wisdom. Unity had so submerged its own connection
with the magazine that the neighbor was not even aware
that Unity was the publisher.

The most popular single item ever published by Unity
School first appeared in *Wee Wisdom*. This is *The Prayer
of Faith,* by Hannah More Kohaus:

> God is my help in every need;
> God does my every hunger feed;
> God walks beside me, guides my way
> Through every moment of the day.
>
> I now am wise, I now am true,
> Patient, kind, and loving, too.
> All things I am, can do, and be,
> Through Christ, the Truth that is in me.
>
> God is my health, I can't be sick;
> God is my strength, unfailing, quick;
> God is my all; I know no fear,
> Since God and love and Truth are here.

For years, this prayer-poem has been circulated on cards
and in booklets and in the Unity periodicals. Today millions
of people are familiar with its message. Adults and children
write to Unity School to tell how during some crisis of their
lives they clung to one of the lines of this poem and found
it a life line—their "help in every need."

Because of the faith of Myrtle Fillmore, thousands of
children have learned to think of God as their help when
they have things to meet in their life. They have learned to

meet life courageously. They have learned to pray. They have learned to value honesty and kindness and co-operation. They are better, stronger, happier children; and they grow to be better, stronger, happier adults.

How much Myrtle Fillmore's insistence on taking care of the children has influenced the Unity movement was shown when work on Unity Temple, the present home of the Unity Society of Practical Christianity on the Country Club Plaza in Kansas City, was begun in the 1940's. As construction proceeded, it became apparent that the entire building could not be completed at one time as it was going to cost over a million dollars. This was an immense sum of money for an organization to raise that had no wealthy backers but depended for its income on small contributions. It was finally decided to build only part of the building and wait before finishing the rest. It was not the Sunday-school rooms but the sanctuary that was left unfinished.

The vision of the Fillmores found expression in many ways. It was not only through the things that they themselves wrote and said and did that they accomplished good. From the beginning of the movement, they showed a talent for calling forth the talent of others.

Among those whom they inspired to write about Truth was a doctor by the name of H. Emilie Cady. She had been a teacher in a little school in Dryden, New York, but had left to study medicine and had been a practicing physician in New York City for several years before the Fillmores heard of her. A little book that she had written fell into Myrtle Fillmore's hands. From that time, Doctor Cady was to have a tremendous influence on the Unity movement although she never visited Unity School and the Fillmores never saw her until 1926 when they met her in New York.

76

The title of the booklet that Myrtle Fillmore found and was impressed by is "Finding the Christ in Ourselves." Mrs. Fillmore passed it on to her husband to read, and he also was impressed by it, so they wrote to Doctor Cady and asked her permission to print and distribute the article in booklet form. They also asked her for contributions to their magazines. In the January 1892 number of *Unity,* the first article by H. Emilie Cady, "Neither Do I Condemn Thee" appeared. In ensuing numbers, there were a number of articles written by her, as well as some personal letters to the Fillmores. In August 1894 she wrote:

"My heart leaped within me when I read some time ago in your answer to a correspondent: 'We do not need to battle for the right or for Truth. We do not need to resist evil. There is a higher way; just be still and know,' and so forth.

"I was so glad to have that thought given to the hundreds of persons who maintain that they must resist evil in order to overcome it. 'This is the victory that hath overcome the world, *even* our faith,' and faith does not need to strive or battle.

"And then all my soul blessed you when you said, 'We will no longer print ads or personal puffs.' Will not Spirit do its own advertising if trusted? If Spirit desires to heal through me, does not the same Spirit live in those it would help through me, and will it not bring the supply and demand together if fully trusted? Surely.

"Oh, how the mortal needs this lesson of being willing to sink out of sight if only Spirit is manifest! How hard it is for this John the Baptist to say, 'He must increase, but I must decrease.' God does abundantly bless you for having taken the stand. Fear not. With great desire He has desired from the beginning to manifest Himself through you as your supply of money, without intervention of human hands outside of yourself. 'Faithful is he that calleth you, who will also do it.' "To me the same call came four years ago, and well have I known ever since that that is my work in the world: to prove to the multitudes that the God within them is their supply, and that it must come forth from within to each one, independently, as his very own supply. I know that we are free today from the law of poverty and want, and further, from the law of work-and-get-pay-for-it. We are freely justified by His grace (or free gifts). Let us stand if all the world turns the other way, for thereunto has He called us. . . .

"I am going to write again. May I send some little message through *Thought?*"

At the same time, the Fillmores printed a letter from a subscriber suggesting a simple course of lessons:

"There are some who are taking your paper for the first time and do not as yet even understand the principles of divine healing. Would you be so kind as to have one of your clearest writers, one who understands the principles, and the uninformed mind of a student, write an explanation of this grand Truth in very simple form and in simple, clear words. It would be a great help to some I know of. H. Emilie Cady or Mrs. Militz or Mrs. A. W. Mills, I am sure, would respond most gratefully if you would request them."

Following this suggestion, the Fillmores wrote to Doctor Cady and asked her if she would undertake such a task. At first, she was reluctant to do so. She explained to them that she was a practicing physician as well as a metaphysician and that because her practice kept her so busy she had little time for writing. Also she doubted her ability, but the Fillmores had no doubt. As a Unity booklet, *Finding the Christ in Ourselves* had been extremely popular with their readers, as it had been popular with them. They felt that this woman had the ability to present simply and clearly the fundamentals of the Jesus Christ teachings that they were endeavoring to propound in their magazine. They recognized in her a deep spiritual insight and they called forth from her, as they were to call from many others, the inspiration and talent that were innately hers. They persisted in asking her to attempt this work, for they knew how much it was needed by their readers. There was at that time no simple set of lessons that presented the principles that they were teaching.

In September 1894, this letter by Doctor Cady appeared in *Unity* as an announcement of the forthcoming series of lessons:

> *"Dear Mr. Fillmore:* Yours, asking me to write a consecutive course of lessons for *Unity,* received. These are the words given to me in reply: 'Now therefore go, and I will be with thy mouth, and teach thee what thou shalt speak.'
>
> "So there is nothing left for me to say but yes. I will send you the first one in time for the October *Unity* if you will let me know when it has to be in for that.
>
> "I shall not give any stilted or set form of lessons, but just the utter simplicity of the gospel in words that the wayfarer, 'though a fool,' may understand; for I believe that to be the need of the hour. Will this be satisfactory to you?"

The first lesson appeared the following month. It was titled "Statement of Being," now the first chapter of *Lessons in Truth.* In subsequent months, eleven other lessons were published. There had been other attempts to present some of the fundamental teachings in *Unity,* but they had never before caught on. These lessons caught the readers' interest as nothing else that had been published in the magazine.

The response to them was immediate and great. The people who read them felt that here was a simple expression of the ideas they were endeavoring to assimilate. Here was something they could understand. Here was something they could pass on to friends and neighbors that would explain their belief for them.

Mr. Fillmore decided to print the lessons in booklet form. Shortly after the last one appeared in the magazine, he issued three booklets, each containing four of the lessons. These booklets sold for twenty-five cents apiece, or all three for seventy-five cents.

It was several years before the lessons were printed in book form and appeared as *Lessons in Truth*, as we know it today, the most popular book ever published by Unity. It has been translated into nine languages, and a million copies of it have been sold. Back in 1894, when the aspiring editors of the humble magazine *Unity* asked the homeopathic physician in New York to prepare a series of simple lessons presenting the fundamentals of Truth, they did not foresee the multitudes who were to be led by *Lessons in Truth* to a source of healing for their bodies and a light for their minds; neither did they foresee how the little magazine that after five years of publication still had a circulation of only five thousand subscribers would some day be expanded into the battery of magazines that today flow into more than a million homes.

But diligently, faithfully, they wrote about Truth as they saw it and inspired others, like H. Emilie Cady, to do likewise; and month in, month out, with little thought of personal remuneration but with the divine urge to serve, they sent their words out to all who would read them. Today because of their steadfastness these words echo around the globe.

CHAPTER VI

Silent Unity

"Pray One for Another"

I N THE April 1890 number of the magazine *Thought,*
Myrtle Fillmore announced the opening of a new de-
partment that she called at first the Society of Silent
Help. She wrote:

"All over the land are persons yearning for Truth,
yet so dominated by the surrounding error that they find
it almost impossible, without a helping hand, to come
into harmony with the divine Spirit. To open a way
for those and to help them overcome their sins, ills,
and troubles is the object of the Society of Silent Help.
The wonderful success of absent healing demonstrates
that bodily presence is not necessary to those in spiritual
harmony. Jesus said: 'If two of you shall agree on earth
as touching anything that they shall ask, it shall be done
for them of my Father who is in heaven.' Those who
have had experience in asking understandingly know
that this is absolutely true.

"Hence a little band in this city have agreed to
meet in silent soul communion every night at 10 o'clock
all those who are in trouble, sickness, or poverty, and
who sincerely desire the help of the Good Father.

"Whoever will may join this society, the only requirement being that members shall sit in a quiet, retired place, if possible, at the hour of 10 o'clock every
night, and hold in silent thought, for not less than fifteen minutes, the words that shall be given each month
by the editor of this department. The difference in the
solar time between widely separated places will not materially interfere with the result, for to Spirit there is

81

neither time nor space, hence each member should sit
at 10 p. m. local time."

The words that were given to be held in silent thought
every night at 10 o'clock from April 15 to May 15, 1890,
were these:

"God is all goodness and everywhere present. He is
the loving Father, and I am His child and have all His
attributes of life, love, truth, and intelligence. In Him
is all health, strength, wisdom, and harmony, and as
His child all these become mine by a recognition of the
truth that *God is all*."

The little band that met in silent soul communion at
first consisted only of Mr. and Mrs. Fillmore and a few
friends and neighbors who had become interested. They
met every night at 10 o'clock in the Fillmore home to pray
together and to give a blessing to all who tuned in to them
in thought. Sometimes to open the meeting they sang a
hymn or two to get themselves into a spirit of worship,
then Charles or Myrtle led the others in affirmative prayer.

"Take with you words, and return unto Jehovah," said
the prophet Hosea. This is exactly what the first members
of the Society of Silent Help did. They became quiet and
meditated on the idea of God until the idea became a living
reality in their minds and hearts and they felt Him as a
living presence in themselves. When they had gained a
sense of oneness with Him, they affirmed that His goodness
was being brought forth in their minds, bodies, and affairs.
They made these affirmations for one another; they made
them for others who had asked them for special prayers. If
someone during the day had asked one of this little band
to pray for him, they all spoke his name and declared Truth
for him; that is, they affirmed his oneness with the goodness
of God, with health and love and wisdom and harmony and

any other blessing they felt he needed. All that they asked of the one for whom they prayed was that he join in silent prayer with them wherever he might be.

From the time that the Fillmores had started Unity, they had been praying each evening for those who came to them personally and asked for prayer. At this time, they enlarged the field of their service.

> "The Society of Silent Help," they wrote, "is open to everyone. If you are sick, troubled, or unhappy from any cause whatever, sit in the silence with us every night and for a short time forget all your external thoughts. Give yourself up to the Spirit within for but a little while, and we assure you your heart will be lighter at the end of thirty days, if not in less time."

In establishing the Society of Silent Help, the Fillmores took a great step forward. From the beginning, they had been teaching that God is omnipresent and suddenly they realized that if it were true that God is everywhere, that His power is everywhere and can be called into activity anywhere, it was not necessary for people to come to them for personal interviews in order to receive help. God's presence was not confined to the little room of their home where they prayed, or to their office; He was not something that only acted in their presence or when they spoke a word of Truth into the ear of someone sitting near them. God was omnipresence, God was everywhere, God was principle. The principle of God was not limited by space or time. The only limitation that there could possibly be was the limitation that existed in those who were attempting to work with the principle. "Whatsoever ye shall ask in prayer, believing," Jesus had said; and so they asked in prayer, believing. Like the Master at the tomb of Lazarus, they declared with perfect faith: "Father, I thank thee that thou

83

heardest me. And I knew that thou hearest me always."

Because they felt that God's will is always good, they had come to the conclusion that all that keeps man's blessings from him is his own thoughts, his own lack of faith. They realized that if men can get their thoughts right, change their attitude, their consciousness—as they called it—into one of receptivity, God's good flows into their lives.

They felt that there is power in united prayer, that when several persons with a high degree of faith in God's goodness join together in affirming Truth a channel is cleared, as it were, through which His blessings may flow forth more freely and abundantly. Therefore, they felt that the location of those for whom they prayed did not matter. Though miles might separate the persons concerned, if they were together in thought, they were together in the true sense of the word. If one person prays in a spirit of love and faith and lifts himself into oneness with God, then all who are attuned in thought with him are lifted into that oneness, no matter whether they are sitting side by side or are on opposite sides of the earth.

This was a great discovery by Charles and Myrtle Fillmore, that people did not have to live in Kansas City in order to commune with them in prayer. "And I, if I be lifted up from the earth," said Jesus, "will draw all *men* unto me." They could pray in the house on Elmwood Avenue in Kansas City or in their office downtown and if they could be lifted up in consciousness to an awareness of the Christ presence, all who prayed with them, no matter where they might be, would be lifted up into that same awareness. It was upon this idea that Silent Unity was founded and it is through this faith that Unity has grown.

At first, the department of Silent Help was supervised

by Mrs. Fillmore, but in a short time, as this department grew rapidly, both she and Mr. Fillmore were thoroughly engrossed in it.

There was something about the idea of the little band meeting together in silent soul communion every night at 10 o'clock to help all those who were in trouble, sickness, or poverty, wherever they might be throughout the land, that appealed to the imagination. People began at once to write for prayers. Mrs. Fillmore wrote:

> "This department is not intended for trained teachers, although many of them might be benefited by sitting in the silence each evening, but the object is to start into spiritual unfoldment those who are so situated that they cannot have personal teaching."

Charles and Myrtle Fillmore were in tune with their time. They knew that men had come to the place where they were seeking to find Truth within themselves. They knew that all over the earth there were people hungering for silent soul communion, people in need, people sick and troubled, people looking for God. They sensed that these people were not finding in the churches the help in their trouble or the communion in their loneliness that they desired. It was for these people that the Society of Silent Help was formed, and it was these people who stretched out their hands to the Fillmores for help through prayer. From the beginning, no charge has been made for this help. The Silent Unity ministry has always been conducted on the freewill offering plan.

In the May 1890 number of the magazine, Mrs. Fillmore wrote:

> "Although the Society of Silent Help [as an organization] has been in existence but thirty days, it has in that short time demonstrated its efficacy as a factor in

the new dispensation. Its potency in opening the way for the Spirit of truth will increase in proportion to its membership—purity and persistence of individual thought being always understood. At the end of one year, there ought to be at least five thousand people in this country alone who will give fifteen minutes each evening to the silent communion with the Spirit of God. With that number of earnest souls holding the thoughts of Truth, every member should be lifted above sickness, sorrow, and poverty."

From lonely farms and little villages, and from the loneliness of big cities, the letters began to come almost at once, from the people who were sick and the people who were unhappy and the people who were seeking the unfoldment of their own spiritual powers. In a short time, all over the land, people were sitting down at 10 p. m. and joining in silent soul communion with the little band in Kansas City. From thousands of isolated rooms, isolated no longer, voices were declaring longingly and prayerfully:

"God is all goodness and everywhere present. He is the loving Father, and I am His child and have all His attributes of life, love, truth, and intelligence. In Him is all health, strength, wisdom, and harmony, and as His child all these become mine by a recognition of the truth that God is all."

In May 1890, the hour of prayer was changed from 10 to 9 at night. "This change," wrote Mrs. Fillmore, "is made to accommodate a number of persons living in the country districts who have written us that they should like to become members but were prevented by the lateness of the hour of communion."

Each month in the magazine a new affirmation, or prayer, for the members of the Society to hold together in thought was printed. These were called "Class Thoughts." These were general statements like the first one printed above, but in a few years two "Class Thoughts" were printed each month, one to cover healing and one to cover prosperity. Today when a person writes to Silent Unity for help he almost always receives a prayer statement printed on a leaf or card, but for many years this was not the case. If a person wanted Silent Unity's help he wrote a letter to the Society and at the same time began to use whichever one of the "Class Thoughts" best fitted his need. The "Class Thoughts" printed in *Unity* were the only prayers that the members of Silent Unity used.

At one time, the "Class Thoughts" were printed on a sheet that could be taken out of the magazine so that the subscriber could carry it with him wherever he went. For a few years in the early 1900's, this sheet was colored red and became known as the "red leaf." Some of Unity's subscribers began to apply this leaf literally to various parts of their bodies that needed healing, like a kind of charm. Charles Fillmore wrote that the "red leaf" was of value not because of any mysterious physical virtue it possessed but only because the diligent use of the affirmative prayer printed on it might quicken the one who used it into a realization of his oneness with the healing life of God. Many of his students, however, went on applying the red leaf to their bodies, and Unity received hundreds of letters telling of good results obtained by this method.

In time, the "Class Thoughts" came to be supplemented by other affirmations composed by Silent Unity to meet specific needs of correspondents. Today there are hundreds of different affirmations, affirmations to fit every conceivable need.

In the beginning, the prayers of Silent Unity were almost exclusively concerned with the healing of physical

87

ailments, and later with financial supply. It was only after several years that people began to feel free to write about other things. Today, of the more than six hundred thousand requests for prayer that are received every year, although many are still concerned with a need for healing and prosperity, the majority of requests deal with emotional problems, problems involving human relationships.

In the beginning, there were no special prayers sent out and letters that were received in connection with the Society were not always answered. Myrtle Fillmore wrote:

> "In reply to the many letters to the editor of this department, we would say that our duties are such that we cannot personally answer each one, but that we do hold the writers in thought for what comes to us as their special needs. We are glad to hear from everyone who takes an interest in this society and every letter will be filed in the archives and become a part of our storehouse of good."

Today almost every letter is answered, and an affirmation especially fitted to the correspondent's need is sent. Also Silent Unity has prepared several hundred booklets that take up the various problems that people write about, and usually one of these is inclosed.

The new organization did not long have the name of "Society of Silent Help." In the spring of 1891, less than a year after the organization was formed, Charles Fillmore had his revelation that the new movement should be called "Unity," and the first *Unity* magazine was published in June of that year. It was published as an organ of the new Society, the name of which was now changed to "Society of Silent Unity," of which Charles and Myrtle Fillmore were listed as the central secretaries. As the Society of Silent Unity, it has been known ever since. Through the years, the name of Silent Unity has come to mean much to millions of persons (many of whom were not yet born in the spring of 1891 when the Fillmores gave it that name). It has come to be a symbol of love and service and help in time of trouble.

Most of those who have written to Silent Unity for help have never been in Kansas City. They have never talked with a Silent Unity worker. Yet to them the name Silent Unity stands for the "silent soul communion" of which the Fillmores spoke in the very first notice that appeared in the magazine about the formation of this new department. It stands for the outstretched hands of prayer, outstretched in love and service, outstretched in faith in God. It stands for help in every need, for healing for the sick and supply for the needy, joy for the down-in-spirit and freedom for those in bondage, companionship for those who are alone.

Relatively few who have turned to Silent Unity have ever visited Unity headquarters; but even if they have not, they know that there is today (as there was sixty years ago) a band of faithful workers praying with them, thinking of them, taking their needs to God in prayer each day. They know that if they should go to Unity headquarters, whatever the hour of the night or day, they would find someone in prayer, someone keeping the vigil of faith that began over sixty years ago. And they know that they do not need to go in person, they only need to go in thought, only need to turn in heart and mind to Silent Unity to find the "silent soul communion" that is their need.

The infinite potentialities of the idea of Silent Unity revealed themselves almost at once. From many places, numerous people not only wrote for prayers for themselves, they wrote that they were having some of their friends who were interested in spiritual matters meet with them at 9 o'clock at night and form another Society of Silent Unity. The Fillmores could see that Silent Unity, with little groups of persons in harmony of thought and purpose joining together all over the land to pray for themselves and for one another, might be developed into one of the most potent spiritual forces that had ever been created. They could see that in a short time they were going to have thousands praying together, uniting their spiritual effort in a common aim, and they could see that through this common effort a tremendous spiritual force was going to be unleashed. They could see how Silent Unity would grow into a great far-flung movement of mutual help.

"For where two or three are gathered together in my name, there am I in the midst of them," said Jesus.

In Silent Unity, there would be not two or three gathered together, but thousands. What immeasurable spiritual power must this united prayer release! In their magazine, the Fillmores wrote directions for forming Silent Unity Societies:

> "Start a society at once if you have but two persons to begin with. Do not seek numbers, but harmony in those who meet with you. Meet regularly every Tuesday night, and the Spirit will eventually draw to you those desired. Two persons in perfect harmony will do the work of the Spirit more effectually than a hundred in discord.
> "Begin with music and sing frequently during the entire time of the meeting. Immediately after each song, hold in the Silence for a moment some thought of Truth. You cannot overdo this feature of the meeting. It is always uplifting and harmonizing to hold in unison some high spiritual thought. 'Speech is silver, silence is golden.'
> "The early part of the evening may be passed in a general discussion of matters spiritual. When the clock

90

strikes nine, go into the silence and hold in consciousness a few moments: 'Be still, and know that I am God.'

"Then after music hold the class thought for the month, in unison, for a few moments. It is sometimes advisable to repeat it audibly, then silently, until the mental vibrations become harmonious. In holding these universal thoughts, let your consciousness go out and take in all the minds of men. Feel that you are talking to every soul in the universe and that all are listening to your call. This mental drill will center your thoughts, and those of you who are spiritually alive will sense the vibrations of Spirit. Then is the time to do effective work. Take up those you desire to help and hold them in thought by name separately.

"The only object and aim of this Society is to get people to listen to the 'still small voice' and know that God will lead them into all wisdom, health, and happiness if they will spend but a few moments each day in His company—the silent realm of Divine Mind. Rules are but temporary leading strings and must eventually all be put aside. 'Behold, the tabernacle of God is with men, and he will dwell with them, and they shall be his peoples, and God himself shall be with them, *and be their God*: and he shall wipe away every tear from their eyes; and death shall be no more; neither shall there be mourning, nor crying, nor pain any more: the first things are passed away.' "

All who desired to be identified with Silent Unity were invited to send in their names with a brief description of their troubles. No answer by letter was assured the writer, but he was assured that Silent Unity would respond in prayer. He could have a certificate of membership if he wanted one. If he wanted help for a friend, he could have that, but he had to promise to pray for the friend himself.

In a short time, the Fillmores decided that the nine o'clock prayer period was not enough and members were asked to sit in the silence not only in the evening but also from 12:15 to 12:45 p. m. and join in prayer at that time. Today people join in prayer with Silent Unity at all times of the day and night.

The day begins in Silent Unity at 8 o'clock in the morning with a prayer service based on the prayer that is given in *Daily Word* for that day. (This is done also in all other departments at Unity.) At 11 o'clock a record of the Lord's Prayer made by Charles Fillmore is broadcast from loudspeakers throughout the buildings. At this time, the Silent Unity workers who have established a high healing consciousness meet in the prayer room for a healing service based on the "Class Thoughts." Before a worker is permitted to take part in this healing meeting, he has been instructed in the principles of healing as taught by Unity School. Usually a worker has had about three years of service and instruction in Silent Unity before he takes part in the healing meeting.

At noon, there is another special period of prayer based on the Prosperity Thought. At two-thirty in the afternoon, the workers meet again to study and pray. Most of the workers go home at 5 o'clock, but a small group comes on and remains all night long. They conduct the nine o'clock prayer service, which is centered on the Healing Thought, answer telephone calls, and pray.

Every worker who handles a letter from a correspondent, even if he is only filing it, gives it his blessing. Every half hour of the day, a worker goes into the prayer room alone to pray. Today prayer is truly continuous in Silent Unity.

The growth of the organization was rapid. In 1891, Mr. Fillmore asked for Societies of Silent Unity to be formed "in every town, city, and hamlet in the land. No formal organization of any kind is necessary—no creed, no leader, no authority but God." In a short time, there were hundreds of these groups. In five years, more than six thousand memberships were issued. By 1903, there were ten thousand members; by 1906, fifteen thousand; today Silent Unity receives more than six hundred thousand requests for prayers each year.

For several years, Charles and Myrtle Fillmore did all the work in Silent Unity. They called themselves "central secretaries" and they handled all the letters themselves, though often unable to answer them all. Occasionally, when there were many letters that had to go unanswered, Myrtle Fillmore printed in the magazine a general letter to all the Silent Unity correspondents who had not been answered personally:

> *"Dear Friends:* Your loving words make us strong and glad. We never tire of them. The inspiration of them goes with us through all of our work. They shine out to us from shadows that sometimes seem. They refresh and bless us. God measure to you again increasingly.
>
> "No less dear to us is your sacred confidence, dear hearts, who believe yourselves overshadowed by sorrow and disease. God loves you! We would rather be able to speak the word that hurls you from these mountains of belief than charm all earth with our eloquence.
>
> "It is because so many ask for words of help and comfort that we have not been able to make our pen fly fast enough to get round to each. Our thoughts are not so slow. You have all, each and every one, been held in strong and loving Truth by us."

It was several years before the Fillmores were able to hire someone to help them with the Silent Unity correspondence. By the early 1900's, they had a half dozen helpers working with them to answer the letters from Silent Unity correspondents. About one hundred letters a day were coming to the department, and Charles Fillmore was prophesying that the time would come when there would be twenty-four workers in Silent Unity.

To one looking back from the present when there are about one hundred and twenty workers in Silent Unity, that may not seem like much of a prophecy, but at the time it took courage and faith to make the statement, and to those who were working with him it seemed like a grand leap of the imagination.

At that time, the work was conducted on the third floor of the new building that Unity had built at 913 Tracy. Here at the top of a narrow stairway, Silent Unity had its prayer room into which no one was permitted to enter save those who through years of silent meditation and consecration to the Christ ideals had unfolded spiritually to the place where they maintained themselves in a high consciousness of faith in God. Here the requests for prayer were brought, and here the members of Silent Unity met each day to take those requests to God in prayer.

The workers of Silent Unity have always claimed that they have no special power that is not also latent in everyone else. "It is not I, but the Father within me, he doeth the works." When they meet in the prayer room, this statement is always in front of them. It is printed at the top of the lists of names that they take into the room. But those who take part in the healing meetings have consecrated themselves to the service of God and their fellow men through years of preparation in prayer and obedience to the teachings of Jesus. To this day, Silent Unity workers feel that their prayer room is a sacred place, a place apart, a place that like the "secret place of the Most High" within themselves is to be kept inviolate and consecrated. Few persons outside of the members of Silent Unity are ever admitted to this room.

From the beginning, the prayers of Silent Unity produced results. In one of the first issues of *Unity* magazine, there were two letters from correspondents. The first was from a woman in Dundee, Illinois, who wrote:

"My husband, a strong, healthy man of two hundred pounds, got out of bed perfectly well to all appearance, after a good night's sleep. All at once, he grew blind and fell forward. The fall awoke me, and I hastened to him. He was trying to arise, and I helped him onto the bed.

"Oh, the looks of him would have scared me a few months ago. The pulse was gone, and the heart's action was imperceptible. I said not a word but quietly lay down beside him, and burying my head in the pillow to shut out the terrible seeming, I mentally affirmed 'Life, life, eternal life,' over and over again. I said, 'God is in that heart, and its action is perfect.' I said it with all my might and soul.

"Soon the heart resumed its action, the body became warm, and he slept, oh, so sweetly in those loving arms of healing mercy. I want to sing praises to God all the time.

"I will just say that my husband was able to be about and do some work the same day."

And the other was from a Kansas City doctor, who said:

"Last Tuesday night, I was watching at the bedside of an apparently dying woman. I had exhausted every resource. She was surely passing away, when I thought of Silent Unity. I prayed that I might have your help in saving my patient. It was about 9 o'clock, and I knew you were in session, so I shut my eyes and asked that the Spirit of truth might be poured out upon the dying woman.

"Instantly the room seemed ablaze with a bright

light, and I saw a stream of what seemed a luminous ether poured upon my patient. I saw it just as plainly as I could the sunlight coming through a window. Just how long it lasted, I do not know. When I opened my eyes, I found the woman sleeping. In about half an hour, she awoke greatly improved. Again she went to sleep. The next morning, I was satisfied she would live. Yesterday she started on a long journey.

"It was to me the tangible evidence of an invisible healing principle of which our medical science is still quite ignorant. I can only say it must have been the power of God."

At first, the Fillmores were reluctant to print testimonials, but in succeeding issues under a column with the heading "Apples of Gold in Pictures of Silver" were printed stories of the healing of many diseases. Through the years that Silent Unity has prayed with those who turned to God for help, the magazines published by Unity have contained letters testifying to the healing of almost every known physical ailment, including cancer, tuberculosis, blindness, deafness, insanity, arthritis, and so forth. There have been letters from those who found through Silent Unity new faith in life after they had come to the place where they had decided to make an end of it. There have been letters testifying to the gaining of freedom from bondage to habits and false states of mind of many years' standing. There have been letters that have told how families have adjusted their lives and grown out of chaos and bitterness into harmony and happiness. There have been letters that have related seemingly miraculous openings of employment and income where before failure had appeared to be certain. There have been letters proving over and over thousands of times that with God all things are possible.

When they were the central secretaries of Silent Unity,

Charles and Myrtle Fillmore were close to those who worked there. Every day, Mrs. Fillmore went from desk to desk among the workers, bringing encouragement and words of cheer, perhaps leaving some small gift that she wished to share with the worker. Mr. Fillmore sat at his desk at the head of the department. When a worker had some particularly difficult letter to answer that he was not sure of, he took it to Charles Fillmore and received advice and inspiration. Together these two led the healing meetings and taught most of the classes in Silent Unity that prepared the workers to conduct the ministry aright. They were the mind and heart of Silent Unity. Their prayers were at the core of it. Their ideas were the inspiration for it.

Today the spirit of these two still moves through the Silent Unity work. The same spirit of devotion to the healing ministry of the Christ burns in the hearts and minds of those who serve there. Letters that go out declare as reassuringly as ever the truths discovered by Charles and Myrtle Fillmore: that God is life, that God is love, and that His life and love are accessible through prayer to heal, to prosper, and to bless.

This year all over the earth, from city and village and farm more than six hundred thousand people will call on Silent Unity for spiritual help, more than six hundred thousand people will find a faith that they would not have found had it not been that sixty years ago in Kansas City a man and woman named Charles and Myrtle Fillmore "agreed to meet in silent soul communion . . . all those who are in trouble, sickness and poverty, and who sincerely desire the help of the good Father."

CHAPTER VII

First Years of the Ministry

"Pastors and Teachers"

ONE OF THE great needs of the Fillmores was a suitable place in which to conduct their ministry. The first office in the Journal Building, where Mr. Fillmore had conducted his mining and real-estate business, proved almost at once to be unsatisfactory, and he moved to the Deardorff Building, where several other persons who were interested in the metaphysical movement had their offices. Here, with the help of some of these friends, he was able to establish a circulating library of books on metaphysics.

Visitors who were interested in any phase of the metaphysical movement were invited to drop into the offices regardless of what school of thought they might represent.

A few months later, the Fillmores moved their offices again, this time to the fifth floor of the Hall Building, on the corner of Ninth and Walnut Streets. The Fillmore boys loved these rooms because from the windows they could look "way down" to the street, and across the street was a fire station. A parking lot is now located on the site of this building.

This move turned out to be a fortunate one, not only because of the more commodious quarters, but shortly after the move the Deardorff Building burned to the ground. Several of Mr. Fillmore's friends who had remained there lost all the records of their work. One of them, Dr. J. S. Thacher, inserted a notice in *Thought* asking those who had been his patients to communicate with him again because he had lost even their names.

The offices in the Hall Building consisted of a double room with a kind of archway connecting them. Meetings were held in the east half of this room. The Knights of Pythias hall in the same building was used for Sunday services.

Mr. Fillmore was not the only speaker at the meetings. Often some friend of the Fillmores who was active in the work was the speaker, or some lecturer on metaphysics who was passing through town was asked to conduct the meeting. At one time, on Sunday evenings, a course of lectures known as the "No Name Series" was given, the subject being announced ahead of time but the name of the speaker being kept secret. The Fillmores were not working to gain personal acclaim. They did not believe that they had sole title to Truth or sole access to it. They believed that each person had in him the potentialities of a son of God and they put their belief into practice by letting various persons who felt that they had something worth saying deliver addresses. Several persons who had taken classes under Emma Curtis Hopkins took charge of the "No Name" meetings.

Emma Curtis Hopkins came to Kansas City several times and taught a series of classes. Tall, slender, and good-looking, wearing a big picture hat while she spoke, she was a dynamic and eloquent teacher. Eighty-seven students attended one of her classes, the largest Truth class in Kansas City up to that time. When she came to Kansas City, arrangements were made so that students coming from a distance could find room and board in the same house with her. The times spent with Mrs. Hopkins were joyous times for the Fillmores, for they found with her and with the students that surrounded her the meeting of minds that as much as any other thing is conducive to happiness in human affairs.

In 1890, the Fillmores went to Chicago to attend a class review at Mrs. Hopkins' school. Both of them made speeches. There were over one hundred and twenty of Mrs. Hopkins' students and graduates assembled at the seminary, and for ten days they threw themselves into classwork, prayer meetings, and joyous visits with others who spoke their language.

When they returned home to Kansas City, Mrs. Fillmore wrote a letter describing the visit to Chicago:

> "There are so many things I wanted to tell you about our Chicago experiences. I got my black dress made up so that it is very stylish and becoming with velvet sleeves and collar and the front of the waist is velvet. The Rays fixed me up a velvet hat out of that velvet of your bonnet; they furnished a wing and trim. There were lots of beautiful dresses there but one didn't think much about such things.
>
> "Of course we met all those whose names are so familiar in the literature: Ida Nichols, Nellie Anderson, Julia Twinchester, and so forth. A finer set of people I never met.
>
> "We were fortunate enough to have a room under Mrs. Hopkins' roof. She is just lovely to be with. There were over a hundred at the Review and all ate at her tables. It was the happiest, most harmonious family meeting on earth—for that's what it seemed—everything seemed as free and natural as air.
>
> "You can see from the program how we spent most of our time. Tuesday was a day off, for they were getting the seminary ready for ordination services. Charles and I wandered about the city, went to see 'Jerusalem on the Day of the Crucifixion.' It is a wonderful cyclorama.
>
> "At night, we all went over to C. I. Thacher's—and such a time! Never was there such a jolly, happy set.

He had cleared out the basement and decorated it and had an orchestra down there as a surprise to the party. You ought to have seen Doctor Gibbons and another old minister there trip the fantastic toe. Can you imagine John Thacher, Sullivan, and Barton dancing? I laughed till I could hardly stand up, it was so funny. As they closed about the fourth set, Charles rushed into the middle of the floor and shouted out: 'I can't dance, but I can sing. Let's sing "Praise God from Whom All Blessings Flow."' And before the orchestra could change its tune to fall in, the house trembled with the old hymn; it was powerfully sung. Then followed a healing song, and next the dancing was resumed. The musicians looked funny. I suppose they thought they had struck a lot of lunatics. A nice supper was served about 11 o'clock.

"Charles and I were invited out there the Sunday before to dinner. Doctor Gibbons, Miss Rix, Miss Austin, and several others were there. I tell you, they have an elegant home and things are served up in grand style. They keep three servants all the time, two girls and a man. And after our eight o'clock dinner, we sat in the silence, and such a wonderful power came over us. We gave it direction, and those we have heard from were wonderfully benefited. It was then our baby was named and blessed."

Up until this time, the youngest boy of the Fillmores had been known simply as "Baby," but at this party he was given the name "Royal."

The Fillmores knew many of the people who were interested in Truth, and whenever they could afford to, they went to gatherings of those friends. In the summer of 1893, they were back in Chicago, where a group of New Thoughters held a congress at the World's Columbian Exposition. In 1895, they were back once more for the meeting of the International Divine Science Association. There, much to their delight, it was voted that the 1896 congress should be held in Kansas City under the sponsorship of the Fillmores.

This congress opened on May 12, and the Fillmores were so busy seeing to the needs and the pleasures of their visiting friends that they did not even take time to publish the May 15 number of *Unity,* but omitted it and put out an extra large one on June 1. This was the first issue that contained small-sized pages such as in the present *Unity.* It gave an account of all the meetings.

The meetings were held in the Academy of Music, which was located on McGee Street, about four blocks from the Unity rooms, which were then in the Hall Building at Ninth and Walnut Streets.

The first act of most of those who attended the congress, when they got off the train at the Union Station, was to take a cable car to Ninth and Walnut Streets. The Fillmores had arranged for rooms and boarding places for most of them. Good room and board cost four dollars a week.

Most of the well-known metaphysical leaders and teachers in the United States were there. Many of those who did not attend sent papers that were read at the meetings.

This organization that met in Kansas City in 1896 later became the International New Thought Alliance, and during the next few years the Fillmores' association with this group was a close one, for they knew and liked many of the teachers personally. They attended several conventions, but in 1905 in an article in *Unity* Charles Fillmore wrote:

> "So far as the Unity Society of Practical Christianity is concerned, we must candidly say that its teachings are widely different from those of the majority of New Thought doctrines, and we do not feel at home in the average gathering under that name, although we try to harmonize with all Truth seekers."

Charles Fillmore went to the convention of the International New Thought Federation, as it was then called, held in Chicago in 1906, but he was disappointed. The turnout was small, and the ideas that he heard expressed were a far cry from the ones that he had come to hold. He wrote:

"I asked several people to give me a definition of New Thought, and they differed greatly in their concepts. It dawned on me that the name 'New Thought' had been appropriated by so many cults that had new theories to promulgate that it had ceased to express what I conceived to be absolute Truth. The New Thought Federation is attempting to carry this load of thought diversity, and I can see no success in it. There are too many lines of thought to harmonize. When I hear what to me is rank error set forth by New Thought speakers, I protest, and say, 'If this is New Thought, I must find a new name for my philosophy.' In the face of these facts, I have decided that I am no longer a New Thoughter. I have a standard of faith which is true and logical, and I must conform to it in my teaching without compromise. We call it Practical Christianity, and under this name we shall henceforth do our work."

From that time, Unity and the New Thought movement began to go their separate ways. The Fillmores continued to be personally friendly with many New Thought leaders, and many of them who came to Kansas City were invited to speak before the Unity Society, but there was no official connection between the two movements until 1919 when Unity returned to the International New Thought Alliance. At this time, Royal Fillmore and E. V. Ingraham, of the Unity staff, were added to the executive board of the Alliance.

Unity invited the I.N.T.A. to hold its congress in Kansas

City the next year. This invitation was accepted, and the meeting was like a joyous reunion. But this connection did not last long, for in 1922 Unity left the I.N.T.A. once more. It has never gone back.

Many times in his magazines, Charles Fillmore affirmed that he was not trying to establish another church or sect; he was trying to establish an educational institution where people of all faiths could study the laws of life as given by Jesus and learn how to apply them in order to establish a more abundant life for themselves.

For several years after the founding of Unity, the Sunday meetings were not held at 11 o'clock in the morning as they now are, but at 3 o'clock in the afternoon so that they would not conflict with regular church hours. Meetings were also held on Wednesday at 3 in the afternoon. Before the Sunday meeting, Myrtle Fillmore conducted a Sunday school for children.

The meetings were as much like discussions as they were like church services. There was singing and prayers much as there is in churches today. But for the main part of the service, copies of *Unity* were distributed to the members of the group, and the Bible text for that Sunday was read aloud, the leader reading the first verse and the congregation the next. After that, each verse was taken up in a general discussion directed by a leader who had been chosen by the group.

Myrtle Fillmore was in charge of the Wednesday afternoon services, but she usually appointed someone else to lead the silence and give a short talk. This was followed by a discussion of the subject in which everyone present participated.

When the Unity Society of Practical Christianity was incorporated July 29, 1903, it was incorporated not as a church but as a "society for scientific and educational purposes, viz: the study and demonstration of universal law." Such it still is.

Charles and Myrtle Fillmore never thought of themselves as preachers, but as teachers. They did not want a church, although from the beginning they envisioned suitable quarters from which they could carry on their work and to which people in need of healing and spiritual help could come.

In one of the first issues of *Modern Thought*, Charles Fillmore wrote that he thought that Jackson County was intended to be a great spiritual center:

> "That a peculiar psychic atmosphere prevails here is plain to everyone who has made any attainments whatever in the unfoldment of the spirit. Metaphysicians from all parts of the country have sensed it and observed its harmonious effect upon them. We have carefully noted their separate testimonies as to its quality, and they all agree that they have here a sense of freedom and peace which they do not feel elsewhere."

He quoted several spiritual leaders in corroboration of his intuition about Jackson County and Kansas City. He wrote that Emma Curtis Hopkins had intimated that the city might be the site of a great temple "which should heal of sin and sickness all who step over its threshold." From the beginning of their work, the Fillmores had a vision of such a temple, a great institution where Christian metaphysics would be taught.

Two rooms in an office building were unsatisfactory quarters for the spiritual work that Charles and Myrtle Fillmore were doing. As soon as they were able, they found a house that provided more room in which to do the things that they had to do to carry on the expanding Unity work.

In 1898, they moved into a house at 1315 McGee Street, which had belonged to a steamboat captain on the Missouri River. This house was situated a block from the cable car and was a homey place built of brick. It was set back from the street, with a steep terrace in the front, a large shady yard, and vine-covered porches on two sides. There were two large rooms with folding doors between them that could be used as offices during the week and for meetings on Sundays. Folding chairs were placed in these rooms to seat about one hundred. In two years, however, this room proved to be too small, and for the Sunday meetings a larger hall had to be rented.

On McGee Street, Unity entered a happy period. It was not rich in the world's goods, but the poverty of the first years had now been overcome and there was enough money coming in so that the Fillmores could live comfortably. The organization was not large but it was large enough to support the work and at the same time all the members could know one another. The Fillmores were gregarious people, they loved to have their friends around them; and on McGee Street, there were gay and wonderful social events. In the summertime, there was always the Fourth of July picnic in Budd Park, a small park in the northeast section of the city, to which the members of the Society could all go by cable car or horse and buggy. Usually about two hundred of them would turn out. Everybody brought his own lunch basket, and they would all eat together on tables under the trees. The lemonade and the ice cream were supplied by the Society.

At Christmas, the Sunday school had a Christmas tree with toys for the children and food for the grownups. On Valentine's Day and Easter and Thanksgiving and at other times throughout the year, there were parties and Charles

107

Fillmore was always in the center of them, cracking jokes and making quips, enjoying himself and helping everybody else to enjoy himself too. There were songs and recitations and games at the parties. Charles Fillmore loved to recite and he could usually be prevailed upon to render a poem.

It was one of these entertainments put on by the Unity Society that caused Mr. Fillmore to shave the beard that he wore in the early days of the movement. He had to deliver a dramatic monologue in which he dressed up as an Irish washerwoman who takes her little boy to get a job. Because his beard spoiled the effect, he shaved it off.

There was a warmth about the Fillmores that drew friends to them. When people came for help, the Fillmores took them into their hearts. They were even likely to take them into their home. It was not unusual for them to take into their home someone who had no means and had come to them for help. The boys often had to double up for sleeping because one of their beds was occupied by someone who had come to the Fillmores for help and remained to live with them for a while.

There was a kind of family feeling about Unity. The group was growing but it still remained a family. Even the meetings that the Fillmores held were more like family gatherings than they were like church services. If someone felt like disagreeing with something that Mr. Fillmore said, he got up on the floor and did so. Charles Fillmore liked to have people think for themselves and he invited discussion. Sometimes he turned the meeting over to others, and when they said something he did not agree with he, too, felt free to express his disagreement.

Once Elizabeth Towne, the editor of "Nautilus," the most popular Truth magazine of that time, was in town, and Charles invited her to speak at a Unity meeting. When she said something with which he disagreed, he shook his head as if to say "No."

"I see Charles Fillmore shaking his head," said the speaker, and forthwith challenged him to discuss the subject. He arose and refuted her point.

To the Fillmores for help, came not only the halt, the lame, and the blind, but also the peculiar, and as these were often the ones who demanded the floor, the meetings sometimes produced exciting surprises.

The joyous informality of his meetings delighted Charles Fillmore. He was a teacher and a thinker; he wanted people to think and to learn and to grow; and he found as he tirelessly and joyously presented his ideas of Truth that people were thinking about them and were growing. His movement grew too, for in a short time it was too large for 1315 McGee Street.

By 1900, a hall had to be rented for the Sunday meetings. This arrangement was not satisfactory, however. The Fillmores wanted a place where they could house all the activities of their growing movement under one roof. In 1902, Charles Fillmore suggested at a meeting of the Society that some committees be appointed to supervise the activities, among them a building committee. During the first year of its existence, this building committee was considered to be a joke. One of the Board members jokingly started the building fund by giving a one-cent piece. But the one-cent piece was not a joke to Charles Fillmore. He took it, gave thanks to God for it, and blessed it. To him, the building was on its way. The fund grew very slowly. By the end of 1903, there was only twenty-five cents in it. Nevertheless, in February 1903 in *Unity* magazine, Mr. Fillmore gave his subscribers "the privilege and opportunity of contributing any sum from ten cents to one thousand dollars, or more," towards the purchase of a site and the erection of a building. By 1905, only $601 had been raised. Some people might have lost faith and given up the project of a new building to house the work, but not Charles Fillmore. The financing of the Unity work had always been a matter that took a great deal of faith. As Charles Fillmore wrote: "The way has not always been strewn with roses . . ." Charles and Myrtle Fillmore had the required faith.

CHAPTER VIII

No Price on Their Prayers

"They Made a Covenant"

FROM THE BEGINNING, the Fillmores had traveled the road of faith. In 1888, when the bottom fell out of the real-estate boom, Charles Fillmore was left not with assets, but with debts that he had to pay off. When he began the publication of his magazine, he had only a few hundred subscribers. After several years, this had grown to a few thousand, many of whom were careless about paying for their subscription.

The Fillmores had set a nominal price of one dollar a year for a subscription to *Unity*. This price is still charged. They had to set a fixed price on the magazine in order to conform to postal regulations.

In January 1891, an editorial in the magazine under the heading, "There Is Only God," explained the attitude of the Fillmores about charging for the magazine:

> "This publication is turned over to and is now under the full and complete control of Principle. Personality has stepped aside in this, as it must in all matters connected with divine science.
>
> "The nominal subscription price is $1 a year, but this is nominal only, as the value of Truth cannot be measured in dollars and cents, and no specific charge can be made for it. 'With what measure ye mete, it shall be measured unto you,' is the law which is affirmed for this paper. It will trust that law, and go far and wide freely and generously to all who are seeking Truth.
>
> "All matters of whatsoever nature pertaining to

this publication are referred to Principle, and no personality is responsible for any action which is taken in its conduct."

In April 1891, when the Society of Silent Unity began, it was decided to make no fixed charge for its services, but to conduct the Society on the freewill offering plan. When Myrtle Fillmore had been healed, people immediately began to come to her for healing for themselves. She prayed for them and worked with them spiritually with no thought of charging for her services. She was on fire with the idea that had come to her; she wanted to help everyone who needed help. It never occurred to her to set a price on her services. Later when more and more people were coming to the Fillmores and rooms were rented downtown to carry on the healing work and publish the magazine, the Fillmores still did not charge for their prayers and time although most of the metaphysical teachers and healers of the time did charge a fixed price for their services. Sometimes this price was very high, but from the beginning, the Fillmores were not led to follow such examples.

It is probable that at first they did not think of metaphysics as a way of earning a living, for Mr. Fillmore continued in the real-estate business as his means of livelihood. They began to help people because they wanted to help them. As they continued in the work, however, they found that it was taking more and more of their time. Finally the demands people were making on them became so great and so continuous that they had no time for anything except the spiritual work they were doing; then the Fillmores realized that they had to be recompensed for their services. It would have been easy at this point to set a fixed charge for these services, or, because the recompense was very small, to get out of the work. Charles Fillmore said:

NO PRICE ON THEIR PRAYERS

"Encouraged by my wife, I persevered when almost at the point of failure; and if there comes any universal success out of this continuous effort, she should have the greater share of the credit. Had I been alone I would more than once have thrown the whole thing over and gone back to my real-estate business."

Little money came in. The Unity movement grew very slowly at first, and many who came for help had little to give. Mr. Fillmore has related that he was ready to relinquish the love offering idea. Mrs. Fillmore, however, prevailed on him to continue it. "This is the right way," she said, in effect, "and God will support us in it; He will carry us through to success if we will follow as He leads us." Jesus said: "He that followeth me shall not walk in the darkness, but shall have the light of life."

Although they did charge a nominal price for their magazine in order to conform to postal regulations, they continued to set no price on the ministry of Silent Unity, nor did they set a fixed charge for personal consultation.

"The Spirit," they wrote, "moves members to contribute, and it is observed that those who manifest gratefulness either in money, in love, or in works, are helped more rapidly than those who are neglectful."

The practice of making no fixed charge for classes or prayers is rigidly followed today. Unity firmly believes that if it trusts God and gives good service its needs will be met and it will not constantly have to ask for money or to charge high prices. This faith has been justified. Today Unity sends out at nominal prices millions of attractive, well-printed magazines and books; gives away thousands more; carries on a correspondence with hundreds of thousands of persons; broadcasts programs from fifty radio stations; and to do all this trusts in God as the source of supply!

113

In the first few years of the Unity work, the Fillmores must have needed money desperately. In 1889, they had written in their magazine that they could not even afford to hire a stenographer although they were so busy that they could not answer all the letters that came to them.

There were six in the family and little money to meet their needs. The first Christmas after they started the magazine, for instance, looked as if it might turn out to be a bare occasion.

> "I had about decided," wrote Mrs. Fillmore in a letter, "that we must go without buying the children Christmas presents when a neighbor we have been praying for walked in and gave me a check for five dollars and insisted upon my keeping it. I got Lowell a two-dollar tool chest, and Rick had commanded me to get him a drum and a gun. I got the drum, a sword, and a military hat, so he is fixed for marching. A friend gave each a book, so all fared well; and your box came Christmas Eve, and the boys were perfectly wild with delight. Lowell was very anxious to help be Santa Claus, so I let him get candy and help fill some little bags I made."

Charles Fillmore's mother was a tremendous asset during these lean years. Her ability with needle and thread kept them all in clothing. Often in these early years, Mr. Fillmore wore the clothing that people who came to his meetings gave him. One time, the boys wore suits that their grandmother had made for them out of old curtains.

Grandma Fillmore was a wonderful cook and could make the simplest foods taste delicious. Years later, when the Fillmores were more prosperous and entertained many friends who came to Unity headquarters, the letters from these visitors had as a recurring theme the excellence of Grandma's meals. Sometimes in the early days, she would buy a soupbone and beans and fix up a huge pot of soup.

114

This might be all they would have to eat for a whole week.

The Fillmores were not only hard pressed at home, but sometimes financial need visited the Unity rooms too. Once Charles Fillmore endorsed a note for a friend; the friend failed to meet the obligation, and Charles was asked to pay. The sheriff threatened to sell out the printing office, and for a time it looked as if the Unity work would come to a sudden end; but the Fillmores prayed and the threat was never carried out.

Another time, one of the men who had been associated with the Fillmores in the Unity work carried off most of the furniture from the rooms to start a work of his own. He claimed that this furniture was as much his as it was the Fillmores'. Instead of threatening him or suing to recover their possessions, the Fillmores went quietly on with their work, praying that they would have whatever they needed. They were able to carry on. In fact, when this man began a magazine of his own a few years later, the Fillmores had forgiven him—if they had ever had any anger against him—to such an extent that they ran a notice in *Thought*, praising him and telling about his new venture. Jesus said: "And whosoever shall compel thee to go one mile, go with him two." They were His disciples and they followed His instructions as well as they were able.

> "We shall make this," they wrote in January 1892, a time when they must have needed money badly, "a grand co-operative brotherhood in which the severe chilling methods of the financial world will have no part. How glorious it will be when we can send our books and pamphlets to all freely and have just enough coming in without solicitation to meet the expense from day to day. This is to be a feature of the new—the old must surely pass out with its 'pound of flesh.' "

When someone asked Charles Fillmore, "Will you send me a paper and wait until I can pay for it?" he replied, "Certainly we will. We know that it will bring to you before the year is out that which will pay for it many times over. . . . It will pay its own way. If you do not feel before the end of the year that it has much more than paid its own way, you need not send us a cent, and you will never be dunned. No bills are ever sent out from this office. If you do not pay your bill freely and gladly, it is evident that you have not had value received, hence you owe us nothing."

And a little later he wrote: "Many think that we are doing a work in which our compensation in some way comes out of the air. To dispossess this idea we find it necessary now and then to make very definite statements of our position on the compensation point, but we are striving to relieve this work of commercial bondage. We send no bills and hold no one in our debt. We only ask that the just and equitable law be established."

The entire Unity work has always been based on "the just and equitable law," "Give, and it shall be given unto you." In the beginning, the Fillmores set the standard that Unity follows today; they decided that they and their movement were to be dedicated to the Spirit of Truth, that the object of their existence was to be the service of God, not personal reward.

In 1942, while looking through some old papers, the librarian at Unity uncovered among papers of Myrtle Fillmore's a document in Mr. Fillmore's handwriting that had remained a secret of Charles and Myrtle Fillmore's for fifty years. The document had remained a secret, but the spirit of this covenant—as it has become known in Unity since its discovery—had shown itself time and time again in the half-century that had passed since the Fillmores had signed it on December 7, 1892, for it is the spirit that motivated their life and work. A facsimile of this covenant is given here:

Dedication and Covenant.

We, Charles Fillmore and Myrtle Fillmore, husband and wife, hereby dedicate ourselves, our time, our money, all we have and all we expect to have, to the Spirit of Truth, and through it, to the Society of Silent Unity.

It being understood and agreed that the Said Spirit of Truth shall render unto us an equivalent for this dedication, in peace of mind, health of body, wisdom, understanding, love and an abundant supply of all things necessary to meet every want without our making any of these things the object of our existence.

In the presence of the Conscious Mind of Christ Jesus, this 7th day of December A.D. 1892.

Charles Fillmore.
Myrtle Fillmore

The Fillmores held to their ideal. They were doing God's work. They were not doing it to enrich themselves; they were doing it because they believed in God and wanted to help others to find Him and His blessings. They wanted to do this work in a way that would enable them to help the most people, to help people when they were in need. They did not see how they could set a price on their work, for that might result in the exclusion of some of those who needed help most of all; and it was not they, but God, who did the work. Then, how could they put a price on God's work? Jesus helped those who came to Him freely and with no thought of charge. They could do no less. If they put a price on their work, it might be that the very time someone needed help most would be the time when he could not afford it. At the beginning of their work, they established the principle of no fixed charge for their prayers.

> "The work of this Society," they wrote of Silent Unity, "is wholly voluntary, and no fees or dues of any kind are imposed upon members. Those who have been helped through its ministrations, or those who feel that it is a worthy cause, contribute for its support as they are moved."

This principle has been adhered to in the Silent Unity work throughout its history.

In the early days, the financing of the Unity work was a continual struggle, but God could not have chosen people more ideally suited than the Fillmores to make that struggle. They believed what they taught. They believed that if they really sought the kingdom of God and His righteousness, the things they needed would be added to them. They did not doubt God's promises. When they made a covenant with Him, it was in complete expectation that the covenant would be fulfilled. They intended to do their part and they had perfect faith that God would do His.

The Fillmores taught that prosperity is governed by the same laws that govern physical health. They thought that if they could maintain themselves in a prosperity consciousness, an awareness of God as the source of their supply, prosperity could not fail to be theirs. If the money did not come in, it was not because God had failed; it was only because they had not maintained a high enough consciousness of their supply in Him, and they redoubled their efforts in prayer. They felt that their supply depended on their maintaining the right consciousness. "Only be strong and very courageous, to observe to do according to all the law . . . that thou mayest have good success."

The Unity work has always been conducted on this principle. For many years the workers in Silent Unity were compensated on a freewill offering basis. No fixed salaries were paid. It was up to each worker through prayer to maintain a consciousness of prosperity. Each one had his share in that responsibility. As the supply came in, it was divided among them accordingly.

The Fillmores were publishing a magazine for which they received only one dollar a year. Besides this, they were trying to issue a magazine for children that cost them much more to publish than they received from it. They were conducting meetings and holding private consultations with those who came to them personally. They were carrying on by means of letters a prayer service of silent communion that was being given to people all over this country and even in Europe. The only immediate source of their supply was voluntary contributions. Yet the Fillmores applied themselves to their ministry undaunted.

They promised, "We will send literature to anybody anywhere any time there is a possibility of benefit resulting to the recipient." That promise has been kept.

With nothing but the freewill offerings of friends to support their efforts, the Fillmores began to send their publications out to everyone who wrote and asked for them. By November 1894, they were writing:

119

"We hope our good friends and helpers will appreciate our position as regards the many appeals for free literature, and be sparing in their requests for free yearly subscriptions for their acquaintances. Our free list now costs us over ten dollars per week, and is growing very fast. We are not backed by a rich Bible society, and please remember that the dimes count fast into dollars where so many are looking for aid."

In 1910, The Silent-70 was organized, and through it Unity literature was sent free of charge to everyone who asked for it, some of whom at the moment were not in a position to pay. Soon a stream of Unity literature was going without charge to individuals and into libraries, prisons, hospitals, and other public institutions.

Many times the Fillmores must have wondered about the direction from which funds would come to carry on their work, but they never wondered about the source—God. Always they prayed. Always prayer worked. Always, however impossible it might appear to be, the funds materialized. They moved out of the little office in the Journal Building into a larger office in the Deardorff Building and they moved from it into still more commodious quarters in the Hall Building. From there they were able to move into the house on McGee Street. Still the work continued to grow. Still it needed more space. In the early 1900's, the Fillmores decided that the Unity movement was prosperous enough to justify them in thinking about buying property and erecting a building in which to conduct the work.

This was a goal set for the Unity Society. The penny with which the building fund began had grown by 1905 only to $601. Nevertheless, the Fillmores did not relinquish their goal. At 913 Tracy Avenue, the building committee found a lot and an eight-room house that were for sale.

This seemed an ideal place to buy. But the money to buy was not forthcoming.

At a meeting of the Board of Directors of the Unity Society of Practical Christianity several men pledged a hundred dollars apiece toward the purchase of the lot and the erection of a building. This was still far from enough. The Fillmores prayed and prayed, yet enough money did not appear. Then one evening, one of the members of the Board arose and announced quietly that he had decided to mortgage everything that he owned in order to provide Unity with the funds needed to buy the lot and begin the erection of a building.

He was not a rich man and he had a wife and four little children to provide for, but he had been attending the meetings for several years, and the Fillmores had inspired in him the same kind of faith that they had. He believed in their ideas and felt that it was important that those ideas be carried to as many people as possible.

His business associates tried to dissuade him from taking the step. To them Unity was not a good risk. But he was not to be dissuaded. Through him, Unity obtained the money needed. The house and lot at 913 Tracy Avenue were purchased. The plans for the new building were pushed ahead.

The man who had mortgaged his property did not lose one cent because he had been willing to stand behind Unity in its need and in a short time he was the owner of a much more successful business than he had had before. "Give, and it shall be given unto you; good measure, pressed down, shaken together, running over . . . For with what measure ye mete it shall be measured to you again."

In September 1905, the house was moved to the rear of the lot, and work was begun on a two-story brick building.

While Unity carried on its work from the house, the work on the building pressed forward. There were no funds on hand with which to complete it, but there was the faith of the Fillmores and of those who were associated with them.

By August 1906, over six thousand dollars had been received, and the rest of the money needed was contributed in the next few years.

On August 19, 1906, Unity students gathered from all over the country for a week of celebration, which was climaxed on Wednesday afternoon by the laying of the cornerstone of the new building. Several hundred persons, one of them from India, gathered to watch Mr. Fillmore lay the cornerstone, the inscription on which read: "Built upon the foundation of the apostles and prophets, Jesus Christ himself being the chief cornerstone." There was a choir and several soloists. Charles Fillmore made a short talk. A copy of the first number of *Thought*, of *Unity*, and of *Wee Wisdom*, the August 1906 *Unity* and *Wee Wisdom*, a copy of the convention program, a copy of the "Kansas City Post" containing a write-up of the new building, and a list of the names of contributors were placed in the cornerstone. Jennie Croft (one of the most faithful and versatile of the early Unity workers) tossed in a rose, and Charles Fillmore took a bouquet from his buttonhole and added it to the contents.

After the ceremony was finished, most of the group ate in Unity Inn, a vegetarian cafeteria that Unity had started for its workers. The Inn at that time was located in the house that had been moved to the rear of the lot. Inside were signs: "All the expenses of this house are met by the freewill offerings of its guests. 'Freely ye received, freely give.'" In keeping with Unity custom, the guests at that dedication ceremony paid for the dinner by freewill offerings.

On that August day in 1906, as Charles and Myrtle Fillmore stood in the new building, they must have felt that truly this was a reward of faith.

How ample the building must have looked to them then! It was forty by seventy feet, three stories high in front. The chapel would seat more than two hundred. The printing shop would handle the magazines. The reception room and offices were furnished in the latest style. There was a special healing room for the use of Silent Unity.

When the Fillmores had started the work seventeen years before, there was no beautiful new building to move into. There was a real-estate office in a downtown building —and their faith. They had started the work on faith; they had carried it on by faith. They had trusted in God as the source of their supply, and their trust had been justified. They had built this building and the work of which it was a physical representation, and except for the magazines, they had never made a fixed charge for the service they gave.

People had laughed at them; people had said it was impossible. Paying no attention, they had gone ahead—on faith. On this August day, they stood in the building faith had built, while around them milled a happy throng called together from all over the earth by the power of their faith.

They looked about them. They looked at the chapel, at their offices, at the printing shop, at the Silent Unity rooms and they knew that all this had been brought about because of their trust in God. As they stood there on that August day in 1906, it must have seemed to them like the culmination of their fondest dreams. Yet it was not a culmination. It was only a beginning.

CHAPTER IX

Growth and Expansion

"He Shall Build the Temple"

ALMOST AT ONCE, the building at 913 Tracy Avenue was too small. In less than four years, an even larger building was going up on the lot next door, at 917 Tracy Avenue. The September 22, 1910 issue of *Weekly Unity* reported:

"The Unity printing plant has been moved to its new quarters at 917 Tracy. . . .

"A new Optimus press, thirty-nine by fifty-five, has been added to the pressroom equipment, making it quite complete. . . . This number of *Weekly Unity* is the first piece of printing done in the new building."

The first number of *Weekly Unity*, with Lowell Fillmore as editor, appeared May 15, 1909. Unity School had taken another step forward. Years before, Charles Fillmore had thought about making *Unity* a weekly, but the idea had not seemed practical then.

The new magazine had grown out of the weekly bulletin that described the activities of the Unity Society of Practical Christianity in Kansas City. People in other parts of the country had expressed an interest in these activities, and it was decided to publish a magazine that would tell about them. *Unity* announced:

"*Weekly Unity*, containing all items of interest to the Society, reports, readings, and so forth, will be mailed to any address fifty-two times a year for one dollar."

The popularity of the new magazine increased rapidly,

and in the July 10, 1909 issue, the editor told his readers:
"We have one subscriber as far east as New York and one as far west as California, with a sprinkling over the intervening States."

Today there are more than two hundred thousand subscribers, living in many countries.

The new building proved to be no more adequate to contain the rapidly growing Unity work than the one at 913 Tracy had been. It had to be enlarged. The original three-story section of the building had been placed far back on the lot. Now a front section was added to this, and a fourth floor placed over all. The dedication of this enlarged structure took place at the stroke of midnight December 31, 1914. Declared *Weekly Unity:*

> "The opening of the Unity administration building was a great success. By 9 p. m., December 31, the Unity auditorium was full to overflowing. The Guild [a young people's group] had ready a multitude of talent with which to entertain the assembled guests. Near 10:30 the Unity Inn became a mecca for the hungry. Apples, sandwiches, cakes, cocoa, and cereal coffee were served to nearly four hundred people. By the time everyone had finished his refreshments, the new year was almost ready to be born. At the stroke of twelve the darkened administration building suddenly flashed into light; the front door swung open and the chimes began to ring."

This building, which was later enlarged twice more, was to house most of the activities of Unity School for the next thirty-four years. Its front, which with its massive white columns somewhat resembled a temple, became— much as today the Tower at the entrance of Unity Farm has become—a kind of symbol of the Unity movement. It is still pictured on the front of the prosperity banks.

The prosperity bank plan is one of Unity's most distinctive ideas. It was originated by the Fillmores in 1910.

Often those who wanted to buy Unity literature were persons of small means to whom a dollar, the price of a year's subscription, was a large sum of money. Also many of those who studied the literature liked to order subscriptions for the periodicals and buy books for their friends too. The prosperity bank plan was a convenient way of doing this.

Those who use the prosperity bank plan are provided with a small cardboard bank. The instructions are to drop a coin in the bank at a regular time each day for seven weeks and to concentrate on the statement printed on the bank. A typical statement reads:

"The Spirit of the Lord goes before me and my health, happiness, prosperity, and success are assured."

Bank users are expected to do their best at all times to feel that the statement expresses the truth about them, whatever appearances may indicate. His repeating the bank statement daily reminds the user that God is the source of his financial supply.

From the first, the bank plan was popular as a means of saving for subscriptions. Also users found it a convenient way to save for their offerings to the Unity work. The bank plan has been popular because through the years those who have used it have felt that they were truly helped and prospered by its use. There are many Unity students who are never without a prosperity bank.

It was fitting that a picture of the new Unity building should be printed on the bank, because it was prayers for prosperity that had built the Unity buildings and the whole Unity work.

Charles Fillmore felt that the main reason for the study

of Truth is to develop spiritual faculties. He wrote that people were too prone to think of Unity simply as a system of healing. He taught that it is not primarily a system of healing. He taught that it is not primarily a system of prosperity either. He taught that spiritual development should bring in its wake both healing and prosperity.

"Some religious teachers," wrote Mr. Fillmore, "have tried to make us believe that it is our Christian duty to be poor. But this is not the doctrine of Jesus." It was not the doctrine of Charles Fillmore either.

Charles Fillmore believed in praying for prosperity. Although he and his wife discovered Truth because they needed healing, they were soon stressing to their students that all people have the infinite resources of Spirit within themselves and they can be successful in all their worthy undertakings. One of the first popular articles that Charles Fillmore wrote was entitled, "Overcoming the Poverty Idea," which was reprinted several times in *Unity* magazine and finally issued as a pamphlet. Silent Unity was not very old before a special time each day—noon—was devoted to praying for prosperity for all who asked for prayers.

Whenever Unity School had a need for money or there was an important decision to be made, the first thing that the Fillmores always did when they called Unity leaders together for a conference was to say, "Let's pray about this matter." Often the whole conference, as they conducted it, turned out to be a prayer meeting. The Fillmores would not only take the matter to God themselves, but they asked everyone else present to speak words of prayer aloud. They believed in the power of affirmative prayer, and they practiced what they believed.

When there is a financial need to be met, the management of Unity School calls on Silent Unity to pray with it exactly as someone on the outside does, and Silent Unity takes up the needs of Unity School in prayer just as it does the needs of others.

Unity School does not have, as some institutions do, wealthy backers. Unity has been supported mainly by the modest offerings of countless persons who have been helped through its ministry. For the most part, it has been the "widow's mite" that has sustained Unity. The workers at Unity feel grateful for every offering that is sent in. They know that it is not the size of the gift but the love in the heart from which it comes that counts.

Even as late as 1910, it was not unusual for the total offering at a Sunday morning service of Unity Society to be no more than ten dollars. One time early in the history of Unity, a subscriber sent in one hundred dollars for a hundred-year subscription to *Unity*. It is hard to imagine the gratitude to God that the one hundred dollars evoked in the Unity office.

The Fillmores did not seek money for themselves, although they felt that it was their right, as it is the right of all the children of God, to have enough to meet their needs. But they sought support for Unity, and they believed implicitly that God would supply the needs of this organization. If they had not believed this, they would never have had the courage to go ahead. Often as they pressed forward, expanding their services, enlarging their magazines, building buildings, there was no apparent worldly source of needed finances. Had they always waited until the funds materialized to do the things they needed to do, they would have been able to do little. They took a step—praying all the while in faith—and the supply came to meet the need. "All things, whatsoever ye shall ask in prayer, believing, ye shall receive."

It has been in this way, praying and working, trusting in God for supply, that the various Unity buildings, one after another, have been built. And the need for more buildings has been continuous.

The building at 917 Tracy, even though it was enlarged, still proved to be too small. Behind it another building was erected to house the radio studio, heating plant, repair shop, and other departments. It was in this building that Charles and Myrtle Fillmore lived in the apartment that she dubbed "Gasoline Alley." Later another building was constructed alongside this one. Also, on the corner of Ninth and Tracy, Unity Inn, a vegetarian cafeteria that became one of the most popular eating places in Kansas City, was erected in 1920.

Finally Unity grew so large that it began to think of moving from Tracy Avenue. The center of population in Kansas City had shifted far to the south and the Unity Society of Practical Christianity needed a location that would be more convenient for those who attended its services. In 1928, it bought the lot on the Country Club Plaza where Unity Temple is now located. Unity School of Christianity, the sister organization, began to think about moving its activities to Unity Farm.

Today it is there, in some of the most beautiful office buildings in the country, in a setting so perfectly landscaped that it is becoming famous throughout the world, that Unity School is located. There almost six hundred workers carry on the work that Charles and Myrtle Fillmore began. There every year come hundreds of students to study and to learn the teachings the Fillmores first propounded more than half a century ago.

In the buildings on Tracy Avenue, there was not enough room nor were there the proper facilities for activities of a community nature. The Fillmores envisioned a place apart, a place where Unity workers and students could go out of the bustle of the world's affairs to pray, to work, to re-create themselves physically and spiritually. Unity workers have always been like a big family, liking to do things with and for one another. It was natural that the Fillmores should look for a place suitable for the activities of their "Unity family."

In 1919, shortly after Rickert Fillmore returned home from service in World War I, he and Lowell and their father began a search for such a place. One Sunday, they saw an ad in the paper that listed forty acres for sale a few miles southeast of Kansas City. They drove out to the place but when they arrived they found that it had been sold. The real-estate agent was still there and he asked them what they had in mind. They told him that they wanted a small place that was removed from city noises and confusion and at the same time not too far out for easy travel back and forth.

The real-estate agent replied: "I know just the place you want." He took them out to the location that is now Unity Farm and showed them fifty-eight acres that were for sale. The Fillmores liked it and made a down payment. On March 1, 1920, Unity Farm was born.

Slowly more and more acres have been added to the original fifty-eight until today Unity Farm comprises more than twelve hundred acres. When the first parcel was purchased, the nearest good road was several miles east of the property. Today U. S. Highway No. 50 goes by the main entrance to Unity Farm and another concrete highway, Colborn Road, runs through the Farm.

The first buildings constructed were of the English Cotswold type. Among them was The Arches, which was

131

built for Charles and Myrtle Fillmore about 1925. It stands near the farmhouse that was on the property when it was bought. After it was built, Mr. and Mrs. Fillmore would go out to The Arches on Thursday evening and stay overnight, going back to "Gasoline Alley" on Friday morning. Then on Sunday after the service was over, they would return to The Arches and stay until Monday morning.

Myrtle Fillmore called The Arches her dream house. Rickert Fillmore had built it for his mother exactly as she had dreamed of a house. Set in the middle of an apple orchard, with a high peaked roof of many gables and casement windows, the house was like one out of a fairy book. Myrtle Fillmore spent a great deal of time in it.

It had no kitchen, as she had wanted "a fairy home without kitchen or care." When the Fillmores were staying at The Arches they took their meals with Grandma Fillmore, who lived in the farmhouse just across the road.

> "Charles," wrote Myrtle to a friend, "is doing his best to get some sort of impromptu kitchen into our fairy home. But I say, 'Not while we have Grandmother's kitchen so close.' We have entertained, doing our share, I think, in the past; and I do wish the fairy home to remain as it is, filled with food for thought and inspiration and blessings, but not the kind that makes stacks of dishes to wash."

Grandma Fillmore was the center of the life on Unity Farm. Resourceful, generous, energetic, she had been born for such a role. Although, when the Fillmores began to spend time on the Farm, she was nearly ninety, she was still as capable of running a household as she had ever been. She was always happy and never seemed to run down. One of her friends once said of her: "She should have been sixteen years old all her life."

In her late nineties, she fell and broke her hip, but she re-fused to use a wheelchair. A wheelchair suggested "invalid" to her. That she never was. She had some rollers attached to a rocking chair and got about on that. Myrtle called this contraption "a roller skate motor."

"It is really a rocking chair with rollers," she described it to a friend, "like those on roller skates, and, my, how Grandmother does ride around on it. She 'motors' all over the house, and she's the engine, the gas, the chauffeur, and the backseat driver all combined in one."

The first office building finished on Unity Farm was the Silent Unity Building, which was designed in the Italian Renaissance style. It was completed in 1929.

In the summer of 1928, a great meeting of Unity leaders was held on Unity Farm to bless the buildings and to make plans for the future. A tent city was erected. There hundreds of Unity leaders, not only from the United States but from foreign countries, lived for eight jubilant days through rain and fair weather.

It turned out to be mostly rain, and of creature comforts there were few. When it rained hard the water streamed through the tents between the cots; the only available shower baths were in the unfinished Silent Unity Building; the only place to eat was in the chapel in this building, which had been converted into a cafeteria serving fifteen hundred meals each day. But everyone sloshed through the rain to the meetings with sunshiny spirits that the weather could not dampen. There was no criticism, no complaint. There was little comfort, but a lot of consecration.

Meetings were scheduled from 8 o'clock each morning until 10 o'clock at night. Sometimes there were several at the same hour, so that it was impossible for one to attend all the events. One person was heard to say that he was kept as busy as if he were at a three-ring circus. And at the center of the celebration, greeting their friends, taking part in the meetings, sharing the meals, joining in the prayers, were Charles and Myrtle Fillmore.

At one meeting, more than four hundred workers from headquarters on Tracy Avenue formed a procession, passing in front of the assembled leaders, singing hymns while they marched. On the last Sunday, the whole conference came to its climax with the dedication of the Silent Unity Building, which more than two thousand people attended. The leaders returned to their homes rejoicing in the vision of the expanding Unity work and of the building rising on Unity Farm to house it. The following spring, Silent Unity moved from Tracy Avenue to its new building on the Farm.

It was a triumphant moment for the Fillmores. It must have seemed to them then that one of their fondest hopes, the dream of a great spiritual center, was about to be realized. There were many years of prayer behind them, many years of trusting God for supply, many years of holding to their high purpose when there seemed little but their trust to hold to. But the lean years had changed into years of accelerating growth and prosperity. Not only had subscriptions to *Unity* and *Weekly Unity* and *Wee Wisdom* been soaring, but the last six years had seen three new magazines established: *The Christian Business Man* (later *Christian Business,* now *Good Business*), *Unity Daily Word* (now *Daily Word*), and *Youth* (later *Progress,* now *You.*) Subscriptions to these were pouring in. Silent Unity was growing. New centers were being opened in various cities. After almost half a century of strenuous spiritual effort, in that jubilant moment it may have looked as if Unity's prosperity was assured and Charles and Myrtle Fillmore could rest on their laurels.

But this was not to be. In the fall, the 1929 depression began. By 1930, Silent Unity was back on Tracy Avenue in Kansas City, and its building on Unity Farm stood empty.

In the 1930's, the Fillmores' vision of a great spiritual center on Unity Farm from which the Unity message would go out to all the world and to which students would come for spiritual instruction may have seemed to some almost a shattered dream. Unity has never had a large reserve fund. Its income has always consisted largely of offerings sent in day by day. Since it has followed exactly the instruction of Jesus, "Be not therefore anxious for the morrow," and has immediately employed in the expansion of the work whatever money it has received, it has not built up any surpluses.

In the 1930's, when great industrial empires with carefully hoarded reserves were going bankrupt, it might have seemed to an onlooker that an institution like Unity, that had no source of income except the literature that was sold for a nominal price and the freely-sent offerings of people who were not even members of the organization and whose only connection was often only that of a letter and a prayer, could not possibly survive. But the casual onlooker could not have perceived the real source of Unity's strength, for this was invisible; it was faith, the faith of the Unity workers, the faith of the Fillmores, the faith that had stood adamant in the beginning when there was almost no income at all; the faith that had stood adamant when the first small building on Tracy Avenue had to be built and there seemed to be no funds with which to build it; the faith that had been tested over and over throughout the years; the unalterable faith that God is the supply of those who trust Him. "Prove me now herewith, saith Jehovah of hosts, if I will not open you the windows of heaven, and pour you out a blessing, that there shall not be room enough *to receive it.*"

Now this faith triumphed as it has always triumphed; Unity not only weathered the depression but began to grow again. Although for ten years no further buildings were erected on the Farm, the Fillmores held steadfast to their vision of the Farm as the center of the work. In 1940, they began to build again.

Rickert Fillmore was in charge of this building program, and he quickly proved that he had in him the same spirit as his parents, a spirit ready to use that which is at hand, quick to see and utilize every natural advantage, and willing to strike out on new paths and try the untried.

Beauty and utility have gone hand in hand in the development of Unity Farm. The Amphitheater, for instance, is as lovely a thing of its kind as can be found in America. This is how it came into being:

"We needed a garage," said Rickert Fillmore, "to take care of the cars of the workers at the Farm. There was a steep bluff at the most convenient location, so we built the garage up against this almost perpendicular bluff. When later we wanted a place for an open-air gathering, we found that we could use the flat roof of this garage as the floor of a platform or stage. The gentle rise of the ground eastward from this point made it possible to use it for outdoor meetings, and seats were set out. When we wanted to use it for larger gatherings, we graded it and built a regular stage, which rises about four feet above the front level of the ground."

The land itself provided limestone for buildings, retaining walls, and roads. Oak and walnut trees, killed by the drought that ravaged the Middle West in the 30's, were turned into a blessing instead of a loss when the lumber was salvaged for cabinet work in the new buildings. Even the Tower, which was completed in 1929 and rises one hundred sixty-five feet above the ground, was not constructed for decorative purposes alone. Rickert Fillmore says:

> "We needed water to operate the Farm, and every time we drilled for water we got oil and gas. So across the railroad tracks on our property we made an artificial lake. The lake covers about twenty-two acres, and has a drop of fifty feet at the dam. We did all the concrete work on the dam ourselves, and it is the only one of its kind in Jackson County. This was in 1927. Then we had the water, but we had to get the elevation and the pressure in order to distribute it where needed. So we built the Tower with its huge water tank at the top. It is a symbol and a delight to the eye, of course, but it also makes available a continuous supply of one hundred thousand gallons of water without which the Farm could not be run and provides seven stories of rooms for office use."

An amphitheater stage roofing a garage, a tower that masks a water tank, chimneys that look like bell towers, mirror pools that are really part of the air conditioning system—such things as these reveal the imagination that has gone into the development of Unity Farm.

In 1940, when it became possible for Unity to build again, it was well that there was such an imaginative spirit in charge of the building program. The shortage of labor and material caused by the war made the usual type of construction out of the question.

Rickert Fillmore turned to a new type of construction —prefabrication. Tests proved that the idea was not only practical, but economical. The result is that all the new buildings have been cast in sections in the casting building on the Farm, the sections hauled to the place they are to stand, and there put together in a process that might better be called "assembling" than "building." Almost everything

137

in the buildings is precast; even the "antique cut-stone trim" is only colored concrete made in molds. The result has been a tremendous saving with no sacrifice of beauty.

In 1947, the printing department moved into its new quarters. In the fall of 1949, work on the building that houses the administrative, publishing, and editorial departments reached the place where it was ready for occupancy. On a week end in late October, a huge fleet of trucks backed up to the dock at 917 Tracy and moved all the departments of Unity School except Silent Unity and the Editorial Department out to the new quarters. On Monday morning, the work in the new building went on almost as if no move had been made. A week later, Silent Unity moved into its building that it had occupied for a brief time twenty years before.

For the first time since 1906, passers-by on Tracy Avenue at night saw no light shining from the rooms where workers in Silent Unity had kept so long the constant vigil of prayer. The buildings on Tracy Avenue, however, were to continue to be identified with the work of Jesus Christ, for after several months they were sold to The Salvation Army.

When Unity School with its vast facilities and hundreds of workers moved out and occupied its new home, it could no longer be appropriately called a farm. It is difficult to find a word that tells exactly what it is. It is the center of a big publishing business. It is a place of prayer, a shrine to which hundreds of thousands of people all over the earth turn in their thoughts when they are in need of spiritual help. It is a garden community where Unity leaders and workers live. It is a recreational center to which they go for physical activities that build and refresh the body and mind: to swim, to play golf and tennis, to picnic, to hike, to dance, and to get together with one another. It is a school and

138

a retreat to which hundreds of people come every year from all over the world to study and meditate and pray. It is a farm with orchards, vineyards, and crops in cultivation. It is all these, and yet it is more than all these, for it is a place of God—it is Unity.

To Unity School of Christianity, Lee's Summit, Missouri, come increasing streams of mail, and from there increasing streams of magazines pour out. From the Silent Unity Building shines more brightly than ever the light that shows that Silent Unity workers are always praying, a light that was lit over sixty years ago in Kansas City where two sincere people began to pray for those in need.

Sixty years ago, Charles Fillmore prophesied that Jackson County was to be the center of a great spiritual work. Today, like faith in concrete, the expression of the enduring faith of Charles and Myrtle Fillmore, stand the buildings of Unity School. And still the dream is not complete. More buildings are going up, the plan for developing Unity School is being pushed ahead, the work of Jesus Christ grows and grows. "And of his kingdom there shall be no end."

CHAPTER X

The Spirit of the Fillmores

"Whosoever Would Become Great"

A UNITY CENTER LEADER once asked Charles Fillmore for an affirmation to use as a blessing for herself and for those who worked with her in her center. He was probably not aware that it was a description of himself that he gave her: "I am dignified and definite, yet meek and lowly in all that I say and do."

Other people recognized the greatness of Charles and Myrtle Fillmore and sought to honor them, but neither Charles nor Myrtle Fillmore sought honor. "We have never cared to interest folks in our individual lives," Mrs. Fillmore wrote. "It makes no real difference to others what we have done, who we are." Their dream had been not of personal advancement, but of the growth of Unity.

Once a group of students arranged a program, the purpose of which was to honor the Fillmores, who had not been told the reason for the meeting. Many flattering words were directed toward them before they understood the purpose of the meeting. Then Charles Fillmore arose and said: " 'Why callest thou me good? none *is* good, save one, *that is,* God,' " and he forthwith turned the meeting into a song service of praise to God.

When visitors came to Unity School, it was not unusual for Myrtle Fillmore herself to show them through the building. The first time people wrote to Silent Unity, she answered their letters personally, until the work grew to the place where she could no longer do this. After that, she did answer personally as many letters as she could. Once a picture of Charles Fillmore was wanted for use on a Unity letterhead at Christmas time. It took two years to get it. "I don't believe in glorifying personality," he said. It was only after many friends had pleaded with him that he reluctantly agreed to let his picture be taken. However, once he had consented, he let the photographers turn him this way and that and sat patiently while the various props were arranged.

> "I remember the first photograph I ever had taken for *Unity*," he chuckled. "It was back in the 90's. There were about six workers in Unity at the time, as I recall. The photographer was fiddling around the way you are now, so I went into the silence. I was sitting there with my eyes half-closed; suddenly the photographer said that he was ready to take the picture; then he added, 'I wonder if the gentleman on the left (he was referring to me) could look just a little more intelligent.'
> "A short time before having the picture taken, I had shaved off my beard, and in commenting on the picture in the magazine, I mentioned the fact that this was the first picture I had had taken without a beard. One subscriber wrote in: 'If cutting off your beard makes you look like that picture, I hope you will let it grow again.'"

Charles and Myrtle Fillmore did a serious work, and other people took them seriously. This was right, for often their words meant life itself to those who came to them for help. But Charles and Myrtle Fillmore had a sense of humor that ran through all they said and did, as a little melody sometimes runs through a great symphony and gives it life and light. Charles Fillmore was a born storyteller and he loved to inject humor into his sermons. He had the gift of all natural speakers to sense the moods of an audience; he could tell when the people were getting restless and he knew when to inject a story. "I do not mind your looking at your watches," he told his audience, "but when you look at them, then put them to your ear to see if they are running, that is too much."

It was this sense of humor that enabled Charles Fillmore to be undisturbed by criticism. Sometimes secular publications ran articles that were unfriendly to Unity, but he refused to let this disturb him. If he felt that they were amusing enough, occasionally he even reprinted them in *Unity* with comments of his own. Once the "New York Times" ran an article ridiculing Unity, entitled "Christian Science Outdone." "This is a good piece, with very good testimonials," wrote Mr. Fillmore, and proceeded to reprint the entire article. He thanked the author for writing it, commenting that he had received numerous letters from people asking help who had never heard of Unity until they read the article in the "New York Times."

Over and over the history of Unity has shown this to be the case: the main effect of critical articles has been to interest people in Unity.

Charles Fillmore was always ready to laugh and if the laugh was on himself he did not mind. There were many typographical errors in the first issue of *Modern Thought,* so in the second issue he wrote:

> "We may not be able, outside a printing office, to convince our Christian Science brothers and sisters that matter really exists, but shall have no trouble in backing our position when once its portals are passed. What outside was a dream, a shimmering illusion, the 'Maya' of the Bhuddist, becomes cold, metallic facts within, endowed with a creative power that coins words and phrases, and plays such fantastic tricks before high heaven as make the angels weep. In the face of such

facts it were useless to beg our readers' pardon for the many typographical errors in our last issue."

In the early days of Unity, someone brought some "hot dogs" to a Sunday-school picnic. This would not have been important if one of them had not been put on Mr. Fillmore's plate. He was a strict vegetarian. Instead of acting displeased, he took the "hot dog" and with a great show and much laughter nailed it to a tree.

While on a lecture trip in Texas, he had a cold and could hardly talk. He started his speech with the words: "It ain't my brother and it ain't my sister, it's me, O Lord, that's standin' in the need of prayer," and he had the whole audience joyously join him in prayer for himself.

Myrtle Fillmore had the same love of gaiety as her husband and at Sunday-school parties would dance with the children. Sometimes she would get off a witticism that it would have pleased Charles Fillmore to make. Once, during a Unity conference, all the center leaders were present at the Wednesday evening healing meeting, which Charles and Myrtle Fillmore were leading. Although the chapel was packed with people, Mr. Fillmore announced toward the end of the meeting: "When this program is over you are all invited to come over to our place for a bite to eat." As he stepped back, Mrs. Fillmore rose and declared quietly: "If you do, there had better be another expression of the miracle of the loaves and fishes."

In the early days, the family did not have much money, but their hearts and their house were large and they found room in both for those who needed help. Grandma Fillmore could always be counted on to conjure up enough of her delicious food to fill an extra plate. They all prayed about their needs—and they had a wonderful time.

One time, when they were children, Lowell and Rickert

played with a little boy who said that he was lost. When they went home that evening they told their parents about him. Mrs. Fillmore sent their father out to find him.

Soon Mr. Fillmore returned with him, and he was a little Negro boy. He was very dirty, and his clothes were in rags, so Mrs. Fillmore took off his clothes and burned them, replacing them with some of Rick's and Lowell's. She heated some water on the kitchen stove and gave him a bath in the tin tub that served the family.

While she was bathing him, she talked to him and tried to give him some Unity ideas about God. "God is everywhere," she told him. "God is in this very room." At that moment, Mr. Fillmore came through the room and went upstairs. The little boy's mouth fell open. "Is that God?" he asked.

The Fillmore family lived in the northeast section of Kansas City. They moved often, but finally settled in a house on Elmwood Avenue where they lived for several years. This was then far out in the suburbs. The barn on the lot was moved forward and joined to the rear of the house, and in this back part, which they called "the den," Lowell, Rickert, and Royal lived. Rickert painted the walls of "the den" with pictures of the Katzenjammer kids. Lowell was the gardener and filled the yard with flowers. There was a huge elm in the back yard, and in this tree Rickert built a series of platforms and ladders that enabled one to climb up high. Often his mother and he would climb up together, and he would play his guitar while she sat and meditated.

The Fillmores were a neighborly family and soon were good friends of most of their neighbors. Many of these became stanch followers of Unity.

To Charles and Myrtle Fillmore, life was a joyous and wonderful experience, and they were not content merely to make their own life wonderful; they tried to live so that some of the wonder spilled over into the lives that touched their own. To them, people were not merely followers, but lovable human beings in whose personal adventures as well as spiritual welfare they were interested.

A woman who now works at Unity told how, when her mother had given birth to her children, Mrs. Fillmore stayed up each time until she was informed by telephone that all was well. One time, the mother was unusually worried about some physical symptoms that had appeared. Before she went to the hospital, Myrtle Fillmore insisted that she be called as soon as the baby was born. No matter what time it came, she would be waiting up for the call. It was not until 3 o'clock in the morning that the baby was born, and when the Fillmore house was called Mr. Fillmore answered the telephone. He and Mrs. Fillmore had stayed up praying for the mother and child.

Myrtle, especially, had a way of making people feel that she loved them. She was always putting her arms around the people she knew; her conversation overflowed with compliments. She had a gentle smile that made her callers feel that she had been looking forward to seeing them especially. And on terminating an interview, she had a way of half-rising, sometimes going to the door, as if to say, "Oh, I wish you wouldn't go." Usually when she had visitors she gave them some gift. She herself received many gifts from everywhere; as she could not use all of them she passed many of them on to other persons. She was not afraid either in her conversation or her letters to say, "I love you."

"How I wish I could write this letter to you right from my heart without waiting for this typewriter to form the words," she began one letter. It was right from her heart that she wrote—and felt.

Although she carried on a voluminous correspondence,

and many of the letters were answered by secretaries, she was able to remember intimate details in the lives of the persons to whom she wrote. The letters her secretaries wrote for her, she always read. Usually she added to them in her own hand a postscript or a word in the margin, perhaps inquiring after a father or a daughter whom the correspondent had not even mentioned in the letter that was being answered.

Charles Fillmore, too, had this faculty for remembering people. One woman wrote to Unity that two years after she and her husband had met Charles and Myrtle Fillmore at a Unity conference, the couple paid another visit to Unity and on entering the building on Tracy Avenue happened to encounter Mr. Fillmore. When he greeted them personally, the woman said, "I believe you are mistaking me for someone else."

Mr. Fillmore replied, "No, a good shepherd knows his sheep," and told her how shepherds have their sheep named. "The shepherd doesn't forget the names of the sheep," he said. "You were here two years ago with your husband, you are from Peoria, Illinois," and he called them by name.

To the Fillmores, people were important, all people, whether important in the world's eye or not. All people were important because they were God's children. The Fillmores loved them, great and small. A young girl who once sat next to Charles Fillmore at a banquet later said, "He made me feel as if what I had to say was of great importance."

One time, a Negro woman came to study at the Unity Training School. She ran out of funds before the term was over. She heard that the Fillmores wanted to hire someone to pick berries on their farm, so she went over to apply for the job. She was instructed to go out and bring in a large bowlful of the berries for Mr. Fillmore's dinner. Then instead of hiring her to work, Charles asked her to eat with him.

Years later, the woman described the incident: "When dinner was served, Mr. Fillmore, like any father serving his little girl who was hungry, took a spoon and served half his dish of berries to me. Then, when I was about to leave, without my asking, he let me have twenty dollars to help me with my expenses and carried me back to Kansas City in his pretty new red car. I loved the twinkle in his eyes. He did his good like a bad boy slipping things over on one."

The Fillmores did not believe in amassing wealth for themselves; they believed in passing it on. "Sometimes I have a very definite place for all my allowance, before I even begin on my own individual needs," wrote Myrtle. They carried no life insurance, made no financial provision for the future. They never copyrighted any of their writings; they wanted people to be free to reprint anything they wrote. People sent them many gifts of money, most of which they turned over to Unity.

> "My husband and I have put ourselves into this thing which God has given us to do, year after year, without personal returns beyond our 'daily bread' and clothing," wrote Myrtle Fillmore. "I work here in the Unity buildings every day, and receive a salary just as several hundred other workers do. I think a very capable businessman or woman would not consider working for my salary."

Charles and Myrtle Fillmore thought of themselves as Unity workers. They were "Papa Charley" and "Mama Myrtle." They felt that every person who worked at Unity, everyone connected with the movement, everyone who wrote to Unity, everyone who even visited the buildings, was a member of the Unity family. They felt a oneness with them all, a kinship with all people everywhere. When Unity workers were having financial trouble, they sometimes found money left on their typewriters. It was from Myrtle.

The offerings in classes taught at Unity School in the early days were likely to be very small. Myrtle Fillmore knew this and she would often have her secretary slip into a class that some worker was teaching and put something for the teacher into the collection plate.

Charles and Myrtle Fillmore often went with the other workers for picnics on Cliff Drive, a scenic spot in the neighborhood. They would build a fire and cook their meal and after they had eaten they would repeat Truth statements together or sing some of the Truth songs they loved.

Mr. Fillmore loved to conduct what he called "joy times" for the workers. He would tell funny stories, and so would some of the others. Long before most places of business were having recreational periods during working hours, the Unity workers were given time to tell funny stories, to sing songs they liked, and to meditate and pray.

The Fillmores wanted their workers to enjoy themselves and to improve themselves. Interesting speakers who came to Kansas City were often invited to speak to the Unity workers. Once an adult educational program in downtown Kansas City sponsored a series of lectures called "University Extension Lectures." Although these lectures were held during working hours, the Unity workers were given the privilege of attending. Today the hours of young people who come to train for the Unity ministry have in some cases been arranged so as to enable them to attend college.

The Fillmores believed in joy and wanted others to be joyful. They had a large tent erected on top of the building at 913 Tracy where Unity workers and students who lived in the neighborhood could sleep out of doors on hot nights. For several years on this roof, Charles Fillmore on his birthday, August 22, had a watermelon party for the workers.

Sometimes, on holidays or at other times when there were only a few workers in the office, he would invite the whole group into his office to have lunch. There he had a little hot plate. Sometimes all he had was soup and crackers. The workers would sit in his office and sip soup from cups or glasses, or any other kind of small container they could get.

A room on the roof of 917 Tracy Avenue was called "The Tower Room" and was used for night work. Often Charles and Myrtle Fillmore would come up to this room to have the nine o'clock healing meeting with the workers who were on duty there. In the winter there would be a coal fire in the fireplace. Sometimes Mr. Fillmore would come up alone and sit in the rocking chair in front of the fireplace. Sometimes he would not say anything, merely sit in the silence; sometimes, when the workers were not busy, he would sing. He loved to sing, especially songs that had amusing words, and he always smiled as he sang. One of his favorite songs was from "The Mikado," and his voice would ring out on the final words of the refrain,

"Let the punishment fit the crime—
The punishment fit the crime."

Mr. Fillmore did not believe in punishment. At one time, a number of Unity workers were won over by another teacher. This alone would not have disturbed him, for in the early days of his ministry, when some visiting lecturer would come to town with a lot of publicity and most of his congregation would go to hear the visitor, Mr. Fillmore would just proceed as always, blessing the lecturer and blessing the people and saying to any friend who was concerned: "Leave them alone, they'll be back." And they came back.

But this time, the other teacher not only tried to win away the workers, he tried to get them to procure for him a copy of the mailing list of Unity's correspondents. These names, of course, are considered inviolate. (The names and needs of all those who write to Unity have always been considered strictly confidential. All the workers are impressed, when they come into the service, with the fact that they are not even supposed to talk among themselves about the correspondents; and some months after the letters are answered, they are burned.) But even when Charles Fillmore learned of the attempt to destroy the loyalty of his workers, he did not become angry. He did not even dismiss the workers. He merely told them that they were free to stay, or go, as they felt led. If they wanted to follow the other man, they were free to do so, only he felt that they should serve in the other man's organization. On the other hand, if they wanted to stay at Unity and be loyal to Unity, he was happy to have them stay; they were his friends.

The Fillmores had faith in people. They had faith in them because they saw them as God's children; they did not see the defects and shortcomings, they saw the spiritual potentialities, they saw the Christ Spirit. Most persons lack faith in themselves. The Fillmores knew this. They had the gift of instilling in people faith in their own abilities. Few persons have love's eyes to see and love's heart to feel the unspoken need and the hidden talents of another. The Fillmores were such persons.

Myrtle Fillmore, especially, was sensitive to others' undeveloped possibilities. No small part of her influence on the Unity movement was the work that she did with the Unity workers. She was always among them, stopping at their desks, praising them, encouraging them, drawing out of them some good quality that they themselves perhaps did not know they had. For example, for years Myrtle Fillmore went every day to the bindery to conduct the blessing of the mail.

The woman who was in charge of the bindery was a timid person; she felt that she could never lead the workers in prayer. But one day, Mrs. Fillmore turned to her and said, "You know, today I would like you to give the blessing. I'd like to hear what it sounds like." The worker was hesitant as to how to begin, but heartened by Mrs. Fillmore's smile, she started out. Before she knew it she had led the workers in a prayer service that she had had no idea she was capable of. After she had finished, Mrs. Fillmore lifted her hands over the mail and said, "There is nothing more to be said. God bless you." From then on the workers in the bindery gave their own blessing to the Unity mail.

Blessing the mail is still a Unity custom: Every morning when the mail from the post office reaches the mail-opening room it is blessed. Every day when mail is ready to leave Unity the workers in the mailing room gather around and place a blessing upon it.

Many who became successful Unity leaders felt that the encouragement given them by Myrtle Fillmore was in large measure responsible for their success. Some of them might not have stayed in the Unity work had it not been for her appreciation and understanding. She helped them to find exactly the right place for themselves. One young man came to work at Unity about the time of World War I. Brilliant and restless, at first it did not seem that he would be able to find a place in Unity where he could use his talents. Myrtle Fillmore, however, recognized that he was a gifted person and encouraged him to stay and to have faith that he would find in Unity the right avenue for the expression of his gifts. In 1924 this young man, Frank B. Whitney, encouraged by Myrtle and Charles Fillmore brought forth *Unity Daily Word,* which has since become the most popular of all the Unity publications. He became the first editor of this magazine and one of the best loved of Unity's writers.

Charles Fillmore, too, knew how to call forth the talents of others. Many workers in Silent Unity remember an experience they had when they first came to work in that department: A difficult letter came to them that they did not know how to answer; they took it to Mr. Fillmore and asked him how to answer it; he told them. This happened perhaps three or four times; then they took a letter to him, and he told them: "The Spirit that is in me is in you. Go back to your desk and ask that Spirit how to answer this letter. You can answer it." At first, the letterwriter might doubt that he could do it; but always in the end he discovered that he had the ability.

Charles and Myrtle Fillmore were leaders. Because they had courage and faith in themselves as children of God, they inspired those around them to have courage and to dare to step out on their own resources.

Charles Fillmore was a man of action. Everything he had to meet he took to God in prayer. He prayed. He looked for guidance. Then he moved boldly ahead. He once told a co-worker: "Go ahead with an open mind and, if you are not on the right course, something will soon appear that you will see is better."

Knowing almost nothing about the publishing business, he dared to publish a magazine. To a materially minded world, he dared to proclaim a new interpretation of the Jesus Christ teaching. Rejecting approved financial methods,

153

he dared to rely on God and accept freewill offerings as his income. Down through the years when there were changes to be made, buildings to be built, steps to be taken, people to be intrusted with important parts of the Unity work— whenever there was a vital decision to be made—Charles Fillmore was there with a David-brave heart, a Solomon-wise judgment, and an unshakable faith in God.

Charles Fillmore was the embodiment of prayer in action. He prayed about everything that he had to do, then he did it. His daring faith had much to do with making Unity what it now is. He always seemed to say, "Where He leads me I will follow, I'll go with Him all the way."

CHAPTER XI

Their Healing Work

"Heal the Sick"

U NITY BEGAN when Myrtle Fillmore received the idea, *"I am a child of God, and therefore I do not inherit sickness,"* and was healed by the power of God in her. The first fruit of Unity was the healing of the friends and neighbors who came to her with their physical ills and saw these dissolved through prayer. Unity has always emphasized healing through Christ.

When the sick heard, back in the 1880's, that a woman named Myrtle Fillmore had been healed of tuberculosis through her prayers and was having success in bringing healing to others, it was natural that they should start beating a path to her door. They have been coming down that path in increasing numbers ever since.

It was through searching for health that the Fillmores themselves discovered Truth. Although Myrtle Fillmore quickly found her wholeness, Charles Fillmore spent untold hours of the day and night, during the last sixty years of his life, working in prayer for healing for himself and others.

He never accepted the withered leg as a handicap that he would have to put up with all the days of his life; he believed that his leg could be made whole and strong and perfect, and he worked in prayer to make it so. Those who knew him over a long period of time attest that as the years went by Charles's leg responded to the faith of the man, for they saw it grow in strength and vigor; they saw him discard cane and braces; they saw the leg become more nearly like the other. Charles Fillmore practiced the prayer that he taught.

The Fillmores never insisted that those who came to them for help give up medicine or other medical aid. They left their students free, and today Unity is glad to pray with those who are taking medical treatment. H. Emilie Cady, author of the basic Unity textbook, *Lessons in Truth,* was a physician and continued for many years to practice medicine. Other doctors have written for Unity. Many have subscribed for the magazines and have not only put them in their waiting rooms for their patients to read but have advised their patients to subscribe for them and study them at home. The Fillmores knew that people were at all stages of spiritual development and that everyone had to live according to his own faith. They were glad to add their prayers to the ministrations of the doctors. For themselves, however, they felt that prayer alone was enough to keep them whole.

At one time, Charles Fillmore was in an automobile accident. A doctor was called who treated the other persons involved in the accident.

Charles Fillmore was in a great deal of pain, but when the doctor came to treat him, Charles said to him, "Just leave me alone, please, I'll do this my own way" and he motioned the doctor aside.

"There," said the doctor, "is a man." Charles recovered very quickly.

This atmosphere of faith in God as the source of healing pervaded the Fillmore household from the early days of Unity. Once, Lowell had the mumps, and Rick caught them in one jaw. That day his mother found him playing barefoot in the rain. When she reprimanded him, he asked, "Don't you believe what you say?" Of course, Myrtle Fillmore believed what she taught, and Rick suffered no ill effect.

The Fillmore boys did not worry much about getting sick. Their mother wrote: "Yesterday, there were about four inches of snow on the ground, and from my study window I saw Royal with bare feet and with legs bared to the knees taking a run in the front yard. 'Just to see how snow feels,' he said."

When people came to the Fillmores for help, they caught the simple faith of this believing family, and soon a constant stream of the sick were coming to the Unity offices. By the time the Fillmores moved their offices to the house on McGee Street, a crowd was coming every day to see if some of the healing faith of these two praying people might touch and restore their bodies. By the time Charles arrived at 10 or 11 in the morning, there were always at least a dozen persons waiting for him in the reception room, which was used for the meetings on Sundays. He had his office in the front parlor. There he took these persons one by one and listened to them and prayed with them. He knew that he of himself could do nothing, but his whole prayer and his whole life were consecrated to gaining a spirit of oneness with the God of life whose power can bring perfection to mind and body.

All day long, into that little office went aching, often despairing, men and women. Perhaps they had suffered pain for years, perhaps they had been told that they had no chance to live. They went into the office fear-racked and suffering, and they found there a little, quiet, kindly man who invited them to sit down beside him and to tell him what was wrong.

Charles Fillmore said that often it seemed to him that he said very little. Sometimes the patient spent the whole time telling him what was wrong. But this Charles Fillmore always silently denied. And always he prayed. Usually he

157

managed to get the one who was asking help to pray also. They would sit still together and in that creative silence they would speak the powerful words of Truth that, as Charles Fillmore had come to know, carried healing.

When those people rose to go, fifteen minutes or a half-hour later, often they were not the same persons who had come slumped and desperate through the door. Almost always, they went forth renewed in spirit and often they went forth renewed in body too; for in this small office in Kansas City the miracles of which the Bible speaks were coming to pass again: The lame were being made to walk, the dumb to speak, and the blind to see.

At first, the Fillmores did not publish many testimonials of healing in their magazine because, as they said, they wanted to place the emphasis on the teaching and on the spiritual results rather than on physical ones. Finally, in response to many requests for testimonials, Mr. Fillmore began to publish a column of them regularly every month under the title, "The Signs That Follow." At one time, he published a magazine by this name for the sole purpose of printing the testimonials.

Charles Fillmore wrote:

> "It has not been our custom to sound our own praises, nor even to print the tons of good words of help received by those who have co-operated with us. Recently there has been a real demand for a sight of the unsolicited testimonial letters we are so freely receiving. People say it helps them to believe when they see how many are being benefited; so it is for your encouragement that we print a few of the hundreds of letters we are constantly getting."

From that time on, thousands of letters describing the healing of almost every known physical condition have appeared in the pages of Unity's magazines. Since the Unity work is strictly confidential, no names are ever mentioned in the letters and permission to reprint them is requested before they are used.

The number of persons to whom the Fillmores have pointed out the way to health is impossible to estimate. To this day, people are writing to Unity, or sometimes visiting headquarters, who say that thirty, or forty, or fifty years ago they were ill and they came to Charles or to Myrtle Fillmore, or they wrote to them, and were healed through prayer.

Recently a visitor came to Unity School in a taxi from Kansas City. When Lowell Fillmore accompanied this visitor out to his waiting taxi, the driver said: "You probably don't know me, Mr. Fillmore, but my brother came to your mother years ago and was healed through her. He is well and working now." And he gave Lowell his name. It was a name that Lowell remembered well. It was one of the first cases of healing that his mother had had, and Lowell had often wondered what had become of the man.

There were many healings in those early days. One woman had a tumor. The doctors wanted to operate on her, but she kept putting them off as she was afraid that an operation would be fatal. Finally she set a time for the operation—Saturday morning. Friday night, weeping, she called on Mr. Fillmore. "For God's sake help me if you can," she cried. She had not slept for many nights but that night when she went home she fell asleep and slept until morning. When the doctors examined her the next day, they found no tumor.

A woman who had been told that she would not live until fall came with tuberculosis of the lungs. A few months later, she was able to tell Mr. Fillmore: "I am a strong, healthy woman, doing all my own housework."

Her husband was one day brought home with a strangu-
lated hernia and rushed to the hospital where the head
surgeon told the wife he would probably die within three
days from blood poisoning. She wired for help to Charles
Fillmore. As the man went under the surgeon's knife, he
kept repeating, *"I am, I am God."* On the third day, there
was no fever, and on the fourth day, the wound was completely healed.

One woman who had had one operation after another
came to Myrtle Fillmore. After four sessions of prayer, she
was completely well.

Another woman with tuberculosis came to Mrs. Fillmore. While they were praying, the woman had a coughing
spell. They prayed together about that. The coughing
stopped. Then the woman said in a surprised voice, "What
did you do to my ankle?" Several years before, she had
dislocated one of the small bones in her ankle and had not
been able to put her foot flat on the ground since then. While
Myrtle Fillmore and she had been praying about the coughing, she had felt a strange sensation in this foot, and when
she rose from her chair she found that she could walk on
this foot as well as on the other. In less than a year, her
tuberculosis was gone.

There was a state legislator who, on applying for an
insurance policy, had been told that he had an advanced
case of diabetes. He attended one of the classes in Truth
principles taught by Charles Fillmore. During the fourth
lesson, he said that he suddenly received the assurance that
he was healed. From ninety-two pounds, he went up in
one month to one hundred and thirty-two pounds in weight.
He was able to discard the diet he had been following, and
tests showed that the diabetes had disappeared. His right
arm, withered and over one inch shorter than the left, had

been useless for seventeen years. One day, he found to his astonishment that the right arm had become the same length as the left and was almost as well-developed.

By the early 1900's, the Fillmores had become so busy that they could not continue as they had in the past spending most of each day taking up the healing needs of individuals who came to them for help. However, they never entirely ceased this practice, and there were probably few days when they were not praying with someone about his healing needs.

Years later, they were still having experiences such as the following one described in a letter to Unity:

"I was very ill in Kansas City, Missouri where I had been living and doing office work for several years. I had been doctoring for about six weeks but steadily getting worse.

"One morning, when I was very low, my doctor brought a specialist with him, and after consulting together for some time, they told me I had to be removed at once to a hospital and operated on, or I would not be alive twelve hours from that time.

"I made up my mind that I was not going to be operated on and I told the doctors to go away. My sister, who had come from the West Coast to be with me, asked me what I wanted to do. I had myself carried downstairs to the telephone, and they left me alone.

"I called up Silent Unity, and the young lady at the telephone could not understand me, as I could not speak above a whisper.

"In a minute she said, 'Oh, hold on a minute, here comes Charles Fillmore. You are very blessed that you can get him to help you.' I had been to several Sunday meetings at Unity and had heard Mr. Fillmore speak and had faith that he could help me.

"As soon as he spoke, I told him the doctors had told me I was going to die if I was not operated on at

161

once. He asked me what the doctor said was the matter with me. I told him.

"He was very firm, and said: 'You are not going to die.' He had me repeat after him the words of the last verse of *The Prayer of Faith,* although that was the first time I had ever heard it. Many times since then, through the years, that prayer has helped me over a hard place.

" 'Now,' he said, 'you go to sleep and rest.'

"I said, 'O Mr. Fillmore, I haven't slept except by fits and starts for over three weeks.'

" 'Well,'' he said, 'you will now. Just repeat those words I told you, and go to sleep.'

"I went right to sleep and dreamed that I was in heaven and a beautiful angel was bending over me and smiling. I opened my eyes, and it was night. Standing there was a lovely girl smoothing my forehead. I said, 'Who are you, an angel?'

"She said, 'No, I'm not an angel. I'm Myrtle Fillmore's secretary, and we thought you might like to see me.'

"She stayed a little while and left, and I slept fine the rest of the night. In three weeks from that time, I was back at work at my desk in the office and four years later, in another city, I was married. Later, I brought my husband and year-old baby daughter to Unity in Kansas City, and Mr. Fillmore held my baby in his arms and blessed her."

Although they themselves no longer had the time to spend each day handling the healing needs of individuals, the Fillmores had gathered about them a group of devoted persons who they believed had a high spiritual consciousness, and these persons took over this phase of the work. Finally there were twelve of these counselors, or healers, as they called themselves. Myrtle Fillmore herself remained in charge of their activities, and every morning at 10 o'clock, she led this group in a healing meeting.

Mr. and Mrs. Fillmore together often conducted the healing meeting that Silent Unity held each morning at 11 o'clock. Together, too, they conducted every Wednesday evening at 8 o'clock a healing meeting that was open to the public. They always stopped this meeting exactly at 9, when they asked everyone to join them for fifteen minutes in silent healing prayer. This nine o'clock healing service was the one they had asked people to participate in when they first formed Silent Unity. They were faithful to it always.

Charles and Myrtle Fillmore had learned to pray at all times, in all places, and under all circumstances and they never let what was going on around them keep them from praying. Sometimes on Sunday morning after the service, Charles Fillmore would come down from the platform and see someone who was in need of prayer. Right there in the front row of the chapel with people talking and laughing and milling about them, he would have the one who needed help sit down beside him, and it would be as if the two of them were completely alone. In the midst of the confusion, he would sit quietly, close his eyes, and speak words of prayer with the one in need.

Usually the Fillmores opened a healing meeting with a song. After the opening song, Mrs. Fillmore led a silence, which is what Unity calls a period of meditation. She would take up the theme of the meeting, discuss the affirmation that she was having the group use in prayer, lead them in declaring it and in meditating silently on the Truth of it. Then Mr. Fillmore would rise and give a talk based on the healing prayer, after which he would lead the group in further meditation, using the prayer as a basis for it. Usually he gave the benediction at the close of the meeting.

It was not what was done at the meeting, it was not the words that were spoken or the prayers that were used that mattered; it was the spirit of the two who conducted it. As they took turns speaking and as they sat together in the silence, a compelling spirit radiated from the platform that all who were attuned to it felt. As the sick and the lonely and the troubled of heart sat in that small chapel and listened to the quiet words and looked into the gentle faces of the two before them, it was as if the healing Spirit of the Christ passed among them.

Here were two who had dedicated their lives to the living God. With adamant faith, they spoke from the silence of their hearts the words that they believed to be the truest words that could be spoken of a human being, words that proclaimed his divinity, words that affirmed his wholeness in Christ. Earnestly, faithfully, thankfully they prayed and prayed again until the words they spoke were no longer words; they were living symbols of God's healing life, and all who heard them and joined in speaking them in prayer felt the power of them too, felt it not only with their minds but in their bodies.

When, at the end of the meeting, Charles and Myrtle Fillmore passed from the room something of them still remained—the consciousness of life that they had kindled in the minds and bodies of those who had been praying with them. "For where two or three are gathered together in my name, there am I in the midst of them."

CHAPTER XII

The Fillmores as Teachers

"Thou Shalt Teach Them"

I N UNITY MAGAZINE of February, 1897, there appeared an announcement by Charles Fillmore which read as follows:

"Monday evening, March 15, 1897, at 8 p. m., I will begin another class of instruction in practical Christianity at Rooms 510 and 511 Hall Building, Kansas City, Missouri. These lessons are in a large measure the outgrowth of my own experience in the regeneration through which I have been passing for several years, and are therefore very practical. I do not follow any teaching, but give the Truth as I have gotten it from spiritual experiences, which I find corroborated in a wonderful way in the Hebrew Scriptures. Theory has been replaced by absolute knowledge, and I am enabled to give many things that have never before been taught. . . .

"These lessons are twelve in number and will be given one each night, taking two weeks to complete the course. All are welcome, but no new students will be admitted after the first lesson.

"No charge is made for the lessons or treatments that accompany, when needed. All expenses are met by freewill offerings."

Charles Fillmore had been teaching such classes in practical Christianity for several years. At first, there were only a handful of students in the classes. They would all sit around in a circle. Mr. Fillmore would ask one or the other of them questions; then the whole group would discuss the answers that were given. He loved to teach in this way, freely and informally, with a group of students as sincerely interested in Truth as himself, gathered around him.

As the Fillmores said over and over, they were not trying to set up a church, they were establishing a school. When the Unity Society of Practical Christianity was incorporated in 1903, it was incorporated as a scientific and educational institution, not as a church. Later Charles Fillmore even tried to conduct the Sunday services along the lines of the informal discussions that he had had in his early classes. At one time, after the Unity Correspondence Course was begun, he assigned members of his congregation questions from this course, which they answered. Then there was an open discussion of the answers. However, his congregation preferred to listen to him talk, so he abandoned this plan; but his talks always had more of the feel and flavor of a lecture by a scientist or philosopher—and one with a keen sense of humor—than they did of a sermon, although they were based on the Bible and the teachings of Jesus.

Charles and Myrtle Fillmore did not teach an abstract theory; they lived what they taught; they put it into practice. They worked for long hours in prayer and meditation to discover Truth and then they applied to their own bodies and their own affairs the Truth that was unfolded to them. Charles Fillmore once wrote:

> "I spend from four to six hours daily in prayer, blessing the various parts of my body, the centers. At first it was difficult to get started, and I had many backsets, but now it is quite interesting and I often stay up all night intent upon improving my control of these subjective functions of the body."

The Fillmores believed that a man has in him divine

166

potentialities far beyond any that he usually expresses, the potentialities of the Christ. They believed that throughout the body there are spiritual centers and that by concentrating on these in prayer one can release spiritual forces centered in them. This they worked to do. Later Charles Fillmore wrote a book about this idea called *The Twelve Powers of Man,* in which he names and describes these centers.

In an article about himself, he described his experience in unfolding his own spiritual powers:

"The most important phase of my experience how-ever was the opening of my spiritual nature. I gradually acquired the ability to go into the silence, and from that source I received unexpected revelations and physical sensations. At first, the revelations were nearly all through dreams. I developed a dream code through which I could get information and answers of marvelous accuracy to my questions. I do not remember that I asked who the author of my guidance was; I took for granted that it was Spirit.

"Then the mental and spiritual developed into sen-sations at the nerve extremities. I was informed by the Presence that I was beginning body regeneration as taught by Jesus Christ. Neither physiology nor psychol-ogy offers a nomenclature describing it. The first sensa-tion was in my forehead, a crawly feeling when I was affirming life. Then I found that I could produce this same feeling in the bottom of my feet and other nerve extremities by concentrating my attention at the place and silently affirming life.

"I spent several hours every day in this process and I found that I was releasing electronic forces sealed up in the nerves. This I have done for nearly fifty years until now I have what may be termed an electric body that is gradually replacing the physical. It is even more than electric, and when certain spiritual emotions are imparted to it it fairly glows and blends with an omnipresent etheric atmosphere that is highly charged with life energy. My physical organism is being transformed cell by cell, and the ultimate will be an entirely new body having all the perfections of youth in addition to ethereal life.

"This, Spirit tells me, is the transformation of mind and body promised by Jesus. Paul called attention to it—'Be ye transformed by the renewing of your mind'— but he did not attain it. Now at the end of this age, the spiritual and mental conditions of the race are ripe for the entering into this new life of all followers of Jesus in the regeneration. It is through this transformation and rearrangement of the atoms of the organism that the Christ body is formed in man's consciousness. When the light of Spirit is allowed to enter the conscious and the subconscious minds, a great revelation takes place, and it is found to be literal fact that 'your body is a temple of the Holy Spirit which is in you, which ye have from God.' "

The Fillmores were slow in putting down in book form the conclusions they reached. The only book that Myrtle Fillmore ever wrote (although a collection of her letters was published after her passing) is the book for children, *Wee Wisdom's Way;* and Charles Fillmore studied and thought for twenty years before he felt that his ideas were ready to be published in book form.

When they first felt that a book on Truth principles was needed, instead of writing it themselves, they had H. Emilie Cady write *Lessons in Truth.* Meanwhile, they were praying and organizing their thoughts.

The subscribers for their magazines wrote in continually asking them to write a book, but they were not to be hurried. In 1902, Charles wrote in reply to some of these letters, "I wish to attain such command of my organism that I can demonstrate what I write." To him, any spiritual law worth writing about had to be demonstrable. He called his work and he labeled his classes practical Christianity. Part of the reason why he did not, for such a long time, put the lessons into print, but insisted that those who wished to study with him come to him in person, was that much of the course consisted of actually working with the ideas, putting them into practice through prayer and meditation. He wrote:

"My class lessons are not in print, and there is no immediate prospect of printing them, as they consist in part of the practical application of the Word and drills that vary according to the need of the class."

He would have felt that his classes had not been a success if in the course of them some of the students had not proved the laws that he was teaching them by attaining more health or prosperity.

Finally in 1905, he began the publication in *Unity* of some metaphysical lessons that he intended to publish in book form when they were complete. The twelve lessons were not completed until 1909. In that year, his first book, *Christian Healing,* was published. The material in it was the summation of what he had been teaching in the classes in practical Christianity that he had been giving since the inception of Unity. For twenty years, Charles Fillmore had tested in his own body and his own life the ideas he presented in this book and because of the results that he had personally secured, he was sure that the ideas would be of practical value to others.

The book has run through twenty-three printings, and although the wording of it was later changed somewhat, the ideas remained the same. They had been tried, they had been tested, they had been found workable and true. They were clear, high expressions of Truth and Charles Fillmore held to these ideas all his life.

Yet he never stopped looking for new ideas. In his nineties, he was still saying, "I reserve the right to change my mind." He did not believe in the closed mind. Life to him meant new beginnings. He was a pioneer of spirit, an adventurer in faith. He wrote:

"Beware of the circumscribed idea of God! Always provide for an increase in your concept. Don't write down any laws governing your conduct or your religious ideas. Be free to grow and expand. What you think today may not be the measure for your thought tomorrow."

Unity existed for more than thirty years before he wrote, and then only in response to a prolonged and persistent demand from readers for a precise statement of his beliefs, the *Unity Statement of Faith,* and to this he added:

"We have considered the restrictions that will follow a formulated platform, and are hereby giving warning that we shall not be bound by this tentative statement of what Unity believes. We may change our mind tomorrow on some of the points, and if we do, we shall feel free to make a new statement of faith in harmony with the new viewpoint. However, we are assured that there will be no change in fundamentals; the form of words may be clarified and the inner and outer meaning of the Truth may be more clearly set forth."

Often in his classes, a student would be answering a question and Mr. Fillmore would ask, "Where did you get that idea?"

The student would reply, "I read that in such and such a Unity book, Mr. Fillmore."

"Are you sure?"

"Certainly, Mr. Fillmore, that is right out of page so and so."

"You know," he would say, "that is not exactly right,"

and then he would go on to explain the point in a way that clarified it.

Often in his classes, he would interrupt his students when they were quoting him with the question: "But what do *you* think about it?"

The main aim of his teaching was to get his students to think Truth through for themselves. By Socratic questioning, he would draw out his students' minds. He felt that Truth means little as long as it is merely words in a book. He was constantly making a distinction between spiritual understanding and intellectual understanding. Although he recognized the importance of words, he was not content with them. He worked in prayer until he had made Truth part of his very flesh and life.

When a student in one of his classes answered a question, he would ask, "Any comments?"

Perhaps one or two would speak up and say, "Good!" Usually that was all.

Then he would say, "Any questions?" Silence.

"Any criticisms?" Silence.

"Any 'blowholes'?"

Usually there would be a laugh at this. Then the class would begin to discuss the question freely, which was what he wanted. He knew that only out of free discussion would his students arrive at an understanding of Truth that was in their own language. This was his aim, for he knew that nothing means much to a person until he has made it part of his own experience.

It was because Charles Fillmore himself was so certain of Truth that he was able to let his students arrive at Truth for themselves. He had the courage of his convictions; he had faith in their validity. There were certain divine ideas that Charles Fillmore knew, and he knew that he knew them.

He had tested them by the logic of his mind and by application to his life. Nothing could have shaken his belief in them.

"I can remember with what satisfaction I used to imbibe the assumed wisdom of freshmen teachers," he once wrote. "I knew nothing about God because I had never made an effort to get acquainted with Him and in my egotism, I said, 'All these people that think they are in communion with God are deluded; I have never seen God. I believe in things you can see and I will take the testimony of Bob Ingersoll, who says you cannot know God, rather than that of Henry Ward Beecher, who says you can.'

"But a time came when I decided to solve this question independent of any man's opinion. I set about to search for Him with my mind. And right here, I want to add my testimony good and strong with those who have said *I know God.* I talk and think to God, and He flashes His ideas into my mind. I am not deluded. I know His thoughts from the thoughts of men as they pass through the mental atmosphere. He also talks to me in certain dreams. I can distinguish these dreams from the other dreams. Repeated thinking about the presence of God makes Him increasingly plainer to my inner vision. I have thought about Him as the life of my body until every cell is athrill with an energy that I can feel as you feel the shock of an electric battery, and He tells me how to communicate this life to others who have not recognized it as I have. Don't let the fool say in your heart, 'There is no God.' I let that kind of fool talk in my heart and it set up a current of thought that kept me for years speechless in the presence of God."

Charles Fillmore knew God and he knew where he stood in relation to Him, and this was a knowledge not open to argument. He was a man of strong conviction, yet

172

he had no trace of the fanatic. Sometimes people came to his classes to denounce his ideas. When this happened, he quietly turned the discussion to other matters. Although he loved to lead his students in metaphysical discussion, he knew that arguing about religion is fruitless. He refrained from criticizing other religious teachings; he did not feel that it was necessary to defend his own. When people needed Unity, they would turn to it, he felt.

The Fillmore spirit of tolerance permeates Unity today. When people write to Unity denouncing its beliefs, the Unity letterwriters agree with the correspondent in all possible points, and in regard to points of disagreement merely say that Unity leaves every man free to find Truth for himself and that there is some Truth in all teachings.

The Fillmores believed in each man's seeking Truth within himself. They always began and ended every class they taught with a silence, where each student's mind would be free to contact God in his own way. Usually it was Myrtle Fillmore who conducted the silence. She loved this part of the meetings. When she led a meditation, she had a way of speaking as if the words tasted good to her. She usually began her prayers by explaining what prayer is. "Prayer is communion with God," she would say. "God is in you, and you can come in contact with Him there; you can feel His presence in you. Turn within now and let His presence come forth as wisdom so that your words and your thoughts may be filled with His wisdom."

The classes that the Fillmores taught were joyous classes. One of the distinguishing points of their teaching is the emphasis it puts on joy. When Unity began, many churches were teaching that life is a vale of tears, a mere temporary halting place where trials and tribulation prepare the soul for the hereafter. However, the Fillmores taught that it is

173

not necessary to be sorrowful in order to be spiritual.

They taught that God's will is joy. They emphasized the importance of living a full life here and now. "Live in the present. 'Now is the acceptable time,' " they declared.

The Fillmores emphasized not Christ crucified but Christ resurrected. They chose for the symbol of Unity not the cross, which to so many persons represents the suffering of Jesus, but the winged globe of Spirit.

Charles Fillmore did not want his teaching to be connected with symbols associated with suffering. He did not believe that true religion is sorrowful. Although he taught that conduct should be governed by the highest ethical standards, he did not teach that there is any virtue in penitence and suffering.

The determination of the Fillmores to keep their teaching joyful is shown by Unity's manner of observing Lent. Unity's Lenten program, based on *Teach Us to Pray,* one of the most popular Unity books, has taught thousands of persons to observe Lent not as a period of physical denial but of consecration and joyous release from old thoughts and limitations.

The denial that the Fillmores taught is the denial of sorrow, the denial of limitations, the denial of sin, sickness, poverty, and death. They made of their teaching a joyous affirmation of life.

There was never anything gloomy or dull about Charles and Myrtle Fillmore. A new center leader was asked to conduct a funeral service. Never having conducted one, he came to Myrtle Fillmore for advice. She told him, "Just because it is a funeral, you don't have to talk about death, do you?"

"What shall I talk about?" he asked.

"Talk about life," she exclaimed.

174

In all their classes, the Fillmores talked about life, abundant life, joyous life. Both Myrtle and Charles Fillmore loved to sing. If he could find a bit of song that applied to some question, he would sing it out. Myrtle Fillmore wrote a number of hymns. Usually she wrote Truth words to be sung to a familiar melody. One such hymn that was often sung in early Unity meetings to the melody of "Rock of Ages," is the following:

"Burst with praise, O gate of song;
Flow, O voice from sorrow free;
Let thy currents, pure and strong,
Roll in healing melody,
Till in one harmonious voice,
Pain redeemed, shall earth rejoice.

"Break thy bonds, O child of might;
Claim the freedom of thy birth;
Joy and wisdom shall unite,
Health and power claim the earth;
Love and peace, one circling sea,
Compass man in unity."

Also Myrtle Fillmore wrote the following words to the melody of "The Rosary":

"The hours I've spent with Thee, dear Lord,
Are pearls of priceless worth to me.
My soul, my being merge in sweet accord,
In love for Thee; in love for Thee.

Each hour a pearl, each pearl a prayer,
Binding Thy presence close to me;
I only know that Thou art there, and I
Am lost in Thee.

Oh, glorious joys, that thrill and bless!
Oh, visions sweet of love divine!
My soul its rapturous bliss can ill express
That thou art mine, O Lord! That Thou
art mine!"

Charles Fillmore tried his hand at writing brief verses such as this:

"Behold, what God hath wrought!
An ideal man, a mighty man—
A man supreme, who thought by thought
Must demonstrate what God hath wrought."

One song in the *Unity Song Selections* was written by him:

Healed, healed by His power divine!
One, one with His love sublime!
My life now is sweet and my joy is complete,
For I'm healed, healed, healed!

Both he and Mrs. Fillmore loved to write affirmations that rhymed, such as:

"I am praying and blessing my basket and store;
The Christ mind increases my good evermore."

In an early issue of *Unity*, Charles Fillmore jokingly asked his writers to get Satan behind them when they felt tempted to put their thoughts in rhyme. One subscriber wrote in and said that Satan was behind Mr. Fillmore when he chose the poems that he printed in Unity. Charles Fillmore replied that he wished he had a poetry editor who knew something about the "stuff." Actually he was fond of poetry and printed quantities of verse in his magazine. From his earliest days, he had read the works of the great poets; they had been a major source of his self-education.

Myrtle Fillmore, too, liked poetry; she liked to write it as well as read it. In her correspondence with her brother David Page, she sometimes inclosed bits of verse that she had composed, and he in turn sent her many pieces that he had written.

The Fillmores believed in everything that was joyous

and beautiful. "When joy is put back into religion, there will be more religion in the world," Charles Fillmore wrote.

One time when he was in a restaurant, Charles Fillmore told his wife that he thought the waitress was a Unity student.

"Why do you think so?" she asked.

"She looks like a Unity student," he replied, "she has such a happy look."

When the waitress came to the table again, Mrs. Fillmore asked her if she was a Unity student.

"Why yes," she said in astonishment, "I am."

When she found out that she was waiting on the Fillmores, she introduced to them several other waitresses in the restaurant who were also Unity students. In a few minutes, the cook came smiling from the kitchen with a big cake with "U N I T Y" written on it in sugar. He was a Unity student too.

It was one of Charles Fillmore's greatest satisfactions to feel that he had made people happy. He believed that happiness is the divine right of human beings, and that anything less than happiness is due only to our failure to perceive the full Truth for ourselves. This he taught in all his classes and this he expressed in all his life. "Let the old world wag as it will," he loved to say, "I will be gay and happy still."

CHAPTER XIII

A School of Practical Christianity

"Teaching and Fellowship"

XCEPT FOR a few classes taught in Colorado in the early 1900's, Charles and Myrtle Fillmore did little of their teaching away from Kansas City. Yet, all through the land, there were people praying with Silent Unity and reading the Unity publications. These people were hungry for Truth. They were grateful for the opportunity to unite in prayer with Silent Unity and grateful for the publications, but in many cases there was a demand for more. They wanted to probe deeper into the principles that Charles and Myrtle Fillmore were teaching. Many of them were unable to make the trip to Kansas City to study or take the class work.

The Fillmores did not feel that they had time to teach in other cities, but they wanted to help these persons. They knew how avidly they had sought for inspiration when they had first discovered Truth. There was one teacher especially whom they had tried to get to come to Kansas City. This was Ursula Gestefeld, of Chicago, whose books on Truth were among the clearest and simplest written in the last century. She had not come to Kansas City, but finally she had had mimeographed copies of her lessons sent to the Fillmores for them and their students to study.

In 1909, the Fillmores decided that they, too, could teach students in other cities in this way. They wrote about their new service:

"For years, requests for lessons in the science of

Being have been coming to the Society of Silent Unity, but the way never seemed open to take up the work until recently.

"Early in April of this year (1909) we received a letter from a correspondent who asked that we send her immediately the first lesson in our correspondence course. It was one of those faith demands that cannot go unrewarded. She took it for granted that we had the lessons to give, and it was no doubt her unquestioning faith that brought our Correspondence School into manifestation. We had often considered the matter of opening such a school, but there seemed to be so much to do that was more pressing that the school remained merely an ideal to be fulfilled sometime in the indefinite future.

"The faith shown in the friend's letter quickened our faith, and we felt moved to undertake the work at once. So an agreement was formulated and sent to this friend to sign, and in the few days' time required for the return of the agreement, the first lesson was written and was ready to be mailed to her when the signed agreement came back to us.

"And so our first pupil was enrolled, and so the Unity Correspondence School, so long a dream, was at last established in the manifest.

"When the April number of *Unity* went out, April 15, it carried the first announcement of the school, and in a few days applications for membership began to come in. At this writing, June 4, the enrollment is 268."

The original lessons were written by Charles Fillmore. They were sent out on the freewill offering plan.

In a few months, not only were students enrolled in this new school from all parts of the United States, but also from Canada, Cuba, Hawaii, England, and India. By 1911, over two thousand students had been enrolled. Today thousands of persons are receiving their instruction in

Truth principles through the Unity Correspondence School. For several years in the early 1900's, Charles and Myrtle Fillmore taught summer classes in Pueblo and Denver, and in August, 1901, they conducted a school in Manitou called "The Colorado Summer School of Metaphysics." Most of the classes of this school were held in a large tent, which seated about one hundred and fifty persons on its wooden benches. At night, the tent was lighted by coal oil lamps. In the daytime, some of the meetings were held in the open, where the people gathered to hear Mr. Fillmore and the other teachers make their talks.

The Fillmores and some of the students lived in tents set up on the grounds. Grandma Fillmore was along and did her cooking in the Fillmore tent. The three Fillmore boys hiked and played in the mountains. Rick had just become interested in photography. By day, he took pictures of the meetings and the teachers and by night developed his films in the waters of a stream that ran through the grounds.

The Fillmores last taught classes in Colorado in 1902. After that, except for a brief series of lectures that Charles gave in Chicago in 1921 and a short trip to New York that he made in 1926, Charles Fillmore did not leave Kansas City again until after the passing of his wife.

The Fillmores had not named their organization Unity School of Christianity idly. Few weeks went by when they were not teaching classes. They taught classes in Truth principles, in prayer, in healing, in prosperity, in numerous allied subjects.

Most of their students came from Kansas City, but always there were a few from other places. Each summer, they conducted what was known as the "Intensive Training School," which drew students from all over the country. This course lasted two weeks.

This was the origin of the Unity Training School, which today is conducted through the summer months at Unity headquarters and attracts hundreds of students. In 1930, when Silent Unity moved back to Tracy Avenue from Unity Farm, the large building that it had occupied was made available to the Unity Training School.

Today the Training School is like a seminary, with courses in public speaking, comparative religion, center organization, Bible history and interpretation, Unity principles, and other subjects. Students come to it from all over the world, and there is a large staff of teachers composed of workers at headquarters and center leaders from other cities. A single class at this school often has many times more students than sat in an earnest circle around Charles and Myrtle Fillmore in the early days of Unity and discussed with them the principles of Truth, yet it is out of those first small classes in practical Christianity that the larger school has grown. Today attendance at the Unity Training School is a requirement for becoming a Unity minister.

Each term at the Training School consists of four weeks. For this period, the students live on Unity Farm as in another world—and such it is, a world apart. As Jesus went up into the mountain to pray, students go to Unity Farm to withdraw into a spiritual environment. At the end of the four weeks when they return to their homes to give to others the ideas they have learned, they go fortified in spirit and renewed in mind and body.

Students and teachers live a simple life on Unity Farm, studying, discussing Truth, meditating, praying. The intensive study course leaves little time for thoughts of the world of affairs. The students sleep in cottages that have been erected in an apple orchard and they eat their meals together at the Terrace Tea Room. These meals are joyous occasions, though the fare is plain. No meat is served at the Tea Room, as no meat was served at Unity Inn, the cafeteria that Unity School operated in Kansas City.

Charles and Myrtle Fillmore did not eat meat. Soon after the founding of Unity, they decided that a meatless diet was conducive to spiritual thinking, and from time to time in their magazines, they advocated vegetarianism. They felt that it is more humane and more healthful.

In the early days, when Unity was located on McGee Street and there were only four or five workers, these ate together. There was a stove in the house, and one of the workers was appointed to prepare something hot for everyone. The workers discussed food and its relation to the spiritual life and decided that it would be better for them not to eat meat.

Later when Unity moved to Tracy Avenue, the workers still chose to have their lunch together, so lunch was prepared in the house at the rear of the lot. At first, only workers ate there, but other persons who were interested in vegetarianism expressed a wish to eat there too, so Unity bought a larger house on the corner of Tenth and Tracy, and opened a restaurant.

For several years, no set price was charged for the food served there. Those who ate were left free to pay what they wished for their food.

At first, meals were prepared by Unity workers, as had been done on McGee Street. Some of the girls from the office would go over and lend a hand at the noon hour, serving at the steam table, clearing tables, and doing whatever was needed. Myrtle Fillmore acted as hostess, going from table to table, talking to her friends, making everyone feel at home.

In a few years, the house on the corner of Tenth and Tracy became too small to accommodate all who wished to eat there, and in 1920 a large restaurant building, decorated by Rickert Fillmore, was erected on the corner of Ninth and Tracy, to which Unity Inn was moved. Here for thirty years, the public and Unity workers were served meatless meals in cafeteria style at nominal prices.

In regard to vegetarianism—as with most of the things they taught—the Fillmores left their students free to follow them or not as each felt led. The Fillmores were not trying to put forth a creed that their followers had to accept; they were not trying to convert people to a new religion. Those who studied Unity were of all religions (such they still are); they were Methodists and Catholics and Presbyterians; many were not even Christians. To all these, the Fillmores said in effect: "Here are some ideas that we believe to be true. Examine them; study them; accept those that you can use in your life. For the rest, do not let what you cannot accept keep you from accepting what will help you now. The time may come when you can accept these other ideas too. However that may be, if some of our ideas are of practical value to you now, we are happy to be of service."

> "The first step is to grant all people entire freedom to follow their own understanding," wrote Charles Fillmore, "no matter how wrong they may appear to us. If they will listen we may express our ideas, but further than that we should not go. They should be free to accept or to reject, as seems good to them."

It was with a great reluctance that Charles and Myrtle Fillmore set up a fixed procedure for becoming a teacher of Unity. "The doors of Unity," they said, "swing in for all who want to come and study, and they swing out just as readily for those who want to go forth and teach."

184

Charles and Myrtle Fillmore had their own ideas that they believed in passionately. They had even withdrawn from the I.N.T.A. because they felt that their teaching had little in common with that of most of the members of that organization. They felt, however, that everyone should be free to interpret Truth according to his own light. In an early issue of his magazine, Charles Fillmore wrote that the Unity rooms were open to everyone "interested in progressive thought. Teachers, healers, or lecturers passing through the city are invited to make any announcement they wish in connection with their work."

If other teachers wished to sell Unity literature, the Fillmores were happy to have them do so and did not ask what they taught. Their names were listed as Truth teachers at the back of *Unity* magazine at their request. When New Thought lecturers came to Kansas City, many of the regular Unity audience went to hear them. Sometimes the Fillmores themselves went.

Once when a lecturer who had been a fellow student with the Fillmores at the school of Emma Curtis Hopkins came to Kansas City, Mr. Fillmore heard that a number of Unity students were going to hear him. "There's nothing wrong with him," he said. "He's fine, only he doesn't put Truth in as simple language as we do, and he charges a good stiff fee for it."

Nevertheless, the Fillmores found at last that they had to place limitations on what could be taught in the name of Unity. All over the country, little groups of students who were studying Unity literature began to meet together and to start classes in the Unity teachings. Often those who led these groups knew very little of the teaching of the Fillmores. They held seances, cast horoscopes, told fortunes, read palms, and practiced numerology. The Fillmores themselves did not believe in any of these things and spoke out against them in their magazines. Still they were reluctant to tell other teachers what to teach—even when the teachings were put out under the name of Unity.

In the summer of 1925, at a conference of Unity teachers, a group that did not approve of some of the things that were being taught in the name of Unity but were unlike the teachings of the Fillmores, met together in the Pergola Room at Unity Inn one afternoon and formed what they named "The Unity Annual Conference." They adopted a set of rules to govern the teaching and conduct of leaders of Unity centers and classes.

Although Charles Fillmore told them at first, "I can't see why you want to bind yourselves with a lot of rules and regulations; leave yourselves free," he could see presently that the step they had taken was a necessary one.

This step assured those who might attend a Unity center that they would receive the same simple, practical teaching of the Fillmores that they were receiving through the Unity literature. Today this self-governing organization of Unity center leaders is known as the "Unity Ministers' Association." Its members meet every year at Unity headquarters. It sets the standard for more than two hundred centers.

Charles and Myrtle Fillmore did not believe in applying restrictions to the teaching of Truth because they knew that Truth is largely an individual matter: the Spirit of Truth is in every person, and it is only through the awakening of this inner Spirit that anyone can come to know Truth. Books and teachers may be of value along the way, but in the final analysis each individual has to find Truth for himself, within himself. It is this belief that is the basis of Charles Fillmore's teaching about the Bible.

Several of Charles Fillmore's books consist of interpretations of the Bible. As early as 1889, he was printing such interpretations in *Unity* magazine.

"Scripture as mere history," he wrote, "is not profitable to the overcoming metaphysician; what he looks for is practical instruction in mind operation. . . . When we look deeper than the mere historical recital, we find that there is a veiled meaning, which may be understood by one who is familiar with the operations of his own mind."

Few man have thought more about the meaning of the Bible than Charles Fillmore. To him, it shed light on every phase of human existence, and one of the great tasks that he set for himself was the exposition of the Bible's inner light to men. To him, the Bible was valuable not because it is a history of people who lived thousands of years ago, but because when properly understood it sheds light on our own problems and shows us the way to more abundant health, prosperity, and happiness. To him, the Bible was valuable because of its practicality; he thought of it as a guidebook to daily living.

To Charles Fillmore, the Bible was more than the Word of God. The Word of God is the Spirit in man, and the Bible is an attempt "to describe that invisible Word which cannot be described, but must be lived." He wrote:

"Practical metaphysicians do not study the letter of the law . . . They study mind in its original purity as manifest in themselves and all men. Then they find that the Scriptures are written in cipher—that they veil the movements of ideas under the symbols of men and nations. Bible writers were dealing with ideas all the time. . . . These they represented by the things of sense because they were writing for the instruction of a people who, like children, had to be amused by pictures and catchy stories."

187

Charles Fillmore's study of the Bible culminated in 1931 with the publication of the *Metaphysical Bible Dictionary,* the most pretentious work published by Unity School. This work is an analysis of the hidden meaning of all the names that appear in the Old and the New Testaments. Although Charles Fillmore had assistance in preparing it, the original idea was his and most of the interpretations that appear were taken from his writings and lectures.

There was much of Daniel in Charles Fillmore, who spent countless hours in prayer. He delighted in hidden meanings. He loved to dream and to interpret dreams. He wrote that God spoke to him through his dreams. He loved to explore the mysteries of Spirit. Yet always, he was interested in these matters with a practical end in view. He explored the hidden meaning because he felt that it might contain something that could be applied to the everyday world of fact, something that would help men to live more abundantly. He sought arcane truths, and he sought to apply them to everyday problems. On his winged imagination, he made far flights of mind, and always it was in the hope that he could bring back to the footweary world trudging through its workaday existence some idea that would prove to be of comfort, strength, and inspiration.

Charles Fillmore once said that Unity could be defined as pure "Christian mysticism practically applied to everyday living." He was a mystic, as was Myrtle Fillmore; but they were mystics with a mission, and that mission was to help men have healthier, happier, richer lives. This is what made his approach to religion such a scientific one. In him, the scientific and religious approach to life were blended. He felt that the discoveries of modern science were a step toward the abundant life that he was preaching.

At the time when Unity was first founded, Darwinism

and materialism had taken hold of the minds of people. The church was denouncing science as denying the truths of the Bible, and the exponents of science were claiming that the Bible is full of falsehoods. In the very first issue of *Modern Thought,* Charles Fillmore had an article to the effect that science and religion should resolve their conflict. He saw clearly that the only religion that can stand is one based on Truth and that the only science that will not destroy itself is one based on religious principles.

One of the goals of his writing was to show that science and religion are but two different approaches to the same Truth. He felt that modern physicists, with their theories about the ethers and energy, are approaching with a different set of terms the same truths that Jesus taught when He taught about the kingdom of the heavens and the power of faith and prayer.

In an address that he made at a meeting of the World Fellowship of Faiths held during the Century of Progress in Chicago in 1933, he declared:

"My aim is to prove that science, in developing the unseen forces of the ether is merely revealing the mechanical side of that realm which Jesus called the 'kingdom of the heavens.'

"The approach of religion to the 'kingdom' is through Spirit; the approach of science to the same, under the name of the luminiferous ether, is through physics, chemistry, and kindred fields of research.

"That science and religion have not worked in unity is borne out by history. Religion functions in the realm of ideas and science in the realm of facts. By facts we mean anything that may be proved by material tests. Christianity has been very jealous of its revelations and has assumed that they are far more valuable than the discoveries of science. When Saint Augustine proclaimed that 'nothing is to be accepted save on the authority of the Scriptures,' a wall of ecclesiastical authority inclosed Christianity, and the pages of church history testify to the entrenchment within that inclosure of millions of followers of Jesus. There could be no new revelations from God; the slogan of religious authorities was 'Where the Scriptures speak, we speak; where they are silent, we are silent.' Then followed the persecution even to death of anyone who dared to discover anything that seemed to conflict with the accepted interpretations of the Bible. The horrors of the Inquisition are almost unspeakable.

"But the proved facts of scientific research and discovery have bit by bit broken down the wall of narrow dogmatic assumptions reared by Christianity, and we are finding that we have, like the Pharisees of Jesus' time, been making the dead letter of Scripture revelation take the place of the living Christ. Jesus was a demonstration of the fact of God's existence and power in this world, and when charged by the ecclesiastical congress with breaking their law He thundered, 'Ye search the scriptures, because ye think that in them ye have eternal life; and these are they which bear witness of me; and ye will not come to me, that ye may have life.' . . .

"Jesus loved to talk about this kingdom of the heavens and He compared it or said it was 'like unto' this and that in many parables and mind pictures. . . .

"To perform its miracles, modern science draws upon the kingdom of the heavens. It tells us that out of this kingdom come light, heat, power, color, sound, electricity, magnetism, life, and substance; in fact, that everything that exists in this universe came out of this invisible, omnipresent kingdom of the heavens, the luminiferous ether. Scientists tell us that in their discoveries they have merely touched the hem of the garment of a kingdom that, by further discoveries along the same line, will revolutionize our whole civilization."

It is this scientific approach that especially distinguishes the Unity teachings. Charles Fillmore did not believe that God is an arbitrary and extraneous Being who answers or fails to answer prayer according to His changing whim. He taught that God is law. He taught that life is governed by law, every incident in life, and that as we gain an understanding of the divine law, we can use it to change our life.

"The world," said Charles Fillmore, "is governed by the law of mind action." It was through this belief that he came to Unity's unique concept of prayer—the use of affirmations and denials, spiritual decrees rather than petitions, in addressing God.

Affirmations and denials are statements that deny the reality of undesirable conditions and affirm the reality of God and His good, such as *"There is nothing in all the universe for me to fear, for greater is He that is in me than he that is in the world,"* and *"I am a radiant, all-wise, all-loving, all-conquering son of God."*

"Prayer," wrote Charles Fillmore, "is not the beseeching a reluctant God. It is intercommunion with God. 'Ye ask, and receive not, because ye ask amiss.' Not that we ask for what God is not willing to give, nor what we, as His children may not rightfully ask for and claim; but because we beseech and supplicate, as though God were not willing but possibly might be induced to change and grant our petition. This is a false notion.

" 'For I, Jehovah, change not.' 'Jesus Christ is the same yesterday and today, yea and for ever.' If God ever did answer prayer, He always does, being the same God. Therefore, if there seems to be any lack of principle, it is in the one who prays. Misunderstanding of the will and nature of our God prevents prayer from being answered.

"Prayer does not change God, the unchangeable,

but it changes mortals and makes them receptive to that good which is being given without limit. 'God is Spirit: and they that worship him must worship in spirit and truth.' Translate material desires into their spiritual correspondents and then declare that in Truth and in Spirit you receive that which you desire, and then you will have it materially as well as spiritually. 'But seek ye first his kingdom, and his righteousness; and all these things shall be added unto you.' "

Fifty years before the inception of the science of psychosomatics, which treats of the relationship of the mind to bodily illness, Charles and Myrtle Fillmore were teaching that the ills of our body are the result of our wrong thinking, that disease has its origin in negative mental and emotional states. Over and over, in the early pages of *Unity,* they traced physical disturbances to mental causes. Many years ago, Myrtle was writing to a correspondent:

"Perhaps it will help if I tell you that I suffered with a trouble similar to yours for years. And I prayed for healing, many times; and did all I knew to please the Lord; and still my healing did not come. I tried to look over all my faults, and to bring myself into harmony with Truth. After asking the Lord to show me just what was hindering, Spirit spoke to me very clearly, saying, 'You have looked among your faults; now, suppose you look among your virtues.' And I did; and there I found the cause of the deep-seated physical suffering and congestion!

"I had considered it a virtue to control my feelings; to never give way to them, outwardly; to never let anyone know when I was hurt or angered. I kept a calm and pleasant exterior, but inside I sometimes grieved and resented and worried and rebelled. And, my secret thoughts and feelings were cutting and congesting and weakening my vital organs and the walls of my body. As I turned the light of Spirit upon these hidden things, and sought to have Divine Mind transform my very sub-consciousness, so that I should work from an entirely new basis, I was healed and restored to harmony and strength. There were times, after the first revelation, when I would forget and give way to old ways of thinking, and there would come a physical warning. I have found that whatever thoughts I harbor do produce some sort of results in me or my environment; that if I want perfect health, I must let the law of God, the rules of harmony and health, come first, regardless of what they do to old habits and thoughts."

The Fillmores taught that the way for a man to change his physical condition is to change his thinking. "People come to me and they ask me for help," said Charles Fillmore. " 'Ask me to do anything,' they say, 'but don't ask me to change my thinking.' But they have to change their thinking if they want to be well."

Over and over, the Fillmores echoed the words of Paul, "Be ye transformed by the renewing of your mind."

"What can a man do with the thoughts of his mind?" Charles Fillmore wrote. "He can do everything with them. They are under his absolute control. He can direct them. He can coerce them. He can hush them or crush them. He can dissolve them and put others in their place. There is no other spot in the universe where man has mastery. The dominion that is his by divine right is over his own thoughts. When man apprehends this and commences to exercise that dominion, he has begun to open the way to God, the only door to God—through mind and thought."

"The purpose of prayer," the Fillmores taught, "is to change your thinking. God does not change; His will is always, only good. All that keeps you from your good is your failure to unify yourself in thought with the source of all good, God."

Following this line of thought, the Fillmores worked out a new technique of prayer, which they called the silence, using affirmations and denials. They instructed the student to relax in mind and body, to turn to God in his thoughts, to think not about his problem but about God, whose wisdom, love, and power are mighty to solve every problem. To enable him to keep his mind away from the problem and on God's presence and power, they taught the student to use affirmations and denials, repeating them over and over. The words themselves had no magic power, but continued concentration on them brought the student to realize the Truth in them. "Ye shall know the truth, and the truth shall make you free."

Jesus taught, "All things whatsoever ye pray and ask for, believe that ye receive them, and ye shall have them." The Fillmores' technique of prayer is based on this idea of Jesus'—"believe that ye receive"—and those who apply this idea rediscover what many churchmen have forgotten, that faithful prayer gets results.

The Fillmores did not advance new teachings. All that they taught is based on the Bible, and especially on the teachings of Jesus. They saw Jesus as the Son of God, the Master, conscious of His oneness with our Father, demonstrating His Sonship in His life, the perfect channel of God's power and love. They felt that Unity is a return to His original teachings, a return needed for centuries. Before they decided to call it "practical Christianity," they had called their teaching "primitive Christianity."

The Fillmores went back to the original teachings of Jesus, and came forth with a modern, seven-day-a-week religious teaching, expressed in up-to-date, easy-to-understand language. They demonstrated that religion has practical value in helping people handle today's problems.

194

Jesus taught that God is loving and accessible. "The kingdom of God is within you," He said, and Paul told the Athenians, "In him we live, and move, and have our being." But through the centuries, people had come to believe in God as a stern judge, living in a far off heaven to which people went after they died.

The Fillmores re-stated in modern language the great truths that they found in the Bible: "God is within you. You can find Him there. Heaven is a state of mind. You can enter into heaven now."

"God is your loving Father and you are His beloved children," they taught, and repeated as had Jesus the words of the Psalmist, " 'Ye are gods, And all of you sons of the Most High.' "

" 'Christ in you, the hope of glory!' " they declared. "The Christ Spirit is in you, and the Christ power. Claim it now, use it now to remake your life."

The Fillmores lived by the Bible. They studied the misunderstood teachings of Jesus—about the immanence of God, about the love of God, about the power of believing prayer. Jubilantly in their magazines, in their books, in their talks, they proclaimed these teachings until thousands on thousands of people were putting the teachings into practice and proving with quickened bodies, with minds set free, with lives renewed, that the teachings are true.

Charles and Myrtle Fillmore were people of vision. Their vision is expressed in Mrs. Fillmore's first affirmation, *"I am a child of God and therefore I do not inherit sickness."* It was the vision of a way of life better than that which men have so long felt that they are heir to.

The teaching of Charles and Myrtle Fillmore was an affirmation of life. "Live!" they proclaimed. "Live free! Live whole! Live eternally!"

195

CHAPTER XIV

The Later Years

"Unto Eternal Life"

Charles and Myrtle Fillmore did not believe in age. They believed that they had constant access to a fountain of youth, the Spirit within themselves. "Whosoever drinketh of the water that I shall give him shall never thirst; but the water that I shall give him shall become in him a well of water springing up unto eternal life."

When Charles Fillmore was nearing fifty, he wrote in *Unity:*

"About three years ago, the belief in old age began to take hold of me. I was nearing the half-century mark. I began to get wrinkled and gray, my knees tottered, and a great weakness came over me. I did not discern the cause at once, but I found in my dreams I was associating with old people and it gradually dawned upon me that I was coming into this phase of race belief. . . .

"I spent hours and hours silently affirming my unity with the infinite energy of the one true God. I associated with the young, danced with the boys, sang 'coon' songs with them, and for a time took on the frivolity of the thoughtless kid. In this way I switched the old age current of thought.

"Then I went deep down within my body and talked to the inner life centers. I told them with firmness and decision that I would never submit to the old age devil, that I was determined never to give in. Gradually I felt a new life current coming up from the life center. It was a faint little stream at first, and months went by

197

before I got it to the surface. Now it is growing strong by leaps and bounds. My cheeks have filled out, the wrinkles and crow's feet are gone, and I actually feel like the boy that I am."

Early in his study of spiritual principle, Charles Fillmore came to the conclusion that ill health is unnecessary, that old age is unnecessary, that death is unnecessary. The Fillmores believed in reincarnation; they thought that they had lived many times before. Charles even thought that he knew who he had been in previous incarnations. But the Fillmores did not believe that reincarnation is the final answer. They believed that the recurring process of birth and death over and over again is not essential, that it is possible for a human being to come into so great an awareness of his spirituality and of his life in Spirit that he can transform the very flesh of his body into spiritual substance, living energy, so that the body becomes an immortal vehicle of the immortal Spirit of which it is an expression.

"Science," wrote Charles Fillmore, "is proving by experimentation that living cells have within them the elements of continuous life, and scientists are at loss to know why man's body should ever die, if it were properly fed and cleansed."

To the question "Do you expect to live forever?" Charles answered:

"This question is often asked by *Unity* readers. Some of them seem to think that I am either a fanatic or a joker if I take myself seriously in the hope that I shall with Jesus attain eternal life in the body. But the fact is that I am very serious about the matter. . . .

"It seems to me that someone should have initiative enough to make at least an attempt to raise his body to the Jesus Christ consciousness. Because none of the followers of Jesus has attained the victory over this terror of humanity does not prove that it cannot be done. . . .

"I do not claim that Jesus has unconditionally promised me that I shall overcome death as He overcame it. The promise is conditional. 'He that overcometh, I will give to him to sit down with me in my throne, as I also overcame, and sat down with my Father in his throne.' I am trying to come up to His standard. . . .

"No man will ever attain anything unless he attempts attainment."

Charles Fillmore never swerved from this belief. In 1919, he went through an illness so serious that some of those who were close to him did not think that he would survive, even though they were affirming Truth for him. For months, he was unable to deliver the Sunday talks. Yet whenever he was able, he was at his office, doing what he could; and always, steadfastly, whatever appearances might indicate, he was affirming health for himself. He came out of the illness with renewed vigor. Through the 1920's, the growth of Unity made ever-increasing demands on his time and energy, but he was able to meet them all.

In 1923, his youngest son Royal passed on. Charles and Myrtle Fillmore had had great expectations of the part that he was to play in the Unity work. Royal had been a big, good-natured, exuberant person with a host of friends, and active in a score of civic enterprises.

Charles and Myrtle Fillmore felt deeply the passing of their son, but even more deeply they felt the truth of the principles they were teaching and the need to cling to those principles with redoubled courage and faith. They had dedicated themselves to helping mankind find a way of life free from sickness, poverty, and death—and they held to their high purpose.

They knew that the way they were trying to go was

not an easy one. Charles Fillmore often repeated the words of Napoleon, "There shall be no Alps!" He saw the Alps clearly enough; but he knew that great faith would overcome them.

The Fillmores had been pioneers all their lives. They were not dismayed by appearances. They kept on praying in faith. They kept on affirming the Truth they believed. They kept on affirming life. They knew that unless someone tried to make the overcoming, it would never be made. Someone had to make the start. Even if the first ones who tried did not succeed, nevertheless a first step would be made. They dared to try.

The next few years were years of joy and action for the Fillmores. Unity School was growing at an unprecedented rate: new magazines were being established; the old services were being augmented; new centers were opening; the headquarters on Unity Farm was being developed.

At home, they had their family. The Fillmores were people with a warm sense of family ties. Both Lowell and Rickert entered the Unity work, and their parents were able to turn over to them many of the details of running the organization. Today Lowell Fillmore is President of Unity School and Rickert Fillmore is Secretary. Both of them married girls whom they had met at Unity School. Rickert married Harriet Collins in 1919 and had two children, Charles Rickert, born in 1921, and Rosemary, born in 1925. Lowell married Alice Lee in 1926. Frances, Royal's daughter, made her home with them. Today there are six great-grandchildren in the family. Charles Rickert married Ann Jones in 1943. Their children are Harriet Fillmore, born in 1944, and Constance Fillmore, born in 1948. Rosemary married Stanley Grace in 1947. Their children are Stanley Rickert Grace, born in 1948, and Rosalind Fillmore Grace, born in 1950. Frances married Robert Lakin in 1945. They have two children, Robert Fillmore Lakin, born in 1946, and Charles Edward Lakin, born in 1948.

Lowell and Rickert have their homes on Unity Farm, and as their parents spent part of each week at The Arches, they were all often together. Charles and Myrtle Fillmore had many happy times with their family. Like most other grandparents they were sometimes called upon to play the roll of baby-sitter.

"You'd smile," wrote Myrtle Fillmore to her sister, "to see me rushing around, trying to keep up with the many things I find myself 'in for.' First, I want to look after some little thing at home; then meetings; then the letters in the office; then another meeting or two; then a trip downtown; then a nap (if I can crowd one in); then an evening out; then a trip to the Farm, and sometimes the care of one of the little folks; then the trip back, to take up work where I left off! And I just keep getting stronger, and younger, and happier, and more interested in things than ever."

There was scarcely time for a vacation. There was much work to be done, not only their work with Unity School but the spiritual work they were doing with themselves. Mr. Fillmore received many requests to make talks in other cities. As his wife wrote in answer to one such request:

"He just isn't much interested in traveling about, and being looked at, and talked to, or even entertained. If he had been the type who likes to travel about, it would have proved that he thought more of such things than he did the delving into the unseen realms of spiritual ideas—and this school, so far as we are concerned, would never have been successfully established."

March 29, 1931, was Charles and Myrtle Fillmore's

golden wedding anniversary. It was a Sunday, and when they entered the chapel at 913 Tracy Avenue the congregation was waiting to honor them. They were ushered up to the platform, and there as a tribute to their golden wedding, Ernest C. Wilson read the Unity marriage ceremony. Myrtle wrote to a friend, "We were quite satisfied to trust the half-century knot that had held us so well, but the new minister surprised us by making it time proof."

That afternoon in Rick's house on Unity Farm, the family had a party for them. Rick took motion pictures of them as they sat on the lawn outside his house. With their children and grandchildren gathered around them and the Unity buildings rising like a backdrop to their joy, this must have been a moment of fulfillment.

A few weeks later, they opened the Unity Training School. In the new school Charles and Myrtle Fillmore taught a class in "Fundamentals of Practical Christianity."

That had been the title of the first Unity class that they had taught. Around them once more, a group of students gathered, as students had gathered for forty years, to hear them teach Truth and affirm their faith in life. But this was to be their last class together.

On October 6, 1931, Myrtle Fillmore passed to the invisible side of life.

Those who knew her closely felt that in some way beyond their own power to understand, Mrs. Fillmore had willed to make this change. For months, she had had her secretary put everything in order as if she knew that she was going.

Several times, in earlier years, she had told friends that she personally felt that she had accomplished all that she was able to in this lifetime and wanted to pass on, but that it had been revealed to her that it was not yet time.

This time, she had felt strongly that she was going to make the transition.

A short time before her passing, she had been visiting with one of the Unity workers. It was the kind of visit that she liked to make with all of the workers, stopping by his desk to pass a few words and to give him a benediction and a smile. In the course of the conversation, she mentioned that she wanted to make a change.

"That's fine," the worker answered. "What kind of change?"

"I believe that it would be easier to do the work that is ahead of me from the invisible plane," she said.

"Oh, you mustn't do that," he replied. "We need your help and inspiration, your spiritual guidance here."

"You know that you will have that anyway," she said smiling.

On the Wednesday before her passing, she helped Charles Fillmore lead the Wednesday evening healing service and the next day she was around the office all day in a gay mood, talking with the workers, writing letters, receiving callers.

That evening, as was customary with her, she left the office in Kansas City and went to The Arches where she usually spent Friday and Saturday. She spent the evening helping to pick apples from the trees around her home. Some friends who came to visit her found her up on a ladder in the orchard. The next morning, she was ill and, on the following Tuesday, she passed away.

Two Sundays later, Charles Fillmore was in his regular place, conducting the service at 913 Tracy Avenue. For forty years every Sunday, Myrtle Fillmore had led the meditation at this meeting. Now Mr. Fillmore took over this part of the service and said:

"Dear friends and co-workers in Christ: It is not our custom here at Unity even to mention the visits of the 'last enemy,' whom we have resolved finally to overcome, as taught by Jesus.

"But there are certain conditions under which we should exchange sympathy and give thanks for that universal unity which these days of stress and strain have brought. I feel your sympathy and I thank you from the bottom of my heart for your many expressions of comfort in thought and word. This occasion is so pregnant with the absence and the presence of the one who has for years stood in my place at this point in our Sunday morning lesson that I am constrained to speak a few words of consolation and comfort, not only for you but for myself.

"Personality sorrows and grieves when the bodily presence is withdrawn, but the sense of absence can be overcome when we realize that there is a spiritual bond that cannot be broken. We do not look at life as a 'night between two eternities,' as do those who, Paul says, 'have no hope,' because they live and have been educated in a foolish fashion, looking at life as a transitory, material thing; but we who are following Jesus Christ in the resurrection know life as a spiritual thing, and that we live spiritually, if we understand the law of life, and that we shall continue to live in Spirit, 'whether in the body or out of the body.' And we know that this spiritual bond is the only bond that will really endure."

Now where there had been two to think together, to plan together, to work together in the cause of Unity and in the service of the Truth that they had discovered and believed in, Charles Fillmore was alone. Yet he was not alone. He was a man with friends in every part of the world. And the Father abiding in him was a real and living presence in his life.

For thirty years, except for two brief visits to Chicago and one to New York, Charles Fillmore had stayed at work in Kansas City. During all that time, he had never taken a real vacation. Everywhere there were thousands of people who wanted to make his acquaintance, who wanted to see and hear this man whose teachings had meant so much in their lives.

Charles Fillmore began to turn over more and more of the details of running Unity School to the people around him, especially to his sons, Lowell and Rick. Yet he did not retire as active head of Unity. He was like the captain of a ship who turns the helm over to the mate. He was there in the cabin if he was needed, and occasionally he came out on the bridge to keep a weather eye on what was going on. Few steps were taken without his approval.

In December, 1933, Charles Fillmore, after more than forty years of continuous service, retired from the pulpit of the Unity Society of Practical Christianity in Kansas City.

On December 31, 1933, he married Cora G. Dedrick, who had for many years served him and Myrtle Fillmore as private secretary and at one time had been the director of Silent Unity. They were married at Lowell Fillmore's home on Unity Farm.

The next day, the two left for California; and Charles Fillmore, who had always been trying the untried, was off on yet another new venture. He went on a lecture tour, the first of many that were to fill the remainder of his life and take him to every part of the nation.

The tour got off to an exciting start. The first lecture was in Los Angeles. Into the Shrine Auditorium, seven thousand two hundred persons jammed to hear him speak, while more than one thousand others were turned away for lack of room.

Charles Fillmore looked the crowd over (many times larger than any he had ever addressed) from behind the red plush curtain. When at last he went out to face the audience, "I feel like a little boy away from home," he began. When the speech ended the crowd rose from its seats and in a wave of applause swept onto the stage to tell this "little boy away from home" how much they loved him and how much his teachings had meant in their lives. He had to be hurried out of the press of his well-wishers.

From Los Angeles, Mr. Fillmore went to San Jose, where the Unity center was in need of funds. He gave a series of talks and turned over the offerings to the center. Then it was on to San Francisco where thousands more thronged to listen to him and to give him an ovation. It was late in the spring of 1934 before he was back in Kansas City, in time to teach at the Training School.

The next winter, Mr. Fillmore was off on another lecture tour, this time through the northeast section of the country. This tour, like most of those that were to follow, was made by automobile. Although at home he was a late riser, when he was traveling he was up early, ready for the day's drive to the next town. He usually stayed in tourist cabins and stopped to eat his lunch by the side of the road from an ice box carried in the car. Often, if he did not have a speech to make, in the evening he would go to a motion picture show, which he loved to attend. Charles Fillmore was a good traveler. Once when his companions thought to fix some pillows in the back seat so that he could lie down, he had them taken out, saying he wanted to sit up and see what was going on.

All his life, Charles Fillmore had unusual stores of energy. He once wrote in *Unity:*

"Complaints are coming in that *Unity* is not being

issued on time. I am the one responsible for this. The
Publishing Department waits on my matter and is de-
layed when I am not prompt. I have undertaken more
writing than I can well accomplish with my other duties. Yet I work twenty-one hours out of twenty-four
and have kept it up at this pace for several years. It is
daylight every morning before I catch the few hours'
sleep that 'knits up the raveled sleeve.' This three hours'
waste will eventually be overcome, and I shall work
right through without a wink."

Later when the Fillmores became interested in radio,
Charles Fillmore would often stay up most of the night in
order to broadcast a talk in the early morning hours.

The Fillmores were among the first to see the possibilities
in radio; Unity was probably the first organization to give
religious broadcasts. In 1924, Unity School purchased radio
station WOQ, the oldest licensed broadcasting station in
the Middle West. Unity speakers had been giving talks over
the station for two years before that time.

The first Unity talks were broadcast by Francis J. Gable
from the window of a downtown store, where a crowd could
gather outside to watch the newfangled contraption in operation. When Unity bought WOQ, the studio was moved
to the building at 917 Tracy.

Charles Fillmore loved to speak on the radio and would
make two or three talks a week. The studio had to be completely closed during broadcasts, even in hot summer weather; use of electric fans was prohibited because it would interfere with the broadcasting. Nevertheless it was not unusual
for Mr. Fillmore, with the perspiration streaming from him,
to deliver an hour's speech over the radio.

Every week or two, he would stay up until 3 or 4 o'clock
in the morning and make an hour's talk at that time. He
would prepare a long time ahead for these speeches. In those

years, there were few stations and none that gave all-night programs, so in the early morning WOQ had the air waves virtually to itself. It was on a good frequency and its programs were picked up all over the country. Charles Fillmore had announcements of many of these early morning broadcasts in the magazines, and Unity students everywhere were able to tune in and receive the program. People wrote from the farthest corners of the country to Mr. Fillmore that they had set their alarm clock and gotten up to listen to him.

Those were the years when owners of radio sets tried to see what distant stations they could receive, and many people had their first introduction to the Unity teaching on these early morning broadcasts. Letters came from night watchmen and fire stations and garages all over the United States.

Charles Fillmore never ceased to be a man of action, a man of decision. On one of their lecture trips to Florida, Charles and Cora Fillmore stopped at a tourist court. Their cottage had a large porch in front of it that caught Mr. Fillmore's fancy. Cora Fillmore owned a piece of land with a small cabin on it near Unity Farm, and they had talked about building a home on it.

"You know, Cora," Charles Fillmore told her, "it would be nice if we had a place with a porch like this." Right then he measured the porch. Late into that night, he was planning exactly the kind of home he wanted. Before he fell asleep, he had sent a night letter to a builder in Lee's Summit describing the house that he had planned and ordering its construction. He wanted it ready, he wrote, when he returned home from the trip.

It was in this house that Charles Fillmore spent most of his last twelve years. It is located in some wooded hills about one quarter of a mile southwest of Unity Farm. Because Mr. Fillmore always loved to have people around him, this house, like his others, was often filled with guests and visitors. Sometimes friends would come and stay for weeks at a time.

He had some apartments built over his garage to provide a place for some of the young people employed at Unity to live. Often late into the night, his young tenants sat around the Fillmore hearth talking and laughing with their host— and also praying.

A few years later on one of his lecture trips to California, Charles Fillmore bought a house in the San Fernando Valley outside Los Angeles. Thereafter, he divided the year between his two homes, writing and lecturing in California in the winter and teaching at the Training School at Unity Farm in the summer.

To those around him, Charles Fillmore never seemed to grow old. Those who were close to him said that throughout the last years of his life his crippled leg was constantly improving, filling out, growing stronger. One of the features that strangers noticed first about him was his radiantly pink skin. "The skin on his face shone," as that of Moses shone as he returned to the valley from Mount Sinai after having received from God the Ten Commandments.

He discovered on his lecture tours that many in the audience expected a large, aggressive man and were astounded at the slight, gentle, twinkling person who came out upon the platform. He liked to tell the story of how on one of his first tours, as he walked onto the platform one evening, he saw two little old ladies sitting down in front peering eagerly up at him. As he seated himself and closed his eyes to enter into the silence—as was his custom when he had a speech to make—he overheard one of the ladies remark to the other: "So that's him, is it?—all washed and pink and powdered like a baby."

Charles Fillmore had a fountain of youth within him, and the waters were forever joyously bubbling up. Life to him was a journey in jubilance. In his eighties, he started taking singing lessons. As his crippled leg improved, he told his friends he was considering taking dancing lessons.

He loved to make up affirmations and would write them on large sheets of paper in heavy black characters. Charles Fillmore had an unusual handwriting. The powerful lines of his signature almost always brought comment from persons who saw it for the first time. At ninety-four, his handwriting was as vigorous as a young man's. He used special writing crayons, and with these he wrote out by hand all his works, books, lectures, affirmations. He left a trail of affirmations wherever he went, like sparks struck from the anvil of faith. A few months before he passed on, he wrote this one:

"I fairly sizzle with zeal and enthusiasm and I spring forth with a mighty faith to do the things that ought to be done by me."

A short time before his passing, he was approached with the suggestion that he get together some biographical material about himself. "Wait another hundred years," was his reply.

Charles Fillmore never gave up his hope of eternal life in the body, in his body. When he was ninety-two he wrote in *Unity* magazine:

> "In my article in the August, 1946 *Unity,* I stated that I had such a vital realization of Jesus' promise 'If a man keep my word, he shall never see death' that I should never pass out of this body. Subscribers are now asking if I mean that I shall live forever in the flesh body. I answered that point in the article as definitely as it can be answered in words. I expect to associate with

210

those in the flesh and be known as the same person that
I have been for ninety-two years, but my body will be
changed in appearance from that of an old man to a
young man with a perfectly healthy body.

"I do not claim that I have yet attained that perfection but I am on the way. My leg is still out of joint but
it is improving as I continue to work under the direction
and guidance of Spirit.

"Some of my friends think that it is unwise for me
to make this public statement of my conviction that I
shall overcome death, that if I fail it will be detrimental
to the Unity cause. I am not going to admit any such
possibility; I am like Napoleon's drummer boy. I do
not know how to beat a retreat and am not going
to learn."

Charles Fillmore worked on as long as his undefeatable
spirit could move his body. In February of 1948, he was
still making speeches at Unity centers in Los Angeles. There
he became ill. It was the same ailment that he had had thirty
years before when some of those around him had felt that
he would not survive.

In April, he came back to his home near Unity Farm.
From then on, he began slowly to slip away. Occasionally
he was able to sit up, but for the most part he lay in bed.

He showed no fear of death. "I am facing it, but I am
not afraid of it," he said.

He never lost his sense of humor. When someone made
a witticism or said something pleasant to him, he never
failed to smile.

Often Cora Fillmore would read him things that he
himself had written. Sometimes he did not recognize
them, as they were the manuscripts of talks that he had
delivered and forgotten years before, but he always liked
them. "That's logical," he would say of some passage as she
read. "I can see that."

Once he asked of a friend who came into his room, "Do you know what the most important words in the world are?"

The friend shook her head. "No, Mr. Fillmore, I don't," she replied.

" 'Christ in you, the hope of glory'—those are the most important words in the world." He lay silent for a moment, then he repeated, " 'Christ in you, the hope of glory.' "

Several days before his passing, he slipped into a coma from which he emerged only for brief intervals. He knew that death was not far away. He said, "I am going to have a new body, anyway, and this time it's going to be a perfect body."

Still he did not accept the necessity of death. All his life he had affirmed life, believed in life, lived to the full. "The last enemy that shall be abolished is death," Paul had said. To Charles Fillmore, this was the goal. He had believed in the divine possibility of its attainment all his life and, though it did not look as though he himself was to attain it, he was not going to relinquish it. He held steadfast to his faith. Even at the end he expressed it.

He would have kept his body, however unsuited it may have been as a vehicle for such a vital spirit. Charles Fillmore could not have willed otherwise. "I do not know how to beat a retreat," he had written. He did not know how to affirm anything else than life.

Shortly before his passing, he began to have a vision. It recurred several times, always the same one, a vision that he had held to all his life, that he had done his utmost to make a reality upon the earth. "Do you see it? Do you see it?" he would ask, staring intently upward. "The new Jerusalem, coming down from God, the new heaven and the new earth —don't you see it?"

212

His son Lowell spent the last night at his bedside. Charles was asleep throughout the night. At 10 o'clock on Monday morning July 5, 1948, he woke, smiled as if at someone that he saw and recognized, and was gone.

Across the way at Unity Farm, the activity had come to a halt because of the Fourth of July holiday. The shells of the buildings that were in process of construction stood empty. The printing presses were idle. The workers were gone from their desks in the building at 917 Tracy Avenue. Only a little group in Silent Unity was keeping the constant vigil of prayer.

The next morning, Unity Farm rang with the sound of men and machinery at work, rushing the buildings toward completion. The presses were thundering out the magazines that bore witness to the faith of the Fillmores. The Unity workers were back at their desks in Kansas City, sending out books and magazines, answering the cry for prayer. From fifty radio stations scattered in many parts of the globe, the Unity Viewpoint was being broadcast. The work of Unity was going right on. It was as Charles Fillmore would have wanted it to be.

Unity Tower

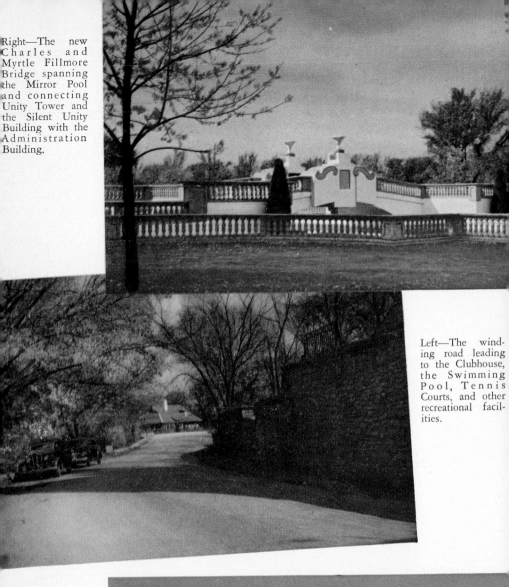

Right—The new Charles and Myrtle Fillmore Bridge spanning the Mirror Pool and connecting Unity Tower and the Silent Unity Building with the Administration Building.

Left—The winding road leading to the Clubhouse, the Swimming Pool, Tennis Courts, and other recreational facilities.

Right—The view from Highway No. 50 showing Unity Tower and its relation to the Administration Building on the right.

Left—Unity Lake and Dam, which supplies water for all the Unity Farm buildings.

ight—A view of the Apartment uilding in early spring, with the rsythia in bloom in the foreground.

Left—The Administration Building and the new Charles and Myrtle Fillmore Bridge.

Above—The Silent Unity Building, in which the consecrated workers of the Society of Silent Unity, through prayer, minister to those who ask for help.

Below—The Unity Printing Building, where the Unity books, periodicals, and other Unity publications are produced. The architecture is in the Italian Renaissance style.

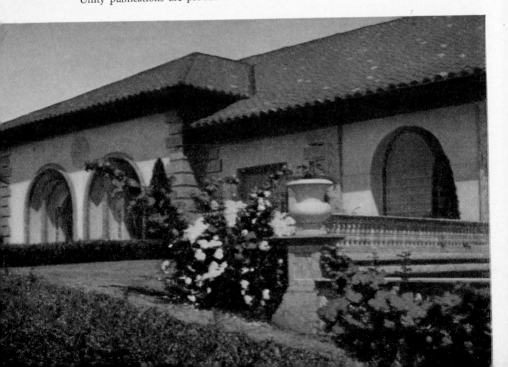

CHAPTER XV

A World-Wide Influence

"That They May Have Life"

THE WORK OF UNITY is going right on. Two decades have gone by since Myrtle Fillmore's passing. Charles Fillmore has been gone for three years. Yet the organization that they built grows on; the ideas that they taught have an ever-lasting influence.

Because Charles and Myrtle Fillmore built on the rock of principle instead of on the sands of personality, they are as much alive today as they ever were. They live in every prayer uttered at Unity School; they live in the words of this book and in all the words of all the magazines and books that go forth in the name of Unity; they live in the lives of all—perhaps you are one—who have changed their lives by using Truth.

How shall we measure the influence of Charles and Myrtle Fillmore? Can it be measured by the Unity literature?

From twelve printing presses, often running night and day, come millions of pieces of Unity literature each month. There are seven English language magazines: *Unity, Weekly Unity, You, Good Business, Daily Word, Wee Wisdom,* and *Unity Sunday-School Leaflet.* There is also a Spanish magazine, *El Sembrador,* which is distributed to Spanish-speaking persons. These eight magazines carry the Unity message into more than a million homes every month. Besides the magazines, Unity publishes dozens of books and hundreds of pamphlets.

Unity's literature has penetrated into the farthest corners of the earth. Sheep ranchers in the interior of Australia and Eskimos in Alaska subscribe for its magazines, read its books and pamphlets. To meet the demand from foreign countries, Unity publishes literature in Dutch, French, German, Greek, Ibo, Italian, Japanese, Portuguese, Russian, Spanish, and Swedish.

During World War II, Unity printed a peace prayer in sixteen languages, but they were not enough to meet the needs of all its students. A letter came to Unity headquarters from a small town in the interior of India. A copy of *Daily Word* containing the prayer had reached there and a man who had read it wrote in to ask why the prayer had not been printed in Hindustani. He sent a translation of it in that tongue.

Although no one from Unity headquarters has ever visited Nigeria, for the many Nigerians who study Unity literature, Unity prayers are published in Ibo, the Nigerian tongue. A Nigerian, visiting the United States, liked the Unity literature, took it home with him, and it turned out to be popular with his fellow countrymen. A few years ago, a geologist making notes in Nigeria wrote that there is even a drum beat that signifies Unity.

Through Silent-70, the literature goes free of charge to about eight thousand public institutions in this and other countries. *Lessons in Truth, Finding the Christ in Ourselves, Daily Word,* and *Wee Wisdom* are printed in Braille and distributed free to the blind. Into leper colonies, into orphanages, into prisons, and into hospitals the Unity message, freely given, goes to bless hundreds of thousands of the sick and unfortunate in every part of the earth.

If we measured the influence of the Fillmores by the scope of the Unity literature, we should conclude that their influence goes far. But their influence goes beyond the printed word.

Their influence goes beyond the spoken word too. To-day in Unity centers in hundreds of cities, classes in Unity are taught, Unity lectures are given, Unity services are con-ducted. In 1934, radio station WOQ was discontinued, but today the Unity message goes out from more than fifty sta-tions, not only in the United States but in Australia, New Zealand, and Cuba, to a rapidly growing radio audience, which is estimated to be more than three million.

Yet the influence of the Fillmores is even wider than this. Countless numbers of writers and teachers and minis-ters have absorbed the Unity idea, and from pulpits and books that have no avowed connection with the Unity move-ment, the Fillmores' idea goes forth.

How then shall we measure Charles and Myrtle Fill-more's contribution to humanity? The contribution of some people can be measured by the buildings they left behind them. Can we understand the Fillmores better by looking at the buildings they built to house the Unity work?

Sixty years ago Charles and Myrtle Fillmore dreamed of having a place where those in need could go to be ministered to in prayer. Today at Forty-seventh and Jefferson Streets, on the Country Club Plaza in the southwestern section of Kansas City, the Unity Temple is the fulfillment of their spiritual vision. The first services in the Temple were held in Fellowship Hall, which is the Sunday-school assembly room, in 1947. This hall has a seating capacity of about eight hundred, and many times that number thronged through the beautifully decorated corridors. The Sanctuary, which seats fifteen hundred, was used for the first time on Easter Sunday, 1950. It was filled to overflowing twice that morn-ing and hundreds were turned away.

Costing more than one million dollars, the Temple has two large auditoriums and numerous Sunday-school rooms. Besides the Sanctuary and Fellowship Hall, there are two chapels. The Charles Fillmore Chapel is a place of beauty, and the small Myrtle Fillmore Chapel is a place for quiet prayer. Charles Fillmore would have loved to have Fellowship Hall with its wonderful equipment, for the games and dinners and parties and shows that the Unity Society put on when he was at its helm. The many spacious and colorful rooms of the Sunday school, especially designed to meet the needs of the children, would have thrilled the heart of Myrtle Fillmore. "Who will take care of the children?" she asked in her vision long ago. This Sunday school is Unity's latest answer.

Yet the contribution of the Fillmores cannot be measured by this temple. It cannot be measured by the more than 1200 acres that are Unity headquarters near Lee's Summit, Missouri.

Walk here among the lanes and paths, across the lawns, through the gardens and the orchards, or pause beside a wayside bench where two students are discussing some point of Truth, and you may begin to catch something of what Charles and Myrtle Fillmore mean to humanity, for there is a tranquil air about this place that blesses everyone who visits it. Here are rock walls covered with rambling roses, and rude stone bridges arching over quiet streams. Flights of stone steps climb up and down green slopes. Lanes wind past slate-roofed cottages, lanes rimmed with poplars that reach up like spires. Fountains laugh in the sunlight, and calm pools reflect the stillness of the trees that edge them round and the peace in the hearts of those who come to discourse or to meditate by their still waters. The sun sparkles on the red-tiled roofs of the many-windowed, cloistered buildings where the spiritual work goes on night and day. Beside the highway rises the Tower, a waymark, a guidepost, a symbol of strength, an emblem of faith, a promise of prayer.

You may come even closer to understanding the contribution of Charles and Myrtle Fillmore if you will drive along U. S. Highway No. 50 some dark night and turn off through the entrance to Unity School. From the windows of one of the rooms in the Silent Unity Building a light will be shining. These are the windows of the Silent Unity telephone room. There workers remain on constant duty, serving and praying, waiting for a call that may come from a home nearby or from the farthest ends of the earth, waiting not only for a call that may come over the telephone or telegraph but also for a silent call that may come from the sick and lonely heart of someone somewhere who in the moment of his need is silently, and from afar, turning in his mind to God through Unity. This year, more than six hundred thousand persons are calling on Silent Unity for help.

The contribution of the Fillmores is more than one of words or buildings. It is one of hearts and minds and lives rebuilt by the transforming touch of their ideas.

Men have always been burdened by the belief that they were born to suffer and die, to be buffeted by evil chance. They have thought of God as far removed from them, willing suffering and death.

The Fillmores dared to set men free. They knew that God is near, as near as one's own thoughts, as near as one's own heart, as near as one's own faith and love and wisdom. They saw that men are bound not by the will of God but by the limitations of their own minds and they dared to strike off the shackles of the mind. They turned people back to the teachings of Jesus—"Ask, and it shall be given you," "According to your faith be it done unto you," "Love one another." They showed that by the application of His simple teachings to daily living men could transform their lives.

If you wish to catch the meaning of the Fillmores, do not seek in printed page and spoken word. Look about you. Seek for their meaning in the lives they have transformed. You may find it in the life of your own neighbor.

On a ranch in western Texas, a rider dismounts from his horse. As he stands looking out across the plains, his thought turns to his wife who is ill. As anxiety starts to surge into his mind, he thinks of the words of the prayer on the card that came from Unity, and for a moment he repeats them silently.

In a room of a London hospital, a mother is waiting. Her daughter has just been taken to the operating room. The doctors have given her little hope. But the mother is not thinking of her fears; instead she has taken from her handbag a little magazine. On the cover is the name *Daily Word*. She opens it and turns to the lesson for the day and she reads: *"I am infolded in the one great Heart that beats for all. My mind is at peace, and I am healed."*

On a ship in the Pacific, a sailor has been reading a magazine called *Unity*. He never heard of Unity before, but he found this magazine among those placed aboard ship for the men to read. He has read it through. Now he is reading it again. He does not know much about religion, but these ideas sound practical. He has a lot of time. He has decided he will see what prayer can do. He quiets his thoughts. *"God is my help in every need,"* he declares silently.

A woman sits alone in a small house in Florida. Her husband went to work disheartened despite her efforts to cheer him up. With the rising prices, they seem to be getting farther and farther behind with their bills. Now she takes out her prosperity bank. She drops a coin into it. She repeats the prayer printed on the back of the bank: *"The Spirit of the Lord goes before me, and my health, happiness, prosperity, and success are assured."* Silently she prays for God's wisdom and love to make their way clear.

In a Roman villa, a countess is preparing to go to sleep. From the drawer of the table beside her bed, she takes out a typewritten letter. It is creased and blurred from many readings; but she reads again, as she has read many times since she received it long ago: "Dear Friend: Silent Unity has received your letter and is praying with you."

In Lee's Summit, Missouri, a worker from Unity headquarters has just turned away from the telephone. When she arrived home after her day's work, she found her little girl ill. Now as she hangs up the receiver, the familiar words are ringing with reassurance in her mind: "Silent Unity will be praying with you; God is with your little girl."

Driving down a highway in California are an elderly couple on their vacation. As they drive along, they turn on the radio. Over it comes a voice: "Good morning, Friends— The Unity Viewpoint . . . "

A prisoner in a penitentiary in New York has been studying a book that he received from an organization called Silent-70. The name of the book is *Lessons in Truth.* He began to read in doubt but as he read something about this book caught hold of his imagination. This is a different kind of religion. He turns to the last lesson. "Bondage or Liberty, Which?" he reads.

If you would find the true message of Charles and Myrtle Fillmore, turn into your own heart and pray. Live for a time by the Unity idea: dare to believe that God is your

221

health; dare to believe that He is your support; dare to believe that you have in you all the ideas that you will ever need for a happy and successful life; dare to be generous, loving, free. Then in your own liberated spirit, in your own liberated life, you will understand what Charles and Myrtle Fillmore came to teach.

"I came that they may have life, and may have *it* abundantly."

"According to your faith be it done unto you."

Selections
from the writings of
Charles Fillmore

To enable Charles Fillmore to speak for himself as a writer and teacher, some excerpts
from his books and articles are presented here.
This section is necessarily limited to the writings of Charles Fillmore, because Myrtle Fillmore wrote little besides her letters, from many
of which this book has quoted.

Books by
Charles Fillmore

ATOM-SMASHING POWER OF MIND
THE TWELVE POWERS OF MAN
MYSTERIES OF GENESIS
JESUS CHRIST HEALS
CHRISTIAN HEALING
MYSTERIES OF JOHN
TEACH US TO PRAY
TALKS ON TRUTH
PROSPERITY

Books by
Myrtle Fillmore

LETTERS OF MYRTLE FILLMORE
WEE WISDOM'S WAY (out of print)

Reform Your God Thought

HIS IS DISTINCTLY the age of reform. Never before have there been such widespread and persistent efforts by both men and women to right the wrongs of religion, society, and politics.

From the hearts and souls of millions goes up the cry "Set us free from our burdens." Every imaginable scheme of release is proposed, and each advocate of a panacea for the people's ills stoutly affirms his to be the only remedy that has virtue. It is observed that the majority of these reformers are clamorous that laws be enacted to force their theories upon the people. In this, they are following the same methods to cure the ills of the body politic that they have followed in curing the body physical, and the results will surely be of like impotency.

Laws, whether natural or artificial, are but the evidence of an unseen power. They are simply effects, and effects have no power in themselves. When man looks to them for help in any condition of inharmony, he is departing from a universally recognized principle of sequence. God, Spirit, or Mind—whatever you choose to name it—is the supreme dictator, and thought is its only mode of manifestation. Mind generates thought perpetually; all the harmonious and permanent affairs of men and the innumerable systems of the infinite cosmos are moved in majestic measures by its steady outflow.

All power has its birth in the silence. There is no exception to this rule in all the evidence of life. Noise is the dying vibration of a spent force. All the clatter of visibility, from the harangue of the ward politician to the thunder's roar, is but evidence of exhausted power. As well try to control the lightning's flash by wrapping the thunder about it as attempt to regulate men's minds by statutory enactments.

All reforms must begin with their cause. Their cause is mind, and mind does all its work in the realm of silence, which, in reality, is the only realm where sound and power go hand in hand. The visible outer world, with all its social, religious, and political laws, customs, and ceremonies, is but the flimsy screen upon which mind throws its incongruous opinions. God's thought is love, the inherent potentiality of the God man, which knows neither persons nor things, mine nor thine, but a universal brotherhood in which perfect equity and justice reign in joint supremacy. All philosophers and sages have recognized this silent cause, this perpetual outflow from center to circumference. Emerson says of Plato: "He was born to behold the self-evolving power of Spirit, endless generator of new ends; a power which is the key at once to the centrality and the evanescence of things." Jesus said: "The kingdom of God is within you." "Seek ye first his kingdom, and his righteousness; and all these things shall be added unto you." Elijah found God not in the whirlwind or the earthquake or the fire, but in the "still small voice."

All men who have moved the world to better things have received their inspiration from the Spirit within and have always looked to it for instruction. God is not a person who has set creation in motion and gone away and left it to run down like a clock. God is Spirit, infinite Mind, the immanent force and intelligence everywhere manifest in nature. God is the silent voice that speaks into visibility all the life there is. This power builds with hands deft beyond the comprehension of man and keeps going, with all its intricate machinery, universe upon universe, one within another, yet never conflicting. All its building is from center to circumference. The evidence for this runs from the molecule and the atom of the physicist to the mighty swing of a universe of planets around their central sun.

Every act of man has its origin in thought, which is expressed into the phenomenal world from a mental center that is but a point of radiation for an energy that lies back of it. That point of radiation is the conscious *I*, which in its correct relation is one with Cause and has at its command all the powers potential in Cause. The conscious *I* can look in two directions—to the outer world, where the thoughts that rise within it give sensation and feeling, which ultimate in a moving panorama of visibility; or to the world within, whence all its life, power, and intelligence are derived. When the *I* looks wholly within, it loses all sense of the external; it is then as the Hindu yogi sitting under his banyan tree with his eyes riveted on the point of his nose, denying his very existence until his body is paralyzed. When it looks wholly without, upon sensation and feeling, it loses its bearings in the maze of its own thought creations. Then it builds up a belief of separateness from, and independence of, a causing power. Man sees only form and makes his God a personal being located in a city of dimensions. This belief of separateness leads to ignorance, because all intelligence is derived from the one Divine Mind, and when the soul thinks itself something alone, it cuts itself off in consciousness from the fount of inspiration. Believing himself separate from his source, man loses sight of the divine harmony. He is like a musical note standing alone, looking upon other notes but having no definite place upon the great staff of nature, the grand symphony of life.

Life is a problem informed by a principle whose essence is intelligence, which the wise man always consults. The ignorant and headstrong trusts to his intellect alone to carry him through and he always is in a labyrinth of errors.

A belief prevails that God is somewhat inaccessible, that He can be approached only through certain religious ordinances; that is, a man must profess religion, pray in a formal way, and attend church in order to know God. But these are mere opinions that have been taught and accepted by those who perceive the letter instead of the spirit. For if God is Spirit, the principle of intelligence and life, everywhere present at all times, He must be just as accessible as a principle of mathematics and fully as free from formalism. When a mathematician finds that his answer to a problem is not correct, he consults the principle and works out the correct solution. He knows that all mathematical problems inhere in mathematical principles and that only through them can they be worked correctly. If he persistently ignored principles and blundered around in a jungle of experiments, he would be attempting to get up "some other way" and he would prove himself a "thief and a robber," for there is but one way. Jehovah God, infinite Mind in expression, is the way, and this Mind is always within reach of every man, woman, and child.

It is not necessary to go in state to God. If you had a friend at your elbow at all times who could answer your every question and who loved to serve you, you certainly would not feel it necessary to go down on your knees to him or ask a favor with fear and trembling.

God is your higher self and is in constant waiting upon you. He loves to serve and will attend faithfully to the most minute details of your daily life. If you are a man of the world, ask Him to help you to success in any line that you may choose, and He will show you what true success is. Use Him every hour of the day. If you are in doubt about a business move, no matter how trivial, close your eyes for an instant and ask the One within yourself what to do, just as you would send a mental message to one whom you know and who could catch your thought. The answer may not come instantly; it may come when you least think of it, and you will find yourself moved to do just the right thing. Never be formal with God. He cares no more for forms and ceremonies than do the principles of mathematics for fine figures or elaborate blackboards.

You cannot use God too often. He loves to be used, and the more you use Him the more easily you use Him and the more pleasant His help becomes. If you want a dress, a car, a house, or if you are thinking of driving a sharp bargain with your neighbor, going on a journey, giving a friend a present, running for office, or reforming a nation, ask God for guidance in a moment of silent soul desire.

Nothing is too wicked or unholy to ask God about. In my early experience in the study of Christian metaphysics, I was told that through the power of Divine Mind I could have anything I desired. I had a lot I wanted to sell and I asked God to dispose of it to a certain man who I thought needed it. That night I dreamed that I was a bandit holding up my customer. The dream showed me that I was asking God to do what was not right, and I thereby gained a lesson. A saloonkeeper came to me for health treatments and was helped. He said, "I also need treatments for prosperity, but, of course, you could not prosper a man in my business." I replied: "Certainly. God will help you to prosper. 'If ye shall ask anything of the Father, he will give it you in my name' does not exclude saloonkeepers." So we prayed for prosperity for the man. He afterward reported that he was out of the saloon business and had found prosperity in other lines of work.

If you are doing things that are considered wicked, you will find swift safety in asking God first, then acting or refraining, as you are moved. Some persons act as if they thought that they could hide themselves from the one omnipresent intelligence, but this is the conclusion of thoughtlessness. God knows everything you do, and you might just as well have His advice. God does not want you to reverence Him with fear. God certainly never can get your confidence if you constantly stand in quaking fear of Him. He will do you a favor just as quickly if you ask in a jolly, laughing way as He would if you made your request in a long, melancholy prayer. God is natural and He loves the freedom of the little child. When you find yourself in His kingdom, it will be "as a little child."

God's kingdom of love and unity is now being set up in the earth. His hand will guide the only ship that will ever sail into the Arcadian port, and the contented, peaceful, and happy people who throng its decks will sing with one voice, "Glory to God in the highest."

A Sure Remedy

HERE IS A mental treatment that is guaranteed to cure every ill that flesh is heir to: Sit for a half-hour every night and mentally forgive everyone against whom you have any ill will or antipathy. If you fear or if you are prejudiced against even an animal, mentally ask forgiveness of it and send it thoughts of love. If you have accused anyone of injustice, if you have discussed anyone unkindly, if you have criticized or gossiped about anyone, withdraw your words by asking him, in the silence, to forgive you. If you have had a falling out with friends or relatives, if you are at law or engaged in contention with anyone, do everything in your power to end the separation. See all things and all persons as they really are—pure Spirit—and send them your strongest thoughts of love. Do not go to bed any night feeling that you have an enemy in the world.

Be careful not to think a thought or to say a word that will offend. Be patient, loving, and kind under all circumstances. You can do this if you are faithful to the silent hour, because there you will be helped to overcome the selfishness of the carnal sense.

There is an immutable law lying back of this healing method. God is love, and love is manifest as life. God is thus manifest in and through all His creations. If we do aught to cut off the love of any person, we are cutting off the love of God; hence, we are cutting off the life that flows through all. When we, by withdrawal from our fellows, in any way cut the cords of love that bind us together as men and women, we, at the same time, sever the arteries and veins through which the universal life flows. We then find ourselves mere bundles of strained nerves, trembling and shaking with fear and weakness, and finally dying for the lack of God's love. But omnipresent Spirit ever seeks to flow into us and to stimulate us in every faculty. We must, however, by our words and acts acknowledge this all-powerful Presence as the moving factor in our life, because each of us has inherent free will, which welcomes or rejects all, even God not being excepted.

Self-condemnation is also a great error, leading to dire results. If you have accused yourself of ignorance, foolishness, fear, sickness, anxiety, poverty, anger, jealousy, stinginess, ambition, weakness, or if you are melancholy and indulge in the "blues," ask forgiveness for each of the loving Father in whose image and likeness you spiritually have perfect life. Say often to this omnipresence:

I do now sacrifice these human limitations unto Thee, O Father! I am obedient unto the law of my being and I know that in Thee I am brave, true, energetic, wise, pure, perfect, strong, rich, and courageous. Thou art my almighty resource, and I do trust in Thee utterly.

The Overcoming Mind

WE BEGIN the new year with our usual inward joy and Christian smile. Regardless of outer circumstances, a real Christian has an inner conviction that all things are working together for good to them that love the Lord.

A Christian is one who has the "mind of Christ," which is the supermind, the mind of the spiritual man. Jesus had the "mind of Christ"; so did Job, who said, "When they cast *thee* down, thou shalt say, *There is* lifting up."

The Christ mind is the overcoming mind. No one ever went down to defeat who in his hour of need declared the almightiness of God through Christ. Many Christians theoretically know and proclaim that Christ saves to the uttermost, but when tribulations come, they think it their Christian duty to play the part of the downcast; like the good woman who, when her friends remonstrated with her for making such a fuss over her troubles, wailed, "When the good Lord sends tribulations, I tribulates."

It is no easy matter to appear helpful and happy in the face of adverse conditions, and no one can, in fact, do it without the aid of a power superior to personality. It is here that Christians who know the truth of man's real spiritual being have the advantage over those who trust in the arm of flesh alone.

We often wonder whether our conduct is pleasing to God. We think we have a monitor in that inner guardian, conscience. But conscience may be seared over by being repeatedly disregarded and may no longer function. Again, the poet moans, "Conscience does make cowards of us all." So some of us are conscienceless and others so conscience-minded that we are haunted by the ghosts of crimes we

233

never committed. Either state brings us to unhappiness, which is not the standard of life patterned for man by Divine Mind.

All the great prophets, poets, and wise men of every age have discerned that this universe is attuned to law and harmony, which has no other issue than joy.

"In thy presence is fulness of joy;

In thy right hand there are pleasures for evermore," sings David. Job says that "the morning stars sang together." Jesus promised, "Your heart shall rejoice, and your joy no one taketh away from you."

No one in mere human consciousness can conceive of the ecstasy that wells up in the heart when the gladness of Spirit floods the soul. It is not like the joy that propitious events produce. There may be no external cause whatever; the situation may even seem to be desperate; as, for instance, that of Paul and Silas, who had been stripped and beaten with rods and cast into a dungeon with their feet made fast in the stocks. Such misery cannot be conceived of in our day; yet, in spite of it, Paul and Silas "were praying and singing hymns unto God, and the prisoners were listening to them; and suddenly there was a great earthquake, so that the foundations of the prison-house were shaken: and immediately all the doors were opened: and every one's bands were loosed."

No external condition or circumstance can hold the soul of man in bondage when he makes mental contact with God. If you want joy to come into your life, begin to rejoice in the things that you know about the goodness of God. We all have many blessings that we have not valued as we should. Begin to praise God for the abundance of all things: your words will crack the omnipresent ethers, and good will flow to you from every direction.

It is written in the 28th chapter of Deuteronomy, "Because thou servedst not Jehovah thy God with joyfulness, and with gladness of heart, by reason of the abundance of all things; therefore shalt thou serve thine enemies . . . in hunger, and in thirst, and in nakedness, and in want of all things."

We make ourself servant of the things we build up in our mind. Thinking and talking about lack or ill-health will lay hold of the etheric living substance in which our mind functions and make it manifest. One who knows this law can blame no one but himself for sickness or poverty.

Begin right where you are to rejoice and to be glad in Spirit. Then, according to Job:

The Almighty will be thy treasure,
And precious silver unto thee.
For then shalt thou delight thyself in the Almighty,
And shalt lift up thy face unto God.
Thou shalt make thy prayer unto him, and he will hear thee;
And thou shalt pay thy vows.
Thou shalt also decree a thing, and it shall be established unto
    thee.

How Should We Pray?

SHOULD WE PRAY in words that imply faith in a sure answer to our prayer or should we ask meekly, leaving the answer to the will of God? This proposition confronts most of us at various times, and our mind wavers between the two attitudes, and the answer is always weakened by the wavering whether we realize it or not.

Whichever way we decide to pray, we quote the Scriptures to fortify our position and usually find enough to satisfy us that we are right. The majority of the prayers of Jesus are affirmations, according to English translations, which are not always in harmony with the original text. For example, the Lord's Prayer, which we so universally use, in the original is a series of affirmations. The translators had no conception of the majesty of man as the Son of God and they twisted His prayer of decrees into a supplication for help. When we realize that we are the outlet of a mind that seeks an adequate expression, we shall cease our begging prayers and elevate our thoughts and words to the high standard set by the Master.

God created man to express Him in the manifest world, and we fall short in our mission when we fail to measure up to our divine authority. Jesus, the representative Son, affirmed, "All authority hath been given unto me in heaven and on earth." When He prayed, things happened, and He expected His followers to do likewise. We are asked why our prayers do not always bring things to pass as His did. The usual answer is that we have not developed faith or assurance equal to that of Jesus. But how shall we go about developing this Christ faith? We have asked for the faith of Christ and even declared it in His name, yet it does not abide with us continually. Why?

236

The answer is that we have not realized and appropriated our princely heritage. We have not trained our mind away from the negative race beliefs but have allowed it to fall into the popular channels of thought, thereby attaching ourself even more firmly to human impotency. Here is a point of which every Christ initiate should be made aware, namely that Christ's baptism has given us a very decided mind expansion and infused into our thoughts and words a power that we did not before possess: "His word was with authority."

Jesus taught His followers to assert the affirmative in thought and word. We do not know the exact words He used in His most radical statements, but judging by the English into which they have been translated from the Greek, Jesus was very positive in His assertion of the power of spiritual man and especially of those who follow Him in the regeneration. He taught and demonstrated that the word could be used to build or destroy. The destructive power was illustrated in the fruitless fig tree. It was in this connection that He laid down the laws through which we can bring forth whatever we desire. What could be stronger in this respect than this? "All things whatsoever ye pray and ask for, believe that ye receive them, and ye shall have them."

We who have studied the sources of the mind know from our experience that the ills of humanity all have their root in thought and the failure of man to express his thoughts in harmony with Principle.

Thought control is imperative, and there is urgent need of teachers on both the mental and spiritual planes of consciousness if the race is to go forward in development. To this end, there needs to be more co-operation between these two schools, because they complement each other. Religion becomes practical and effective in everyday life when it incorporates spiritual psychology as part of its litany. Without religion, psychology is weak in its fundamentals, and without spiritual psychology, religion fails to give proper attention to the outlet of its ideals. The fact is that religion, comprehended in its fullness, includes psychology. Jesus was a profound psychologist.

The fact is that religion cannot be effectively taught in its scientific aspect without applying the higher attributes of the mind. Paul is the outstanding psychologist of the Bible, and none other comes anywhere near him in this respect. He says, "Have this mind in you, which was also in Christ Jesus." He refers repeatedly to the mind of Christ as the model for all Christians. In Hebrews, we are told, "I will put my laws into their mind."

Comparing our mind with that of Christ Jesus, we find many points in which we can improve ourself in thought and word. We may assert that we believe but do we prove it in our mental deportment? Every Truth student may become a disciple and reap the benefits promised by Jesus if he or she will assume the mental attitude of a Christian and practice the power of words.

"They Say, and Do Not"

I N MATTHEW is written, "Then spake Jesus to the multitudes and to his disciples, The scribes and the Pharisees sit on Moses' seat: all things therefore whatsoever they bid you, *these* do and observe: but do not ye after their works; for they say, and do not." Then Jesus tells how the scribes and the Pharisees put burdens upon the people "grievous to be borne"; how they "make broad their phylacteries, and enlarge the borders *of their garments,* and love the chief place at feasts, and the chief seats in the synagogues, and the salutations in the marketplaces, and to be called of men, Rabbi."

Jesus was giving a lesson on "faith without works," that is, on teaching others without doing ourself; on preaching without practicing; on proclaiming a doctrine that we do not demonstrate. Man takes a lot of credit, frequently, for being good, when he has no real enduring good. He sits in the seat of Moses; he understands the law and lays it down for others, but does not follow it himself. It is quite common to hear Truth students say, "I understand the law but I cannot demonstrate." There is a reason for every failure to demonstrate. It is usually found in too much theory and not enough practice. We cram our intellect with great truths; we see the wonderful possibilities of man; but we do not get down to the simple, everyday application of the rules of thought, word, and act that carry out the law of Being. We are like that friend of Emerson's who, he said, "soared into the empyrean heights, and dived into the unfathomable depths—but never paid cash." We look into the heavens and discern in the earth great possibilities, but do not prove the simple law of life in either.

We will always find the key to every problem in some

mental attitude. The Pharisee assumes that his knowledge of doctrine gives him high rank spiritually. But Jesus taught in this same chapter that, instead of wanting the chief place in the synagogue, we should be willing to take the lowest place, even to become servants. We must be willing to take an humble part, like a child learning his first lesson.

The intellectual man comes to the door of the temple of Truth and asks to be admitted because he writes Ph.D or L.L.D. after his name. Do the diplomas of earthly institutions open the door to spiritual understanding? If anything, they bar the door. It does not make any difference how many diplomas you have; they do not help you the least bit in the understanding of Truth. You can be called "Rabbi" by all the religious people in the world, but it will not help you into spiritual understanding. You may be the highest church dignitary in the whole world and yet be outside the pale of Truth. Some simple peasant may know more about Truth than you know. You may have studied many metaphysical books and yet not know Truth, because you have given more attention to the study than to the lowly work of threshing out your thoughts. To get an understanding of what is taught by Jesus and what is taught in the Bible, one must begin at the very lowest round of the ladder and deal with the simple *yes* and *no* of the science of mind.

Many metaphysicians, and often those who think that they are very advanced, are given to this tendency to forge far ahead of their demonstrations. They are talking the highest kind of a philosophy and putting very little of it into practice. Yet these people are not up for condemnation or blame, although in this same chapter, Jesus said, "Woe unto you . . . Pharisees!" He said that the Pharisees compassed both "sea and land to make one proselyte; and when he is become so, ye make him twofold more a son of hell than yourselves." People who understand with their heads what they call Truth are, as a rule, very active in making proselytes. A proselyte is one who is converted to believe what you believe. Religious Pharisees seek converts to their particular form of religion. They tell the convert, "You must believe just as I tell you," or "just as it is written in our book," or "just as our teacher teaches." Is this Truth? No. Truth gives everyone freedom. "Where the Spirit of truth is, there is liberty." If anyone tries to bind you in Truth, you may know at once that he has not found the real thing. Truth is a universal science, like mathematics. There are many textbooks and teachers, but every student must work out his own problems.

If you are not applying the principles taught in Truth to the problems that come up in your life, it is evident that you do not understand Truth or that you are not using the formative power of thought. If you have not demonstrated, get down onto some low place in the synagogue; find the very lowest seat and get hold of some simple statement, such as, *I am Spirit* or *The kingdom of God is within me.* Jesus said, "The kingdom of God is within you." If the kingdom of God is within you, you should realize it. Will one ever find the kingdom of God in the outer world? Will one ever find it by studying books, even the Bible? I tell you, no. It is not the work of man that brings you into the consciousness of the kingdom but it is the work of Spirit. It is first the work of your own Spirit. And if you want really to get hold of the power that regenerates, get still and *feel* the working forces of your soul and body.

It is sometimes a little difficult to get people started in this simple way, because the whole race is overeducated in head knowledge. The doctrines of the different religions have been built up in the race thought, and the minds of most believers are set. If you talk with them, you must discuss your points from the standpoint of their education. So it is a difficult matter to get them off the ecclesiastical high horse that they are riding. As a rule, they think that they know it all. Religious zeal eats up brain tissue, and ministers have nervous prostration like businessmen. "The zeal of thy house hath eaten me up."

The story goes that a mystic in the old country once had a young man come to him to be instructed in spiritual things. This young man had been taught in the colleges—he was a theological graduate—and the mystic master did not know just how to start him in the simple methods of Truth. The mystic said: "Look at your little finger for one year and then come back to me. This will be your first lesson." The young man went away puzzled but obedient. He began to look at his little finger and study it every day and he found that he could look at it in many ways that he had never thought of before, and the more he looked at it, the more wonders he found in that little finger. At the end of the year, he returned to the master and told what he had discerned in his little finger. The master said: That is a good start. Here is your lesson for another year. Look at your other little finger." These simple lessons continued for seven years. At the end of that time, the young man had learned obedience and concentration and was ready to take up deeper lessons.

When I first began the study of Truth, I found that I could warm my feet by centering my attention in them and affirming that they were warm. This encouraged me to try the same process in other parts of my body, and I found that I could stimulate any function to greater activity by centering my attention in it and silently speaking words expressing increased vigor. Now when my stomach, or any

242

other organ, fails to work harmoniously, I can soon restore it to its natural state by telling it what to do.

Suppose that I were to say to you, "If you want to get an understanding of the kingdom of God within you, look at your body." You might respond, "I cannot look at my body except with my eyes." Yes, you can. You have eyes that you know not of. Jesus meant this when He said, "Having eyes, see ye not? and having ears, hear ye not?" The sense man sees with the outer lens of the eyes only. There is a deeper sight than this. Your ears listen without, and you hear but the coarse vibrations of matter. The five senses have their spiritual side, and if we will just let go of the outer and enter into the spiritual, a new world will be revealed. Turn your attention within and you will find that Jesus was telling the truth when He said, "The kingdom of God is within you."

But it is necessary to do a little work every day in developing the spiritual side of your being. Do not make it hard, but see how easy it is to *think* into your body. Not through studying, not through amassing a whole lot of mottoes, or memorizing statements of Truth. Some people in this age have a way of enlarging "their phylacteries." They do not exactly wear Scripture texts on the lapels of their robes, as the old Pharisees did, but they paste them on the wall. "God bless our home" and other mottoes are as thick as daisies in June. Words of Truth are for our education, but before they can quicken us, they must sink back into the spiritual life. There is an inner side to everything, man included.

What we need above all things is to practice concentration; the concentration of thought not upon transitory things, but upon ideas. They are real, and when the mind has grasped them, they manifest ever-increasing power. If there is anything in the external that you want to know about, say to

243

yourself, "I have that within me as an idea. I have within me, for example, the perfect idea of a healthy body." That is the spiritual body idea that we all inherit as part of His image and likeness. Say, "I am healthy, because I inherit a healthy body from my Father." Another truth is: "My Father is good. I inherit, then, goodness from my Father. Then, I see my mind so filled with the good that evil has no reality to me. Then, I see myself as wise, intelligent, knowing. This I inherit from the all-knowing Mind."

These are a few of the lessons that we have to learn. Just begin saying Truth with your mind and insist upon it. You will demonstrate and you will demonstrate in such a wonderful way that it will surprise you. This is real concentration.

I would not advise anyone to quit all reading and all study, because the mind must be fed from both within and without. However, George Bernard Shaw, said to be the wisest man in Great Britain, wrote to a young author, "Keep away from books and from men who get their ideas from books, and your own books will always be 'fresh.' " You must take your ideas and fructify them and build them into the kingdom of God within you. It is only from the kingdom within us that we shall grow into the perfect race, the new race that is soon to begin to be seen in the earth.

Do not get too far away from the everyday little things. Some people are ridiculing Truth demonstrations. They say, "That might occur in the ordinary everyday life of any man or woman." A woman told about leaving a pair of scissors on the car, and she said that she never found those scissors, but in some unknown way, she had got two other pairs of scissors. She called that a "demonstration." Then someone said that it was not. But it was a demonstration to her, if she thought that it was. If she counted that in her mind as the work of God, the mind of Spirit in her was strengthened just to that extent. So if you take in all the little things that seem to you to be the work of Spirit, they will prove steppingstones to higher things. You will begin to have results when you believe in the spiritual side of every experience.

Suppose that you get a raise in your salary. You say, "I earned that." Well, how? By giving attention to your business. By being truthful and faithful. What made you truthful and faithful? Spirit, didn't it? Then why not give Spirit credit for it ?

Follow back every one of your experiences and you will find that there is a cause; keep following back and you will find that there is a spiritual cause for every result in your life.

Then, we say, if you want a continuous enlargement of your activities, if you want them to be perfect, if you want success along any line, study the spiritual cause. Once you get hold of the spiritual cause, you can increase it and through its increase, you will prosper in every way.

Overcoming the Poverty Idea

E VERY LESSON OF Scripture illustrates some phase of mental action and can be applied to each individual life according to its most pressing need at the moment of its perception.

The conflicts between the Children of Israel and the Philistines represent the conflicts that are always taking place in your mind and that are reflected in your body and affairs.

If you are ignorant of the laws of mental action, you get but the mere shell of the lesson in reading Scripture, and it is not of much real benefit. If, however, you consider that the characters in the narrative represent ideas in your own mind and if you follow them out in their various movements, you will solve all the problems of your life through a study of Scriptures. This does not mean that a study of the written Word alone will solve for you the problems of life, but you will see Scriptures as the outward symbol of an inward condition and, through its study and its application, you will come into an apprehension of the real Scripture, the Bible of the ages, the Book of Life within your own consciousness.

In everyone may be found the conflicting ideas represented by the Children of Israel and the Philistines. They are pitted against each other, and the conflict goes on night and day. We call these warring thoughts Truth and error. We stand on the side of Truth and know that its thoughts are the chosen of the Lord, the Children of Israel, but the error thoughts seem so formidable that we quake and cringe in their presence.

We know that Truth must eventually prevail but we say that error is so large and strong that we cannot now cope with it—that we will do so when we have gathered more strength.

Thoughts are not all of the same importance. Some are large and strong and some are weak and small. There are aggressive, domineering thoughts that parade themselves and brag about their power and, with fearful threats of disaster, keep us frightened into submission to their unrighteous reign.

These domineering thoughts of error have one argument that they impress upon us at all times, and that is, fear of results should we dare to meet them and to oppose openly their reign. This fear of opposing error, although we know it to be false, is woven into our whole mental fabric.

This fear is portrayed by the spear of Goliath, and the narrative most aptly states, "And the staff of his spear was like a weaver's beam."

The first step to rid your mind of this giant bugaboo is to get a clear perception of what your rights are as a child of God. You know that you should not be under the dominion of anything in the heavens above or in the earth below. You are given dominion over all. If you are not exercising that dominion, now is the time to begin. You will never find a better time nor a more propitious state of consciousness. If you are in fear of the boastings of this brawny Philistine, seek out the way to "give the dead bodies . . . unto the birds of the heavens." There is a way, a righteous way, and it is the duty of every one of God's children to find it. This way is graphically set forth in the 17th chapter of I Samuel.

The name David means "the beloved of the Lord" and David represents your righteous perception of your privileges as a child of the living God. You are not a slave to anything or to anybody. You cannot be alarmed by the threat of this god of mammon. You have the perception of Truth and you sling it at the center of his carnal thinking, which is the forehead.

This formidable shield and armor of brass do not intimidate you, because you know that they are empty show, that the right idea will reach the vulnerable part in spite of them and the braggart will go down.

Whole armies of good people, righteous people, Christians, the Children of Israel, believe that this power cannot be overcome. They are looking for something larger and stronger in a material way to be brought forth for its destruction. They forget that "the battle is Jehovah's."

Are you cringing in the sight of this Goliath? Does he come out daily and frighten you with his display of strength and his threats? It does not have to be so. There is a little idea in your mind that can slay him: the perception of your place in Divine Mind. You doubtless have not considered it of much importance. You have kept it off on the mountain-side of your spirituality shepherding your innocent thoughts. You have not considered it equal to coping with the affairs of active life. Now let this David come forth. Get a clear idea of where you really belong in creation and what your privileges are. Then that boasting Philistine will cause your perception of justice and equity to say hot words of Truth. You will ask, "Who is this uncircumcised Philistine, that he should defy the armies of the living God?"

Do you think it possible that God has so ordained it that men cannot escape from the servitude of hard conditions? Verily not. This would not be justice, and who dare say that God is not just?

No, it is your privilege at any time to step boldly out and to defy the giant of the Philistines. The Lord has been with us in slaying the fear of sickness and of sin—the bear and the lion of David—and why should He not be with us in slaying this fear of poverty with which the mammon champion so unsparingly whips us?

"The battle is Jehovah's," and He will be with us, and we shall be delivered "out of the hand of this Philistine."

The weapons of the Lord's man are not carnal; he does not wage war after the manner of the world. He does not use steel, brass armor, and coats of mail. These are the protection of selfishness and the weapons of oppression.

The beloved of the Lord is the devout shepherd David, who goes forth in the simplicity of justice, knowing that his own innocence is his defense. His weapons are not those accepted by the world as equal to the occasion—the shepherd's sling and its smooth stones. These are the words of Truth, and it is the will that sends them forth. They are disdained by the Philistine but they do their work, and the great mass of materiality goes down before their sure aim. So the Lord has this day given this financial fear in all its phases into our hands. We know that it is not true that man is servile to the money idea. He does not have to slave for his brother man and cringe to him in order to obtain this universal servant of all. No, we are not bound to this wheel of work day in and day out that the god of mammon may be appeased on his own terms.

We are the children of the living God. The loving Father is here today and always, right in our midst, and it is our privilege to claim Him as our support and resource on conditions and terms that He will reveal to us when we have acknowledged Him and dismissed the fear of mammon.

The five smooth stones chosen by David out of the brook represent five irrefutable statements of Truth. These five statements, slung from a mind confident of itself and its cause, will suddenly crush the forehead of Goliath, error's giant. These statements are covered by the following affirmations and denials:

I am the beloved of the Lord, and He will be with me in all my righteous words, and they shall accomplish that for which I send them forth.

I cannot be deprived of my own and I dissolve in my own mind and in the minds of all men the belief that what is mine can be withheld from me.

My own shall, by the sure and certain law of God, come to me, and I now welcome it in the presence of this clear perception of Truth.

I am under obligations to no one. God, my opulent Father, has poured out to me all resource, and I am a mighty river of affluence and abundance.

My bounty is so great that men marvel at its sumptuous abundance. I own nothing selfishly, yet all things in existence are mine to use and, in divine wisdom, to bestow upon others.

Faith Precipitations

WHEN ASKED what electricity is, a scientist replied that he had often thought of it as an adjunct to faith, judging from the way it acts.

This linking of faith and electricity seems, at first glance, fantastic, but when we observe what takes place when certain substances in solution and an electric current are brought in conjunction, there seems to be a confirmation of the Scripture passage, "Now faith is assurance of *things* hoped for."

Just as the electric current precipitates certain metals in solution in acid, so faith stirs into action the electrons of man's brain; and acting concurrently with the spiritual ethers, these electrons hasten nature and produce quickly what ordinarily requires months of seedtime and harvest.

In the time of Elisha, the widow, so distressed with debt that she had even mortgaged into slavery her two children, appealed to the prophet, who said, "What hast thou in the house?" She said, "Thy handmaid hath not anything in the house, save a pot of oil." He told her to borrow all the empty vessels her neighbors had and then to go into the house and shut the door and to pour the oil in the pot into all those vessels, which she did until they were all full. She then paid her debts and had plenty left.

Jesus fed four thousand persons at one time and five thousand at another by the same means. He also "precipitated" the elements of wholeness many times and healed the multitude. He required co-operation in faith on the part of those He healed in order thus to complete the healing circuit.

Speedy answers to prayer have always been experienced and always will be when the right relations are established between the mind of the one who prays and the spiritual realm, which is like an electrical field. The power to perform what seems to be miracles has been relegated to some God-selected ones; but now we are inquiring into the law, since God is no respecter of persons, and we find that the fulfillment of the law rests with man or a group of men, when they quicken by faith the spiritual forces latent within them.

The reason why some prayers are not answered is lack of proper adjustment of the mind of the one who prays to the omnipresent, creative spiritual life.

Jesus was the most successful demonstrator of prayer of whom we have any record and He urged persistence in prayer. If at first you don't succeed, try, try again. Like Lincoln, Jesus loved to tell stories to illustrate His point and He emphasized the value of persistence in prayer. He told of a woman who demanded justice of a certain judge and importuned him until in sheer desperation he granted her request.

Every Christian healer has had experiences where persistent prayer saved his patient. If he had merely said one prayer, as if giving a prescription for the Lord to fill, he would have fallen far short of demonstrating the law. Elijah prayed persistently until the little cloud appeared or, as we should say, he had a "realization"; then the manifestation followed.

The Bible is treasured as the word of God because it records so many of these apparent miracles; but the fact is that all over this land enough demonstrations of the super-mind are taking place every day to fill many books the size of the Bible. Some of them are recorded, and people read about them; but these are few compared with the many that are happening. All of which goes to prove that there is a restorative law that, if taken advantage of, will heal the world of all its ills.

Many of the old-school faith healers object to the scientific explanation of the healing process. They have believed in a personal God and that all superworld forces are set in motion by His personal intervention. However, it is much more satisfying to logical minds to know that God is the law and that the Spirit that we have thought of as a projection of Him is, in fact, He Himself in His own spiritual identity. This is the teaching of Jesus, and our men of science are proving it to be true. An understanding of this all-accessible Truth is making seers, prophets, and mighty men of God out of pygmies. On every hand, men of mediocre ability are becoming world leaders through exploiting the supermind qualities that they have merely glimpsed as existing within them.

These ephemeral Caesars have gained an inkling of the disciplined mind's dominion and are using it to control the negative mass thought and, through the hypnotic force of words, they evolve chaos and dark night the world over.

When men accept and understand Jesus' teaching about the mastery of the spiritual man, all the evils that arise from these upstart saviors will disappear. But now in the night of mind's eclipse

"We petty men
Walk under his huge legs, and peep about
To find ourselves dishonorable graves."

Then the question arises, If this supermind ability is in every man, why is it not more widely understood and used?

There are several answers to this pertinent question, the most plausible being the lack of human initiative. Men prefer to let others do their thinking for them. This is especially true in religious matters. The race thought has been so

253

saturated with the belief that spiritual revelation must come through some authorized channel that the man without an ecclesiastical degree is timid about expressing an opinion about God or man's spiritual nature.

Jesus broke this hypnotic spell when, without ecclesiastical authority, He claimed to be the Son of God.

We should remember that Jesus included as sons of God all those who, as He said, are "my sheep," that is, follow Him. He quoted the 82d Psalm, in which it is written,

"I said, Ye are gods,
And all of you sons of the Most High."

The church elders and the people cried, "Crucify *him!*" Jesus taught great truths, which were grasped by but a few open-minded followers, and they formed a new church. After doing mighty works for hundreds of years, they, in turn, built an ecclesiastical hierarchy from which the common people were excluded. The Church Fathers gathered and selected certain religious manuscripts and compiled the Bible, which they proclaimed to be the very word of God, to be read and interpreted by those only having the authority of the church.

Here again, we see positive thought submitting to negative thought, thereby keeping the world in darkness for ages.

As Luther started the Protestant Reformation, so we are now at the beginning of another reformation, in which the freedom and power of man spiritually will not only be taught but demonstrated.

The supermind demonstrations that mark this modern religious reformation seem so at variance with nature that they are still looked upon as miracles, notwithstanding the fact that logic and science shout from the housetops the universality of law.

254

The literature of Unity teems with testimonials of persons who have been healed and are grateful to God for renewed health, strength, prosperity, and happiness. Thus, it is not necessary to strengthen your faith by reading about the work of God in ages past; you can personally consult your neighbor, who can doubtless tell you of marvels fully as great as any recorded in the Bible.

The majority of cases that come to us belong to the class of the discouraged woman told of in Luke 8:43, "who spent all her living upon physicians, and could not be healed." Doctors have pronounced them incurable, and, as a last resort, they turn to God. The hardest part of the work in their healing is to get out of their minds the verdict of the doctor that their case is incurable. We have discovered that there are no incurables. "With God all things are possible." Any experienced metaphysical healer will tell you that he has been the instrument through which all the popular diseases have been healed.

I can testify to my own healing of tuberculosis of the hip. When a boy of ten, I was taken with what was at first diagnosed as rheumatism but developed into a very serious case of hip disease. I was in bed over a year and, from that time, an invalid in constant pain for twenty-five years, or until I began the application of the divine law. Two very large tubercular abscesses developed at the head of the hipbone, which, the doctors said, would finally drain away my life. But I managed to get about on crutches, with a four-inch cork-and-steel extension on the right leg. The hipbone was out of the socket and stiff. The leg shriveled and ceased to grow. The whole right side became involved; my right ear was deaf and my right eye weak. From hip to knee, the flesh was a glassy adhesion with but little sensation.

When I began applying the spiritual treatment, there

was, for a long time, slight response in the leg, but I felt better and I found that I began to hear with the right ear. Then gradually, I noticed that I had more feeling in the leg. Then as the years went by, the ossified joint began to get limber, and the shrunken flesh filled out until the right leg was almost equal to the other. Then I discarded the cork-and-steel extension and wore an ordinary shoe with a double heel about an inch in height. Now the leg is almost as large as the other, the muscles are restored, and although the hipbone is not yet in the socket, I am certain that it soon will be and that I shall be made perfectly whole.

I am giving minute details of my healing because it would be considered a medical impossibility and a miracle from a religious standpoint. However, I have watched the restoration year after year as I applied the power of thought and I know it is under divine law. So I am satisfied that here is proof of a law that the mind builds the body and can restore it.

A Scientific Religion

SPIRITUAL DISCERNMENT reveals that we are now in the dawn of a new era, that the old methods of supply and support are fast passing away, and that new methods are waiting to be brought forth. In the coming commerce, man will not be a slave to money. Humanity's daily needs will be met in ways that are not now thought practical. We shall serve for the joy of serving, and prosperity will flow to us and through us in countless streams of plenty. The supply and support that love and zeal will set in motion are not, as yet, largely used by man, but those who have tested their providing power are loud in their praise.

The dynamic power of the supermind in man has been sporadically displayed by men and women of every nation. It is usually connected with some religious rite in which mystery and priestly authority prevail. The so-called "common herd" are kept in darkness with respect to the source of the superhuman power of occult adepts and holy men. But we have seen a "great light" in the discovery by physical scientists that the atom conceals electronic energies whose mathematical arrangement determines the character of all the fundamental elements of nature. This discovery has disrupted the science based on the old mechanical atomic theory but has also given Christian metaphysicians a new understanding of the dynamics back of Spirit.

Science now postulates space rather than matter as the source of life. It says that the very air is alive with dynamic forces that await man's grasp and utilization and that these invisible, omnipresent energies possess potentialities far beyond our most exalted conception. What we have been taught about the glories of heaven pales to insignificance

257

compared with the glories of the radiant rays—popularly referred to as the "ether." We are told by science that we have utilized very meagerly this mighty ocean of ether in producing from it the light and power of electricity. The seemingly tremendous force generated by the whirl of our dynamos is but a weak dribble from a universe of energy. The invisible waves that carry radio programs everywhere are but a mere hint of an intelligent power that penetrates and permeates every germ of life, visible and invisible. Scientific minds the world over have been tremendously moved by these revolutionary discoveries and they have not found language adequate to explain their magnitude. Although a number of books have been written by scientists, setting forth guardedly the far-reaching effects that will inevitably follow man's appropriation of the easily accessible ether, none has dared to tell the whole story. The fact is that the greatest discovery of all ages is that of physical science, that all things apparently have their source in the invisible, intangible ether. What Jesus taught so profoundly in symbols about the riches of the kingdom of the heavens has now been proved true.

According to the Greek, the language in which the New Testament has come down to us, Jesus did not use the word heaven but the word heavens in His teaching. He was not telling us of the glories of some faraway place called "heaven" but was revealing the properties of the "heavens" all around us, called both "space" and "ether" by physicists. He taught not only its dynamic but also its intelligent character and said that the entity which rules it is within man: "The kingdom of God is within you." He not only described this kingdom of the heavens in numerous parables but made its attainment by man the greatest object of human existence. He not only set this as man's goal but attained it Himself, thereby demonstrating that His teaching is practical as well as true.

The scientists tell us that the ether is charged with electricity, magnetism, light rays, X rays, cosmic rays, and other dynamic radiations; that it is the source of all life, light, heat, energy, gravitation, attraction, repulsion; in short, that it is the interpenetrating essence of everything that exists on the earth. In other words, science gives to the ether all the attractions of heaven without directly saying so. Jesus epitomized the subject when He told His followers that it was the kingdom from which God clothed and fed all His children. "Seek ye first his kingdom, and his righteousness; and all these things shall be added unto you." Science says that the electrical particles which break into light in our earth's atmosphere are also a source of all substance and matter. Jesus said that He was the substance and bread that came from the heavens. When will our civilization begin really to appropriate and use this mighty ocean of substance and life spiritually as well as physically?

God Presence

I AM NOW *in the presence of pure Being and immersed in the holy Spirit of life, love, and wisdom.*

I acknowledge Thy presence and power, O blessed Spirit. In Thy divine wisdom now erase my mortal limitations, and from Thy pure substance of love bring into manifestation my world, according to Thy perfect law.

Man knows intuitively that he is God's supreme creation and that dominion and power are his, though he does not understand fully. The I AM of him ever recognizes the one divine source from which he sprang, and he turns to it endeavoring to fathom its wonderful secrets. Even children grope after the truths of Being.

No man knows the beginning of the query, Who, what, and where is God? It is dropped from the lips of the little child when he first begins to lisp the name of father and of mother, and it is repeated throughout the years.

Who made you? Who made me? Who made the earth, the moon, and the sun? God. Then who made God?

Thus, back to the cause beyond the cause ever runs the questioning mind of man. He would understand the omnipresence that caused him to be.

Does an answer ever come to these questionings? Does man ever receive satisfactory returns from this mental delving in the unfathomable? Each man and each woman must answer individually, for only the mind of God can know God. If you have found God in your own soul, you have found the source of health, of freedom, and of the wisdom that answers all questions.

Language is the limitation of mind; therefore, do not expect the unlimited to leap forth into full expression through the limited.

Words never express that which God is. To the inner ear of the mind awakened to its depths, words may carry the impulses of divine energy and health that make it conscious of what God is, but in their formulations, such words can never bind the unbindable.

So let us remember that by describing God with words in our human way we are but stating in the lisping syllables of the child that which in its maturity the mind still only faintly grasps. Yet man may know God and become the vehicle and expression of God, the unlimited fount of life, health, light, and love.

God is the health of His people.

Man recognizes that health is fundamental in Being and that health is his own divine birthright. It is the orderly state of existence, but man must learn to use the knowledge of this truth to sustain the consciousness of health.

Health is from the Anglo-Saxon word meaning "whole," "hale," "well." The one who uses the word really implies that he has an understanding of the law of the perfect harmony of Being. Health is the normal condition of man and of all creation. We find that there is an omnipresent principle of health pervading all living things. Health, real health, is from within and does not have to be manufactured in the without. Health is the very essence of Being. It is as universal and enduring as God.

Being is the consciousness of the one Presence and the one Power, of the one intelligence, and man stands in the Godhead as *I will*. When man perceives his place in the great scheme of creation and recognizes his I AM power, he declares, "I discern that I will be that which I will to be."

Man is the vessel of God and expresses God. But there is a mighty difference between the inanimate marble, chiseled by the sculptor into a prancing steed, and the living, breathing horse consciously willing to be guided by the master's rein.

So there is a wide gap between the intelligence that moves to an appointed end under the impulse of divine energy and that which *knows* the thoughts and desires of Divine Mind and co-operates with it in bringing about the ends of a perfect and healthy creation.

"No longer do I call you servants; for the servant knoweth not what his Lord doeth; but I have called you friends; for all things that I have heard from my Father I have made known unto you."

It must be true that there is in man a capacity for knowing God consciously and communing with Him. This alone insures health and joy and satisfaction. It is unthinkable that the Creator could cause anything to be that is so inferior to Himself as to remove it beyond the pale of fellowship with Him.

It is our exalted ideas of God and our little ideas of ourself that built the mental wall that separates us from Him. We have been taught that God is a mighty monarch with certain domineering characteristics, who wills us to be sick or healthy; that He is of such majesty that man cannot conceive of Him.

Even in metaphysical concepts of God, the impression left us is of a Creator great in power, wisdom, and love. In one sense, this is true, but the standard by which man compares and judges these qualities in his mind determines his concept of God.

If I say that God is the almighty power of the universe and have in mind power as we see it expressed in physical energy and force, I have not set up the right standard of comparison. It is true that all power comes from God, but it does not follow that the character of the thing we term

262

power is the same in the unexpressed as in the expressed.

God is power; man is powerful. God is that indescribable reservoir of stored-up energy which manifests no potency whatever until set in motion through the consciousness of man yet possesses an inexhaustible capacity that is beyond words to express. When that power is manifested by man, it becomes conditioned. It is described as powerful, more powerful, most powerful, and it has its various degrees of expansion, pressure, velocity, force, and the like.

This power is used by men to oppress one another, and there has come to be an idea that God is power in the sense of great oppressing capacity. It is an ancient idea that He can and does exercise His power in punishing His creations, pouring out upon them His vengeance.

But this is not the character of divine power. If by power we mean force, energy, action, oppression, then we should say that God has no power, that God is powerless; because His power is not like the so-called power that is represented by these human activities.

God is wisdom—intelligence—but if we mean by this that God is "intelligent," that His knowledge consists of the judgments and inferences that are made in a universe of things, then we should say that God is nonintelligent.

God is substance; but if we mean by this that God is matter, a thing of time, space, condition, we should say that God is substanceless.

God is love; but if we mean by this that God is the love that loves a particular child better than all children, or that loves some particular father or mother better than all fathers and mothers, or that loves one person better than some other person, or that has a chosen people whom He loves better than some other people who are not chosen, then we should say that God is unloving.

263

God does not exercise power. God is that all-present and all-quiet powerlessness from which man "generates" that which he calls power.

God does not manifest intelligence. God is that unobtrusive knowing in everyone that, when acknowledged, flashes forth into intelligence.

God is not matter nor confined in any way to the idea of substance termed matter. God is that intangible essence which man has "formed" and called matter. Thus, matter is a limitation of the divine substance whose vital and inherent character is above all else limitless.

God is not loving. God is love, the great heart of the universe and of man, from which is drawn forth all feeling, sympathy, emotion, and all that goes to make up the joys of existence.

Yet God does not love anybody or anything. God is the love *in* everybody and everything. God is love; man becomes loving by permitting that which God is to find expression in word and act.

The point to be clearly established is that God exercises none of His attributes except through the inner consciousness of the universe and man.

God is the "still small voice" in every soul that heals and blesses and uplifts, and it is only through the soul that He is made manifest as perfect wholeness.

Drop from your mind the idea that God is a being of majesty and power in the sense that you now interpret majesty and power.

Drop from your mind the belief that God is in any way separated from you, that He occupies form or space outside of you, or that He can be manifested to your consciousness in any way except through your own soul.

We look at the universe with its myriad forms and

stupendous evidences of wisdom and power and we say: All this must be the work of one mighty in strength and understanding; I should stand in awe of such a one and realize my own insignificance in His presence. Yet when we behold the towering oak with its wide-spreading branches, we say it grew from a tiny acorn. A little stream of life and intelligence flowed into that small seed and gradually formed the giant tree. It was not created in the sense that it was made full-orbed by a single fiat of will, but it grew from the tiny slip into the towering tree through the inherent potentialities of the little seed, the acorn.

So God is in us the little seed through which is brought forth the strong, healthy Christ man.

That "still small voice" at the center of our being does not command what we shall be or what we shall do or not do. It is so gentle and still in its work that in the hurly-burly of life we overlook it entirely. We look out and, beholding the largeness of the world of things, we begin to cast about for a god corresponding in character with this world.

But we do not find such a god on the outside. We must drop the complex and find the simplicity of "the most simple One" before we can know God. We must become as a little child.

Jesus said "God is Spirit" not "a Spirit," as in the King James Version. According to Webster, the word spirit means life or living substance considered independently of corporeal existence; an intelligence conceived of apart from any physical organization or embodiment; vital essence, force, or energy as distinct from matter; the intelligent, immaterial, and immortal part of man; the spirit, in distinction from the body in which it resides.

Paul says, "In him we live, and move, and have our being." If we accept the Scriptures as our source of information, there can be no higher authority than that of Jesus and Paul. They say that God is Spirit.

Spirit is not matter, and Spirit is not person. In order to perceive the essence of Being, we must drop from our mind the idea that God is circumscribed in any way or has any of the limitations usually ascribed to persons, things, or anything having form or shape. "Thou shalt not make unto thee a graven image, nor any likeness *of any thing* that is in heaven above, or that is in the earth beneath."

God is life. Life is a principle that is made manifest in the living. Life cannot be analyzed by the senses. It is beyond their grasp; hence, it must be cognized by Spirit.

God is substance; but this does not mean matter, because matter is formed while God is the formless. This substance that God is lies back of all matter and all forms. It is that which is the basis of all form yet enters not into any form of finality. It cannot be seen, tasted, or touched. Yet it is the only "substantial" substance in the universe.

God is love: that from which all loving springs.

God is Truth: the eternal verity of the universe and man.

God is mind. Here, we touch the connecting link between God and man. The essential being of God as principle cannot be comprehended by any of the senses or faculties, but the mind of man is limitless, and through it, he may come in touch with divine principle.

It is the study of mind that reveals God. God may be inferentially known by studying the creations that spring from Him, but to speak to God face to face and mouth to mouth, to know Him as a child knows his father, man must come consciously into the place in mind that is common to both man and God.

Men have sought to find God by studying nature, but they have always fallen short. This seeking to know God by analyzing the things made is especially noticeable in this age. Materialistic science has sought to know the cause of things by dissecting them. By this mode, they have come to say: We must admit that there is a cause, but we have not found it; so we assume that God is unknowable.

To know God as health, one must take up the study of the healthy *mind* and make it, not physical appearance, the basis of every calculation. To study mind and its ideas as health is a departure so unusual that the world, both religious and secular, looks upon it as somehow impracticable. The man who lives in his senses cannot comprehend how anything can be got out of the study of something apparently so intangible.

The man of affairs cannot see what mind or its study has to do with matters pertaining to his department of life, and the religionist who worships God in forms and ceremonies makes no connection between the study of mind and finding out the real nature of God.

Behold, I go forward, but he is not *there;*
And backward, but I cannot perceive him;
On the left hand, when he doth work, but I cannot behold him;
He hideth himself on the right hand, that I cannot see him.

Thus, ever cries the man who looks for God in the external, for health from an outside source.

In mathematics, the unit enters into every problem; and in existence, mind is common to all, above and below, within and without. The secret of existence will never be disclosed before man takes up and masters the science of his own mind.

Man's consciousness is formed of mind and its ideas, and these determine whether he is healthy or sick. Thus, to know the mysteries of his own being, he must study mind and its laws.

Many persons in every age have come into partial consciousness of God in their own soul and have communed
with Him in that inner sanctuary until their faces shone with
heavenly light; yet the mysteries of creative law were not
revealed to them, because they did not get an understanding
of its key, which is mind.

Mind is the common meeting ground of God and man,
and only through its study and the observation of all the
conditions and factors that enter into its operation can we
come into the realization of God as abiding health and
sustenance.

God is mind; and we cannot describe God with human
language, so we cannot describe mind. To describe is to
limit, to circumscribe. To describe mind is to limit it to the
meanings of sense. In our talk about mind, we are thus forced
to leave the plane of things formed and enter the realm of
pure knowing.

We can only say: I am mind; I know. God is mind;
He knows. Thus, knowing is the language I use in my inter-
course with God.

If you ask me about the language I use in communicating
with God, I am not able to tell you; because you are talking
from the standpoint of using words to convey ideas, while
in the language of God, ideas in their original purity are
the vehicles of communication.

But ideas are the original and natural agents of communication, and everyone is in possession of this easy way
of speaking to God and man. Thus, we may learn to use
this divine and only true way consciously if we will but
recognize it and use it on the plane of mind.

But we must recognize it. This is the one truth that we
have to reveal to you: how to recognize this divine language
in your own consciousness and how, through recognition, to

bring it forth into visibility. It is a truth, however, that we cannot reveal to you by a series of eloquent essays on the majesty, power, and wisdom of God and on the everlasting joy that follows when you have found Him; but only by showing you in the simplest way how to come into conscious relations with the source of omnipresent wisdom, life, and love, by taking with you in the silent inner realms the first steps in the language of the soul.

Compared with audible language, communion in mind can be said to be without sound. It is the "still small voice," the voice that is not a voice, the voice using words that are not words. Yet its language is more definite and certain than that of words and sounds, because it has none of their limitations. Words and sounds are attempts to convey a description of emotions and feelings, while by the language of mind, emotions and feelings are conveyed direct. But again, you must transcend what you understand as emotion and feeling in order to interpret the language of God. This is not hard. It is your natural language, and you need only return to your pristine state of purity to achieve it entirely.

You are mind. Your consciousness is formed of thoughts. Thoughts form barriers about the thinker, and when contended for as true, they are impregnable to other thoughts. So you are compassed about with thought barriers, the result of your heredity, your education, and your own thinking. Likewise, your degree of health is determined by your thoughts, past and present.

These thoughts may be true or false, depending on your understanding and use of divine law. You must open the walls of your mental house by a willingness to receive and weigh these thoughts in the balance of good judgment and to drop out of your mind everything except this one powerful idea:

I want to know God's Truth; I am now willing to learn.
If there is not in your consciousness a demonstration that
mind has a language on its own silent plane and that it can
manifest itself in your mind, body, and affairs, then you can
go back to your old convictions.

The fundamental basis and starting point of practical
Christianity is that God is principle. By principle is meant
definite, exact, and unchangeable rules of action. That the
word principle is used by materialistic schools of thought to
describe what they term the "blind forces of nature" is no
reason why it should convey to our mind the idea of an unloving and unfeeling God. It is used because it best describes
the unchangeableness that is an inherent law of Being.

From the teaching that the Deity is a person, we have
come to believe that God is changeable; that He gets angry
with His people and condemns them; that some are chosen
or favored above others; that in His sight good and evil are
verities, and that He defends the one and deplores the other.
We must relieve our mind of these ideas of a personal God
ruling over us in an arbitrary, manlike manner.

God is mind. Mind evolves ideas. These ideas are
evolved in an orderly way. The laws of mind are just as
exact and undeviating as the laws of mathematics or music.
To recognize this is the starting point in finding God.

God loves spiritual man, and that love is expressed according to exact law. It is not emotional or variable, nor is
there any taint of partiality in it. You are primarily a spiritual being, the expression of God's perfection, the receptacle
of His love; and when you think and act in the consciousness of perfection and love, you cannot help being open to
the influx of God's love and to the fulfillment of His divine
purpose. This is the exact and undeviating law that inheres
in the *principle* that God is.

270

God is wisdom, and wisdom is made manifest in an orderly manner through your consciousness.

God is substance—unchangeable, incorruptible, imperishable—to the spiritual mind and body of man.

This substance of mind—faith—does not happen to be here today and there tomorrow, but it is moved upon by ideas, which are as unchanging as Spirit.

In Spirit, you never had a beginning, and your I AM will never have an ending. The world never had a beginning and will never have an ending. All things that are always were and always will be, yesterday, today, and forever the same.

But things formed have a beginning and may have an ending.

But God does not form things. God calls from the depths of His own being the ideas that are already there, and they move forth and clothe themselves with the habiliments of time and circumstance in man's consciousness. We must have firmly fixed in our understanding the verity that we shall have to square all the acts of our life.

God is never absent from His creations, and His creations are never absent from their habiliments; hence, wherever you see the evidences of life, there you may know that God is.

If you are manifesting health, that health has a source that is perpetually giving itself forth. A perpetual giving forth implies a perpetual presence.

There is no absence or separation in God. His omnipresence is your omnipresence, because there can be no absence in Mind. If God were for one instant separated from His creations, they would immediately fall into dissolution. But absence in Mind is unthinkable. Mind is far removed from the realm where time and distance prevail. Mind is without metes or bounds; it is within all metes and bounds; it does

271

not exist but inheres in all that is. Hence, in Spirit and in Truth you can never for one instant be separated from the life activity of God even though you may not externally feel or know of His presence.

God lives in you, and you depend on Him for every breath you draw. The understanding you have, be it ever so meager, is from Him, and you could not think a thought or speak a word or make a movement were He not in it. Your body is the soil in which God's life is planted. Your mind is the light for which He supplies the oil. "I am the light of the world," said Jesus. "Ye are the light of the world."

Intelligence is the light of the world. "Let your light shine." How? By increasing the supply of oil, by increasing your consciousness of life, and by learning how to draw upon the omnipresent God for every need.

Jesus Christ

Quite a few Truth students ask why we emphasize Jesus Christ so strongly in our writings and statements of Truth. Spiritual psychology proves that the name of a great character carries his mind potency and that wherever his name is repeated silently or audibly his attributes become manifest. Jesus knew this and commanded His disciples to go forth in His name. The marvelous works they did prove that they exercised power far beyond anything warranted by their education or previous ability, power springing directly from Spirit.

Every thinker who studies the life and teachings of Jesus readily admits that He attained an understanding of spiritual things far beyond that of any other man who ever lived. His mind touched heights far beyond those of other advanced searchers for Truth. As we unfold spiritually, we see more and more that Jesus understood the finer shades of metaphysical reasoning and related His mind and body to both ideas and their manifestation.

Jesus demonstrated that He understood the healing power stored up in the body, which He said is released through faith. "Thy faith hath made thee whole." Jesus identified Himself and His name with the sacred name of the Hebrew dispensation, Jehovah, and added another link to that long chain of names and events which brought forth the perfect man ideated by God-Mind, Jesus Christ.

As a directive head is essential in an army, militant or spiritual, so in every forward movement of the human family there must be a leader. The leader is chosen because of his ability as a demonstrator of the principles adopted by the group he represents. The religious principles taught and demonstrated by Jesus were not originated by Him, nor

273

did He claim them as a "discovery." He said that Moses wrote of Him and He often quoted Moses, but with an interpretation quite different from that of the popular religious leaders. He told them that they studied the Scriptures, expecting through them to attain eternal life when the only way to attain that life was through Him, and they would not come to Him. Right here, Jesus emphasized the spiritual man, the I AM in man, as the only way by which man can enter the kingdom of God.

Jesus was undoubtedly the greatest of all exponents of the impersonal I AM, which is revealed to man when he opens up the supermind within his own soul. Jesus Christ's real name is Jehovah, I AM. The personal man Jesus is merely the veil or mask worn by the spiritual man Christ or Jehovah. We are all, in our personality, wearing the mask that conceals the real, the spiritual, I AM. Jesus shattered that mask and revealed the spiritual man. He also taught the way by which we may all do what He did and, thus, fulfill the destiny implanted in us by the parent Mind.

There are many distractions to keep us from finding the one door into the inner kingdom and many voices calling to us that they will show us the easy way, but Jesus Christ is the only one that appeals to those who are grounded in principle.

Any declaration man may make, in which the name Jesus Christ is used reverently, will contact the spiritual ether in which the Christ I AM lives and will open the soul and body to the inflow of spiritual healing rays. These healing rays are very much superior to the ultraviolet rays that come from the sun or our best medical appliances, because they minister to the mind as well as the body.

The Last Supper

A T THE LAST SUPPER, Jesus taught that the bread and wine which He consecrated was His body and His blood and He told His followers to partake of them in remembrance of Him. He did not say that these elements were symbols of His blood and body but that they were essentially the same substance and life as His body. This also has been the teaching of the church, as interpreted by the Council of Trent: "Under each species and under each particle of each species Christ is contained whole and entire." This is the doctrine of transubstantiation, that the consecration by the minister of bread and wine changes the material elements to Christ elements without affecting their appearance.

This doctrine has been attacked both within and without the church, the majority of ministers and laymen accepting it on faith as in some way related to the miraculous. But the discoveries of the elemental character of matter by modern science is revealing the universal unity of substance and the possibility of its transformation from one thing to another by changing the number and arrangement of the electrons in the atom.

According to modern science, this whole universe of forms can be dissolved into energy, from which it may again be formed. Science does not say that the directive and formative power is man, but the Bible so teaches and especially Jesus. Jesus said that all power was given unto Him in heaven and in earth. He manifested His power in a small way by multiplying a few loaves and fishes to feed more than five thousand persons. In various other instances, He demonstrated that He had an understanding of the transmutation of substance. He raised His flesh body to an energy level far higher in potential life and substance than any reached before.

As a race, we have for ages been deprived in our consciousness of union with our creative source, and the result has been a gradual decrease in vitality until our body has lost the ability to hold its atoms together and, consequently, has disintegrated. Thus, death has come to be accepted as in some mysterious way a part of the divine plan. Here again, certain biological experiments with cells prove them to be possessed of an ability to reproduce themselves, which at least hints at physical immortality.

There are in the world today men and women who have followed the teaching of Jesus and have developed in their bodies a superenergy or life that not only permeates the physical structure but envelops it in a luminous aura that can be and is felt by both themselves and others. Spirit reveals that spiritual thinking breaks open the physical cells and atoms and releases their imprisoned life, which originally came from Divine Mind. Jesus carried this process so far that His whole body was transformed and became a conscious part of the Father life and intelligence.

In this way, the substance and life of Jesus' body became a connecting link between our body and the body of God. Jesus merged His consciousness with the race consciousness and made Himself subject to our shortcomings in order to lift us up to spiritual life. This is the secret of our Saviour's great sacrifice and sin offering.

Attaining Eternal Life

THESE QUERIES often come to us: "What do you teach about death?" "Where do people go when they die?" A succinct answer to these questions is found in a statement made by Paul: "The mind of the flesh is death." According to the Bible, all men are "dead through . . . trespasses and sins."

Adam, as originally created, was in illumination. Spirit continually breathed into him the necessary inspiration and knowledge that gave him superior understanding. But he began eating (or appropriating) ideas of two powers— God and not-God, or good and evil. The result, so the allegory relates, was a falling away from life and all that it involves. This was the first death.

Men do not think of the first death in its relation to the second death. The latter enters when the soul loses control of the body, when the functional activities permanently cease and the physical organism dissolves. If the scriptural statements given above express facts, sinners (men who believe in two powers, good and evil) are already dead. They do not have to wait until the body stops acting in order to know the conditions that prevail in death. Why should we worry about the condition of men who go through the second death? The first death is death of the light and the life of Spirit in our consciousness, and the result is a withdrawal of the soul from the organism. The soul of the carnally minded does not live in the body but outside of it. Because of his sins, man has been driven out of the body Eden.

What is death? Briefly stated, it is cessation of vital force and action in the body. Jesus referred to the dead as "fallen asleep," as also did Paul. There are various degrees of this sleepy condition into which the body falls. Students of physiology find that the body has unused resources that can be temporarily awakened. Through deep breathing, they bring into action certain centers in the lungs that give additional purity to the blood; by the quickening of other centers in the body weak persons can be made strong. This is not the regeneration taught by Jesus, but it demonstrates that the body is not living up to its capacity in even a material way. Some physiologists say that in our thinking exercises we use only a small part of the brain. Nearly the whole nervous system of man is in a sleepy, inactive state. These material investigators tell us that if some substance could be poured in through our nervous system that would wake us up all over, we should be transformed into a new being.

That is exactly what the new life in Christ does for us. "Be ye transformed by the renewing of your mind." We are to be transformed not by deep breathing or by muscular exercise or by having our nerves shocked by electricity; but by a new process of thought and spiritual energy, we are to awaken our sleepy body, we are to get back to the original state in which we consciously receive the inspiration of Spirit and charge our body with the life of the infinite life.

This is the teaching of pure Christianity, and it is borne out by the discoveries of modern science. Both agree that men must have more life and greater vitality in order to carry forward the demands of mind and its aspirations. Jesus went so far as to claim that men who do not lay hold of the larger consciousness of life that He brought to the race have no life in them.

What shall we do to escape the second death? We must take the life of the Christ man, which is potentially here in every one of us, and concentrate it into this brain and this body of ours. This is accomplished by the power of the word.

To hold negation in the mind is to stamp negation on

the body. There is no duality in God. We intuitively know that God is good and that God is all. We intuitively know that life is the one real expression of God. To demonstrate the God life, we must plant the knowledge of that life in the flesh. To keep on living, we must supply the God substance out of which the body will be renewed.

There is no need of any state or condition called death. The word death is a denial of God's idea of life. If we would accept life as God offers it to us, we are obliged to refuse the conditions that man has attached to it.

If we would realize the larger life, we must believe in it; we must begin to affirm it as ours here and now. And what kind of life do you conceive this eternal life to be? A life that goes and comes? Affirming eternal life, would you say, "I feel tired and weak; I wish I had a little stimulant to tone me up?" Certainly not. You would meet the feeling of weakness with an affirmation of strength; you would meet every evil suggestion with a denial of its reality and a strong word of Truth. Sound words quickly tone up the mind and body, and there is never a reaction of weakness following their use.

It does not make any difference to the loyal Christian how many people "fall asleep." We know that the sleepers awaken again, that what men call the sleep of death is just a long dream. Some people have more vivid dreams than others, so some who fall asleep in the second death may dream of returning life until they quickly take up again the construction of an organism. The early Christians considered it a great advantage to have a knowledge of Jesus before falling asleep.

It is possible to think about the absence of life until death seems real and lasting. This makes the dream dense and dark, and the awakening slow. Christianity shows how to come right back into life, and that is the only salvation for man. If you believe faithfully in Christ life, you will never die. That is the promise of Jesus, and our understanding of the laws of mind substantiates His assurance in this respect. The mind can be so filled with thoughts of life that there will be no room for a thought of death. Death can never take possession of the body of one whose mind is thoroughly charged with ideas of life.

This will answer the question "If a man die, shall he live *again?*" Eternal life means continuous conscious existence in the body. Every man lives just to the extent of his appreciation of eternal life. Not only must we live, but we must live wisely. In the Genesis allegory, it is written that, for fear man would eat of the tree of life and live forever in his sinful mind, the Lord God sent him forth from the Garden of Eden. This means that man does not consciously live in his organism, which is the real Garden of Eden. In his unregenerated state, man reflects his mind into his body. But when the baptism of fire, the descent of the Holy Spirit, takes place, there is a reunion of mind and body, and the thrill of divine life is again felt by Adam. The return of the soul to the interior of the organism is part of the symbology portrayed in the history of Jesus of Nazareth. Man must seek and know the law of life before he can live forever. Living without conforming to that law is tragedy.

The law of life is revealed to the mind of man through conscious thinking. Give attention to the omnipresent intelligence and it will make you wise. The *"light* which lighteth every man, coming into the world" is here as the atmosphere is here. "The light shineth in the darkness; and the darkness apprehended it not." Why? Because men do not realize the truth about Spirit and its laws. Spirit is like mind —in fact, it is the highest realm of mind. There is an ever-present, all-knowing One. Put yourself into conscious unity with this Presence through the power of your thought and your word and you will gradually become mentally open to a world of causes of which you never before dreamed.

Metaphysicians have found that man can light up the body cells by affirming life and intelligence for them. Metaphysicians tell their patients to make affirmations such as these:

I am alive with the life of Christ. I am intelligent with the intelligence of Christ.

Take these words and use them day after day, night after night. Affirm them when you go to bed and affirm them when you awake in the morning; make them part of your consciousness and you will take a very important step in demonstrating eternal life.

Love, peace, and harmony are the only remedies that count. "God is love," and to live in God-Mind, man must cultivate love until it becomes the keynote of his life. We must love everybody and everything, ourself included. Some people hate themselves. Self-hate is destructive. You must love yourself. Affirm infinite love as your love and you will find that there will be generated in your mind and body an entirely new element. Love is the cementing element of all things. You could not have an organism without the help of the cementing power of love. Love is the magnet. You must have love. You cannot live without it. Then begin to live in the thought of love. Personal love is part of the law, but divine love fulfills the law. Center your love thoughts upon God and you will find love for your fellow man growing marvelously.

We must have substance in its purity in our body. All about us are elements out of which, if we knew how to use them, we could make any form that we desire. We have not

281

cultivated faith in the invisible substance idea, and it, therefore, has not been incorporated into flesh. But now that we know that it exists and that through our affirmations we bring it into expression, we begin at once to affirm divine substance. By this practice, we put our body under a refining process, which we may continue until we are transfigured into the likeness of that divine man whom John saw on Patmos.

The pure substance of Being is a universal solvent. Man can take the substance idea into his mind and, by the presence of its native purity, cleanse everything upon which he concentrates his thought.

Jesus said that His body was living substance and He told His followers to eat it. You eat the purified substance of the body of Christ by affirming it to be the real substance of your body.

In the regeneration, we thus daily put on the body of Christ until finally every cell becomes so related to its neighbor that each reflects upon the other, as diamond reflects upon diamond, and the redeemed body literally shines. "They that are wise shall shine." The wisdom that shines is the wisdom of Spirit, the knowledge that life is spiritual Being, complete here and now.

Man is spirit, soul, and body. The spirit is I AM, and I AM is the ego of the Deity. Jehovah told Moses that His name was I AM. Jesus said, "I am the way, and the truth, and the life." Every time that man says "I AM," he is speaking the name of Being.

Soul is the sum total of man's experiences gathered throughout the ages. Soul has its inner and its outer avenues of expression.

The body is the meeting place of the life and substance attributes of Being; consequently, body is an important factor in consciousness. Body is not matter; it is substance and life in expression. Expression takes the character of the presiding ego. When the ego attaches itself to life and substance alone and ignores the higher attributes of Being, it becomes gross and material in thought and in manifestation.

Every form in the universe has within it a thought picture or pattern. The form may be destroyed, but the picture endures. Man's body is first a mental picture imprinted upon the ether or universal substance.

To the oft-repeated question "Where is my loved one who is dead?" there can be no comprehensive answer until there is a broader and deeper understanding of man. If the physical were all of man, then the question could easily be answered. But man is very much more than body, even more than intellect. The most interior and real part of man is spirit; then comes soul; then come intellect and sense consciousness, out of which body is formed. When the body is destroyed, the house of these various component parts of man is no more, and they are left homeless. Then they separate, each going to its own state of consciousness. The spiritual ego reverts to its original essence in the bosom of the Father; soul falls asleep until the next incarnation. Body and sense consciousness are earth-bound and, in due season, they disintegrate. Those who have lived honestly and purely find peace and happiness for a time in the rest that follows sincere observance of the divine law.

But the goal of man is eternal life and, in each incarnation, that goal is brought nearer if Spirit is given opportunity to express itself. When this is done, the true spiritual body will replace the physical body and all men will become like Jesus Christ. This is to be accomplished here in the earth. With the eye of a prophet, John saw the redeemed earth, as described in Revelation 21:1-5, "And I saw a new heaven and new earth: for the first heaven and the first earth are passed away; and the sea is no more. And I saw the holy city, new Jerusalem, coming down out of heaven from God, made ready as a bride adorned for her husband. And I heard a great voice out of the throne saying, "Behold, the tabernacle of God is with men, and he shall dwell with them, and they shall be his peoples, and God himself shall be with them, and be their God; and he shall wipe away every tear from their eyes; and death shall be no more; neither shall there be mourning, nor crying, nor pain, any more: the first things are passed away. And he that sitteth on the throne said, Behold, I make all things new."

Preserving the Unity of Soul and Body

THE WESTERN WORLD in general looks upon re-embodiment, or reincarnation, as a heathen doctrine. Many persons close the door of their mind upon it, without waiting to find out what message it brings when interpreted in the light of Truth. It is the object of this article to set forth the Unity teaching concerning reincarnation, to show why we consider it reasonable, and to explain its relation to and its place in the Christ doctrine.

The teaching of Jesus is that all men shall, through Him, be made free from sin and be saved to the uttermost—spirit, soul, body. But until this salvation is attained, there is death. To give men opportunity to get the full benefit of salvation, life is necessary, and a body through which to express life is also necessary. So, when man loses his body by death, the law of expression works within him for re-embodiment, and he takes advantage of the Adam method of generation to regain a body. Divine mercy permits this process in order that man may have further opportunity to demonstrate the Christ life. But generation and death must give place to regeneration and eternal life. The necessity of rebirth must, therefore, pass away with all other makeshifts of the mortal man. It will have no place when men take advantage of the redeeming, regenerating life of Christ and quit dying.

Re-embodiment should not be given undue importance, because it is merely a temporary remedy to be followed by the real, which is resurrection. The whole man—spirit, soul, and body—must be lifted up into the Christ consciousness of life and perfection.

Through *"the light* [the indwelling Christ] which lighteth every man, coming into the world," the so-called heathen

285

have discerned many truths to which the more material-minded people of the newer countries have been blind. Whenever there has been a nation of thinkers who were not bound in materialism, those thinkers have accepted re-embodiment as a fact. It is rejected only where the craze for wealth and for fame and for the things of the world has darkened the mind with materiality.

The heathen who have not received Truth as revealed by Jesus do not know where and how re-embodiment fits into the race redemption; to them, it is a fixed, unalterable law. They believe in karma, the accumulated effects of the sins of past lives. The burden of karma they have carried for ages, and they expect to carry it for ages more, until they have worked out of it. This makes them victims of a blind fatalism, weary treadmill travelers from birth to death and from death to birth. There is no such hopeless note in the doctrine of Jesus. He came to bring a full consciousness of abundant life, complete forgiveness and redemption from all sin, victory over death and the grave, so delivering man from any occasion for re-embodiment and from all ideas of karma.

The heathen hold that reincarnation is one of the natural evolutionary steps of man's development. We teach, and our doctrine is sustained by the teaching of Jesus, that re-birth is the unifying force of nature at work in its effort to restore man to his original deathless estate. Man, through his disregard of the law of life, brought death upon the body, as taught in the 3d chapter of Genesis. A single span of life, from the birth of an infant to the death of an old man, does not constitute all man's opportunity for life. Life is continuous and in harmony with the wholeness of Being only when it is expressed in a perfect body; hence, man must have a body in order to gain an abiding consciousness of life. Through repeated trials at living, man is finding out that he must learn to control the issues of life. The divine law, as taught by Jesus, must be understood and applied to all life's details, and when this is done, the Eden state will be restored.

Knowing that spirit, soul, and body are all necessary to man and that he cannot truly be said to live except in their conscious union and expression, the error of believing that death is the open door to a higher life, the gateway to heaven, is easily seen. There is no progress in death. Death is negation. The demonstration of eternal life can be made only in life—soul and body together working out the problem and together being lifted up.

The idea of progress in death has its origin in the mortal mind, which reasons from its own limitations instead of from absolute Truth. The mortal mind desires to preserve eternally the personal consciousness and all personal relations. Man, therefore, attempts to make and to people a heaven, or spirit world, where all the old family relations are as he knows them in his present life. He clings to this idea with a tenacity worthy of a better object, and it is usually only after hard experience that he is willing to drop the personal and to say, "Whosoever shall do the will of my Father who is in heaven, he is my brother, and sister, and mother." Eternal life cannot be demonstrated in personal consciousness. The great family of Christ, the redeemed Adam race, are all one, and the little selfish relationships of the Adam man have no place in the new order.

Another illogical belief about the destiny of man is that the patriarchs and the prophets, and all others who have lived, have been lying in their graves, some of them for thousands of years, having no place in the onward movement of the race. Another teaching, unfounded in Scripture or in reason, holds that they who formerly lived are now either in a realm of eternal bliss or in a state of unending torment. It is far more logical to believe that the race is a unit and that all its members grow and develop together as well as individually. Thus, we find it only reasonable to think of every man and every woman as coming onto the stage repeatedly, keeping up connection with the race and its experiences. A definite instance of this is written in the Scriptures concerning Elijah's appearance and work as John the Baptist. "And the disciples asked him, saying, 'Why then do the scribes say that Elijah must first come?' He answering, said, 'Elijah indeed comes, and will restore all things. But I say to you, that Elijah has already come, and they did not recognize him, but have done to him whatever they wished.' . . . Then the disciples understood that he spoke to them concerning John" (Matt. 17:10-14; Emphatic Diaglott).

That you do not remember your past lives proves nothing. Neither do you remember the day on which you were born, but you do not on that account question the fact of your birth. Comparatively little of your present life is remembered. But that does not alter the fact that you have lived. Memory, to the natural man, is a matter of physical brain records, photographic or phonographic in character. The memories of experiences in past lives are not clearly recorded in the new brain structure of the infant. Such memories are usually in the nature of vague impressions; the sense of identity is blurred. But in the book of life, the great Mind of the universe, all identity is sharply marked, and as the individual becomes quickened and raised out of personal consciousness into the universal, he will be able to bridge over the breaks in personal experience. He will come to himself. Realizing his spiritual identity as the son of God, he will not entangle himself with either present or past

288

personality but will claim and demonstrate his divine sonship. He will no longer limit himself to a brief span of life, beginning with birth and ending with death, but will live in the consciousness of eternal life, which has neither end nor beginning.

The Kingdom of Heaven Is at Hand

HAD THE KINGDOM, to which Jesus so often referred, been a city with golden streets in the skies, He could easily have located it; but He did not do so. On the contrary, He again and again gave illustrations to show His listeners that it was a desirable condition, which would be brought about among them through the power of Spirit. He did not speak of it as situated anywhere in particular nor did He say that it could be attained quickly. For instance, He said: "Unto what is the kingdom of God like? and whereunto shall I liken it? It is like unto a grain of mustard seed, which a man took, and cast into his own garden; and it grew, and became a tree; and the birds of the heaven lodged in the branches thereof." And again, "It is like unto leaven, which a woman took and hid in three measures of meal, till it was all leavened."

It is a great mystery how these comparisons of heaven ever came to be construed as referring in any way to a locality in the skies. What relation to a city with streets of gold has a mustard seed, planted in the earth and springing forth into a tree? or a little cake of yeast fermenting a baking of bread?

A remarkably strange lot of comparisons Jesus used, if He had in mind a place where the good were to go after death!

But He never pretended to convey any such meaning. His command to His disciples fully carries out His idea of the kingdom of heaven. Heaven is a condition to be brought about in the affairs of men here on the earth. It is to grow from small beginnings, like the mustard seed or the yeast cake. His disciples were sent forth to sow the seed in a definite way, by carrying into the midst of men the signs that evidence the power of Spirit through which the kingdom of

290

heaven is to be established, right here on this planet. There is no basis for any other view. All the theories about a place called "heaven" are founded on John's symbolical description of New Jerusalem, which was a picture in the imagination of the fulfillment on earth of the very movement that Jesus inaugurated and that He described as having such small beginnings. This city that John saw is among men. "Behold, the tabernacle of God is with men, and he shall dwell with them, and they shall be his people, and God himself shall be with them, *and be* their God: and he shall wipe away every tear from their eyes; and death shall be no more; neither shall there be mourning, nor crying, nor pain, any more: the first things are passed away." This all describes what is to take place here among us. No reference is made to its being among angels or to its being established at the time that John saw the vision; it is to be consummated in new conditions on earth.

If the kingdom that Jesus taught is in the skies, why did He direct His apostles to pray: "Thy kingdom come. Thy will be done, as in heaven, so on earth"?

Now that men are opening up the hidden resources of nature, in earth and in air, possibilities of achievement are dawning on them, and they see that human endeavor will yet make the earth a paradise.

No one should be deluded with the vague assumption that there is a place in the skies or on some faraway planet called "heaven." There is not the shadow of a foundation in either the Old or the New Testament for such doctrine. On the contrary, the teaching is clear that all the heaven which men will ever find will be here. It is here now and it will be revealed to everyone who rends the veil of sense.

The teaching "The kingdom of heaven is at hand," is not alone indicative of the quick ushering in of a new order

291

of things but it states a fact of subjective consciousness in man. Nothing else is so near to man as God and the kingdom of heaven. They exist eternally in the depths of man's own unrevealed consciousness. He has them in the hidden recesses of his mind, exactly as he has the circulation of the blood in the hidden veins of his body. He is not conscious of the blood before he looks for it and he is not conscious of God and of his own spiritual nature before he gets into the deeps of his own soul.

It is the subjective or interior consciousness that is to be made objective or exterior. To the question of His disciples as to when the kingdom of heaven would come, Jesus answered, "when the without shall become as the within" (Apoc. New Testament).

This one passage should forever settle the location of heaven. It is the *within* and it will come to the consciousness of humanity when it is brought forth to the without, when the without conforms to its conditions.

Is There a Hell?

I HAVE LIKED your teaching in most things, but the way in which you explain metaphysically some parts of the Bible has disturbed me very much. There can be but one true interpretation of any word of God. It is a simple, plain word from God to man for his salvation. I may get healing and help from God and do many wonderful works and yet never truly know God to the salvation of my soul. Of course, there is, if Jesus' own words are true, an "eternal fire prepared for the devil and his angels." It cannot be explained away. The one message of the Bible is not to get healing, temporal help, comfort, or power but to make provision to escape the wrath to come, to seek to save men's souls from death, the death that never dies.

"So I am dropping Unity till I get light as to my attitude towards its teachings, which are very true and fine in one way but untrue in the important real facts concerning the soul. . . . I pray that He will lead you to see the great *soul* need—the necessity for first repenting, the remission of sins through the blood of Jesus. Without this cleansing, no one can inherit the kingdom of heaven."—*From a letter to Unity.*

The seeker for Truth will miss the mark if he reads the Bible literally. The Bible is a book of parables, allegories, comparisons. Spiritual things cannot be described in a language that is limited to material names. Jesus' lessons were given, and should be accepted, allegorically. In Mark 9:43, it is recorded that He said, "And if thy hand cause thee to stumble, cut it off: it is good for thee to enter into life maimed, rather than having thy two hands to go into hell" (margin, *Gehenna*).

This statement is plainly allegory. Jesus certainly did not advise the amputation of one's hands to cure sin. Neither did He refer to a place called hell. According to the original Scriptures, He used *Gehenna* to illustrate the state of mind into which the sinner is plunged by his sin. *Gehenna* was the burning refuse heap near Jerusalem. The remorse of sinners may be compared to a fire in the soul. It is corrective and, when the sinner is repentant, purifies both soul and body.

This corrective work of the purifying fire in the soul of the sinner is set forth thus in Ferrar Fenton's translation of the New Testament, Matthew 25:46: "And these He will dismiss into a long correction, but the well-doers to an enduring life."

In the Bible, three different words, either Hebrew or Greek, are translated "hell." *Gehenna* is the only one of these that in any sense means fire. *Gehenna* is the Greek form of the Hebrew *Ge Hinnom* (valley of Hinnom). The valley, lying just outside the city of Jerusalem, was a dumping ground for the city's sewage and filth, and a fire was kept burning continually to consume the waste. From this, we see that *Gehenna* is a fitting illustration of the cleansing fire of Spirit.

In a sermon, Archdeacon Farrar said: "There would be the proper teaching about hell if we calmly and deliberately erased from our English Bibles the three words, 'damnation,' 'hell,' and 'everlasting.' I say—unhesitatingly I say, claiming the fullest right to speak with the authority of knowledge— that not one of those words ought to stand any longer in our English Bible, for in our present acceptation of them they are simply mistranslations."

Jesus taught in parables, that is, in symbols. If this were always remembered and if the guidance of the Spirit of truth were sought in the interpretation of symbols, the great mass of confusing, contradictory interpretations of

His words would be cleared away and all people would see alike in the light of spiritual understanding. No one claims that the parable of the wheat and the tares or the parable of the sheep and the goats is to be taken literally, yet the whole religious world has insisted that hell-fire means a burning lake where men and women shall burn in material fire forever. With such beliefs about God's purpose for His erring children, it is no wonder that people have found it hard to believe that He is love. True understanding of the real character of God, of man, and of the universe in which we live will dispel the darkness of ignorance that has made possible the old concept of hell. God is not an arbitrary man seated on a throne in the skies but He is the everywhere present substance, life, intelligence, and power of the universe. Our recognizing this and obeying the laws of our being place us in harmony with the one life-giving energy, the fire of Spirit, which works in us as our own joyous life and purity. By the nature of its own purity, it begins to consume the abominable works of ignorance and error, but to the extent that its laws are disregarded, the mind and the body are put out of harmony with it.

The Interpretation of Visions

WHEN PAUL TOLD of the vision that had come to him on the way to Damascus, he said, "I was not disobedient unto the heavenly vision."

We all receive visions but we are not always obedient to them. Often our lack of obedience is caused by ignorance or by failure to realize that a vision is a leading, guiding intelligence. By visions, I mean something more than one would see in a special opening of the invisible realms. Every high aspiration, every splendid dream that we have of our possibilities—what we should like to be—is a vision. But most of our visions seem so far removed from our everyday life that we do not give them substance; we do not give them a chance because we are not obedient "unto the heavenly vision."

Obedience comes through spiritual inspiration. Man must make himself obedient. In other words, it is necessary for him to covenant with the Lord that he will be obedient. He does that in Spirit, in his meditations, in his prayers.

All of us have had visions; we have had waking visions and sleeping visions. We have seen things that we could not tell to others for fear they would ridicule us. The visions that we have seen are from the Lord, and if we acknowledge those occult, hidden things as being real and in the silent recesses of our soul become obedient, we shall get something more definite; this, in turn, will lead to a clearer revelation, and soon we shall have the door open between us and our higher self.

One of the most delicate subjects that the metaphysician has to deal with is that of visions and dreams. The practical, everyday man considers them foolish, childish, and valueless. Many religionists put a like estimate on these seemingly meaningless mental pictures. Even those who have a certain faith in visions and dreams are largely in darkness as to their real import. The reason for all this is that the realm in which dreams operate is so far removed from material consciousness that it is difficult to get a right interpretation or a right understanding of the symbols.

Spirit functions in a consciousness in which there is no limitation. It is not a place of things; it is a place of ideas. In order to connect or synchronize with the world of effects, these ideas have to be transposed, changed about entirely. If you take your dream to be what it seems literally, you will fail to understand the message. Spirit talks in ideas, which are presented to man's consciousness as shapes and forms. So when you have the vision or the dream, remember that it is through understanding its abstract or absolute character that you will get the lesson and the right interpretation. If you dream of persons or of things and think that the dreams mean the persons and the things themselves, you are not interpreting scientifically. Men become prophets and seers by seeking to know the meaning of the pictures of the mind.

Today there are thousands of Bible students studying the dreams and visions that Daniel had; and yet if you should say to one of those same students, "Do you ever have dreams?" he would probably reply, "Oh, yes! I have dreams and I see things sometimes, but it is all my imagination."

In the Bible, there is evidence of an inner and an outer interpretation and relation of visions. It is plain that what is called Peter's vision was partly a dream. The narrative says that he fell into a trance. He went into what we call the silence; he was meditating and praying on the housetop. When you meditate and pray, you look toward the realm of the spiritual—not with your eyes but with your mind—and through this looking, this directing of your attention to the spiritual, it begins to open to you. It always follows that those who look spiritually, who pray, who believe in spiritual things, have added to them this other faculty, a spiritual imagination.

The fact is that we are using this imagination all the time. It is the maker in us of forms and shapes. In contour, your body is the result of your imagination. So every time you look into the glass, you can see yourself as you appear or seem to be in your mind.

Cultivate imagination; be true to the heavenly vision. Picture in your mind continually that which you want to be and refuse to judge according to appearances.

Some of our dreams pertain to the individual, and others to matters external. It is difficult sometimes to decide just where to place the dream. I find that my greatest difficulty in interpreting is to know whether the dream applies to me individually or to me as an individual related to persons and to things.

I remember that a good many years ago, when Spirit first began to lead me in dreams, I had some very definite lessons and guidance with respect to things external as well as my individual development. One night, I dreamed that I went into the bank where we were doing business and as I talked to the teller, I saw that his clothes grew shabby; I looked over to where the cashier was sitting, and his desk began to look worm-eaten, and everything grew less and less prosperous in appearance, and, all at once, the place faded away. I did not pay much attention to the dream. I was very busy at the time. I did not attempt to interpret it. After one has had a dream, he should meditate upon it and pray and ask for the interpretation. Spirit will show him. But I did not give any special attention to that dream and, a few nights later, I dreamed that I was standing in front of the office. In the dream, I saw a large bank of dirt flying through the air; it landed with a great crash right in front of me, and out of it came a voice saying, "Now do you understand?" I thought that that was strange but still I did not understand and did not stop to inquire. In about three days after the last dream, the bank failed, and we lost all the money we had. Then I saw the warning that Spirit had twice tried to give me.

On awakening after a dream, lie perfectly still and let the various incidents drift through your mind; then see whether you can connect some of them with some matter or question that you have been considering. Reduce the dream pictures to representative factors and you will have the key to the interpretation.

Pharaoh dreamed that seven fat cattle were devoured by seven lean cattle, that seven full ears of corn were devoured by seven thin ears. Joseph told the king that these simple things represented seven years of plenty to be followed by seven years of famine. That was the true interpretation, as the succeeding years proved, and not only Egypt, but Canaan, and the family of Joseph were all saved by this simple dream.

So you can see how, by taking advantage of these simple lessons, these ordinary dreams that you have, you may get a guidance of importance to you. The Lord uses the simplest things to confound the mighty. Visions and dreams are from the Lord more often than we think, but they need a right interpretation.

When you go to sleep, you simply quiet the outer consciousness. When the body enters into its rest, the external mind rests also. Then the mind of Spirit has its opportunity, and, in your dreams, you get its wisdom. But if you ignore the spiritual mind and fail to inquire into its symbolical messages, it loses all hope of expressing itself, and mortality reigns supreme.

All people have visions and dreams, but there is lack of God interpretation. Nearly all people interpret from the standpoint of form and shape. They take the symbols for what they seem and fail to see the ideas back of the symbols. Joseph said that his dreams and visions were interpreted by God; all who go to the Lord for the interpretation get a lesson entirely different from that given to those who leave out the Deity. The dreamer who interprets in the name of the Lord gets a different lesson and he is growing and developing in an entirely different direction from the one who functions wholly in the intellect.

As to Meat Eating

THE SUBJECT OF DIET is attracting more attention every day among metaphysicians. At one time, it was only necessary to quote, "Take no thought for your life, what ye shall eat, or what ye shall drink," to dismiss the whole matter. But the revised Bible puts an entirely new face upon this familiar passage. It says, "Be not *anxious* for your life, what ye shall eat, or what ye shall drink." It was a treatment for anxiety about God's providence that Jesus was giving and not an injunction to take no thought about food.

Food does have a part in body structure, and the Truth student must take this fact into account if he would demonstrate the higher, finer substance.

In years of experiment, I have tested the effect on mind and body of eating meat and of not eating meat and I feel that I am more competent to judge of the effects than one who theorizes about the question.

When I began the study of Truth, I was told that it made no difference what I ate if I was in the right thought. This seemed to prove true up to a certain point in my experience. While my spiritual development was confined to the conscious mind, there seemed no special need for food discrimination. But gradually a new phase set in. I found that I was having vibrations in the sympathetic nerve centers; the subconscious mind was being quickened, and I was becoming a conscious, vital battery. The vital currents gradually grew stronger and stronger until I could hardly control them. Appetite, passion, emotion were greatly increased. Then my prayers for guidance were answered and a system of communication set up with the higher realms of consciousness. I was shown that the food which entered the organism had to pass through a process of "regeneration" every day before it was in condition to be built into the new body in Christ. Just how to carry on this regenerative process in the various subconscious centers was also shown, and here is where I discerned the effects of food in body building.

The vitalizing element in food is contained in the cell, which may be termed a mind battery vibrating with intelligence, force, and substance. These elements are present in the *living* cell; dead cells are those from which intelligence and force have been withdrawn and in which only inanimate substance remains. Man appropriates these cells, and they become part of his consciousness according to his capacity to use them. Those who have not developed the capacity to regenerate the cells consciously get but a small part of their energies. Sufficient energy is extracted through the automatic functioning of the organism to build up and sustain a physical body for a few years, but the thread of life is frail and its texture coarse.

Personal experiment has proved to me that there is but very little change in the character of the food until it passes through the refining process called regeneration, a process by which, through spiritual meditation and affirmation, the I AM is enabled to appropriate and bless for the use of the body the spiritual elements in man's food. But the process is not well sustained until man consciously works with the law and seeks daily regeneration and purification of all the cells in the organism. Then a system is established and the new body built up as designated by Jesus in the symbology of the New Testament.

With this understanding of body substance and of the physical and psychical process of body building, we can see the necessity of discrimination in choosing foods. If the cells of the food pass into the blood and glands essentially the same as they were when formed, it is highly important that their character be of the highest and purest.

The argument that life is destroyed in eating fruits and vegetables is frequently used to excuse the slaughter of animals having intelligence and affections. It is so farfetched that a moment's sincere thought ought to disclose its fallacy to anyone. The fruit and the vegetable have completed their life course and have apparently been prepared by a wise creator for food, as we are told in Genesis 1:29: "Behold, I have given you every herb yielding seed . . . to you it shall be for food." Here is plainly indicated a vegetable and fruit diet for man. When these plant products are found spread upon nature's green-garnished tables everywhere, why should man dye his hands in the lifeblood of animals that resent the carnage and cry out and bellow in terror when his cruel knife is raised against them? This is in direct opposition to the divine law of freedom and the right to life, liberty, and the pursuit of happiness of all God's creatures. Man is today suffering in his body and mind the results of this transgressed law and he will continue to suffer until he observes in its fullest degree the command "Thou shalt not kill."

INDEX

INDEX

Progress, 134

Prosperity, 9, 10, 118, 126-128, 249-250, 251

Prosperity Bank, 126-127, 221

Psychosomatics, 192

Pueblo, Colorado, 36-37, 181

Radio, 15, 113, 207-208, 213, 217

"Red Leaf," 87

Red Mountain, 38

Reincarnation, 198, 285-289

Residences, 49, 84, 130, 131-132, 145, 201, 208-209

"Rock of Ages," 175

"Rosary, The," 175

Rosicrucianism, 41

Saint Augustine, 189-190

St. Cloud, Minnesota, 19, 26, 27

Salvation Army, The, 138

San Fernando Valley, 209

San Francisco, California, 206

San Jose, California, 206

Sauk River, 19

Science and religion, 188-191, 257

Shakespeare, 25, 26, 40

Shrine Auditorium, 205-206

"Signs That Follow, The," 158

Silas, 234

Silence, the 90-91, 173, 194

Silent Help, Society of, 81-88

Silent-70, 71, 120, 216, 221

Silent Unity Building, 133, 134, 135, 138, 139, 219

Silent Unity, Society of, 12, 14, 67, 71, 81-97, 112, 118, 119, 134, 135, 138, 139, 141, 153,

163, 219, 221

Silverton, Colorado, 38

Sioux Indians, 20, 21

Small, Charles, 37

Spiritualism, 41, 56, 57

Stagecoach trip, 34-35

Stone, Mary. *See* Fillmore, Mary Georgiana

Sullivan, Dr. D. L., 43, 102

Sunday School, 72, 75, 105, 107-108, 144, 218

Taylor, Caroline, 25

Taylor, Edgar, 25

"Teachers and Healers Directory," 70

Teachings

affirmative prayer, 54, 82, 86-87, 191-192, 194, 236-238, 243-244, 249-250, 279, 281

afterlife, 283, 287-288

age, 197

Bible, 56, 186-188, 189, 190, 194, 195, 246, 254

blood and body of Jesus, 275-276, 282

body, 282-283

Christ, 167, 174, 195, 212, 274

conscience, 233

death, 198, 276, 277-284, 285-289

demonstration, 239-245

dream interpretation, 16, 53, 167, 229, 296-300

eternal life, 198-199, 210-211, 212, 276, 277-282, 285-289

UNITY SCHOOL OF CHRISTIANITY

LEE'S SUMMIT, MO.

PRINTED U.S.A.

52-F-25M-6-51